The Strange Career
of Bilingual Education
in Texas, 1836–1981

Number Two:
Fronteras Series
Sponsored by Texas A&M
International University
José Roberto Juárez
General Editor

The Strange Career
of Bilingual Education
in Texas, 1836–1981

Carlos Kevin Blanton

Texas A&M
University Press
College Station

Library of Congress Cataloging-in-Publication Data

Blanton, Carlos Kevin, 1970–
The strange career of bilingual education in Texas, 1836–1981 / Carlos
Kevin Blanton.—1st ed.
p. cm.—(Fronteras series ; no. 2)
Includes bibliographical references and index.
ISBN 1-58544-310-7 (cloth : alk. paper)
1. Education, Bilingual—Texas—History. 2. Mexican American
children—Education—Texas—History. I. Title. II. Series.
LC3732.T4 B53 2004
370.117′09764—dc22
2003016351

To Lee,
Belia, Celina,
Lucas, Herschel,
Annie, Emilio,
and Juanita

Contents

Illustrations

The Strange Career
of Bilingual Education
in Texas, 1836–1981

Preface

The subject of bilingual education makes major historians of United
States policy and politics uncomfortable. In *The Uncertain Triumph: Federal Education Policy in the Kennedy and Johnson Years*, historian Hugh Davis Graham remarks that bilingual education, in addition to being a new thing in American life, was nothing more than a "Hispanic Job Corps" desired not by pedagogical experts but by "Hispanic militants" (p. 219). *The Disuniting of America: Reflections on a Multiracial Society*, by famed historian Arthur M. Schlesinger, Jr., portrays bilingual education today as a false and socially corrosive multicultural ethos without real pedagogical value. Schlesinger, without citing corroborating sources, judges, "Bilingualism shuts doors. It nourishes self-ghettoization and ghettoization nourishes racial antagonism" (p. 108). These assertions are quite far from the historical truth. Such unfortunate ignorance of the history of bilingual education is common. Graham's and Schlesinger's statements embody the dangers of historians who invoke the authority of history in commenting on present controversies without a real understanding of their historical context. However, their mistakes are somewhat understandable in that historians have yet to document the story of American bilingual education. *The Strange Career of Bilingual Education in Texas, 1836–1981*, attempts to fill this void.

Bilingual education's strange career in Texas—from the founding of the Republic of Texas in 1836 to the creation of the most significant and encompassing bilingual education law in the state's history in 1981—is known yet unspoken. Many profess to "know" the story without having any idea of its dimensions or implications. It uncovers a valuable window to the past illustrating the attitudes and daily practices of people who are ignored by historians. There are many ironies to this tale. The late C. Vann Woodward, one of the nation's greatest historians, in his *The Strange Career of Jim Crow* reminded his audience that history lives on in the present, that the questions grappled with in the past never really die. Woodward's gentle doggedness and passionate humility offer an ideal model for anyone seeking to illuminate the past of some present controversy. It is in this spirit that *The Strange Career of Bilingual Education in Texas, 1836–1981,* contributes to the process of uncovering bilingual education's history in Texas and the nation.

This is a work of history, not educational theory or linguistics. It is not the purpose of this study to evaluate the effectiveness or ineffectiveness of today's bilingual education. However, the subject of bilingual education is a creature of other disciplines, and thus some distinctions and definitions must first be made clear. The terms *bilingual education* and *bilingual instruction* will be used interchangeably. Bilingual instruction can be simply defined as the use of more than one language in the education process. However, this is too vague. For the purpose of this study, bilingual instruction means the education of language-minority children in public and private schools with the use of their vernacular language for some kind of communication, whether it be classroom directions and instructions (the medium of communication) or actual lessons (content), while also using English as a medium of communication and/or as a content area.

There are two separate and distinct historiographies concerning bilingual education in the American past: a "useable past" body of work and a "detached accident" strand. First undertaken in the 1960s and continuing through the present day, the "useable past" works were authored for the most part by non-historians such as Joshua Fishman, Arnold Leibowitz, Theodore Andersson, and Mildred Boyer. They sought to use history to bolster the concept of bilingual education with a sense of historical legitimacy. Later in the 1970s and 1980s critics like Shirley Brice Heath and Steven Schlossman sought to discredit bilingual education by casting doubt on its historical legitimacy. While the pro-bilingual activists writing the first draft of history on bilingualism in the American past can be rightly accused of writing poor history, the anti-bilingual activists are, strangely enough, guilty of the same charge from the opposite ideological perspective. Standing completely apart from this debate is the "detached accident" historiographical strand. These writers are historians who, for the most part, note instances of bilingual instruction but pay little or no attention to such phenomena. Historians of ethnic groups, culture, politics, law, and education comprise this body of work. Though problematical, the best marriage of these two historiographical traditions is *The American Bilingual Tradition* by Heinz Kloss. This was originally researched and written in Nazi Germany and not published in English until the 1970s.

The first section of this book examines the period from Texas Independence to the early twentieth century. A definite and unmistakable "bilingual tradition" was particularly vibrant during the earliest days of education in Texas. Chapter 1, "Legal and Policy Aspects of the Bilingual Tradition, 1821–84," examines the basic framework of bilingual education's existence. It is a policy history of bilingual instruction in Texas from the onset of Anglo immigration to the beginning of its demise. In between were many twists and turns; the official language policy shifted from one extreme to another and then back again. The legal status of language in the public schools was, contrary to popular misconception, always a source of great controversy and frustration for policymakers.

Chapter 2, "Tejanos, Germans, and Czechs in the Making of the Bilingual Tradition, 1850–1900," examines the local practices of bilingual instruction in Texas schools. Although public and private schools are examined, special emphasis is given to public education. Archival sources, including unpublished, handwritten reports from local county officials, highlight a number of different types of bilingual instruction. This bilingual tradition was sometimes crude and rudimentary and at other times remarkably similar to bilingual education today. In Texas, unlike other states, this tradition consisted of more than just one ethnic group; Tejanos, Germans, Czechs, and others participated in the state's rich bilingual past, making it an ideal case study for bilingual education throughout the nation. Chapter 3, "The Gradual Demise of the Bilingual Tradition, 1884–1905," analyzes a period when the rise of Progressive Education and the growth of nativism combined to spell doom for the bilingual tradition. Any form of bilingual instruction came to be regarded as pedagogically backward and un-American.

The second section of the book covers the first half of the twentieth century ending shortly after World War II. From out of the Progressive Education philosophy came the advance of Americanization and English-Only curriculum. Chapter 4, "The Rise of Americanization Curriculum, 1918–41," specifically deals with the Americanization movement in Texas from World War I to World War II. A mild, inclusive type of Americanization in the nineteenth century came to be replaced by a harsher, more nativist form in the early twentieth century. By the 1920s that harsher Americanization became ever more focused on one particular group participating in the Texas bilingual tradition—Mexican Americans—with disastrous educational results. Americanization and its curricular adjunct of English-Only language policy became enmeshed with the racist school segregation of Mexican Americans.

Chapter 5, "The Theory and Practice of English-Only Pedagogy, 1893–1941," illuminates the role that language pedagogy played in the demise of Texas' bilingual tradition. Theoretical and scientific writings attacked bilingual instruction and supported its pedagogical opposite in English-Only. Chapter 6, "The Promise and Limits of the Politics of Accommodation and Wartime Opportunity, 1930–47," examines the promise and limitations that World War II held for Mexican Americans, particularly with the Good Neighbor movement. During this time the intellectual foundations of English-Only pedagogy were shaken but remained intact. The Mexican American Generation of political activists labored greatly to end the abuses of English-Only in the schools.

The third section of the book extends through the second half of the twentieth century to the 1980s. This was a time when English-Only pedagogy finally crumbled and was replaced with officially sanctioned bilingual education at both the federal and state levels. Chapter 7, "Mexican American Activism and Language Theory in the Gradual Demise of English-Only, 1947–65," illustrates twin movements: one from the academic community and the other from the Mexican American activist community, which eventually aided in the discrediting of English-Only methods of instruction. Mexican Americans challenged English-Only in the battle against school segregation just as academicians in psychometrics and language acquisition came to find English-Only indefensible.

Chapter 8, "The Birth of the Modern Bilingual Education Movement, 1965–68," examines the brief period of time in which bilingual education came to be federally recognized as a legitimate program to aid in the teaching of language minorities. As part of President Lyndon Johnson's Great Society, the Bilingual Education Act overturned the criminalization of bilingual instruction across the country and was supported by the rising Chicano Generation of activists. Chapter 9, "The Return of Bilingual Education to Texas, 1964–81," analyzes how these national trends affected Texas. The state was an important laboratory for the development of bilingual programs. Although it would go through several ups and downs from the late 1960s to the early 1980s, bilingual education in Texas persevered, reconnecting the state with an old, important thread of history that had been temporarily broken by the decades of English-Only.

The scholarly enterprise of comparing the bilingual educational practices of yesteryear with those of today is difficult and potentially controversial. Throughout the nineteenth century ethnic communities in the United States utilized their native languages in public and private education. Because of the lack of uniformity in all curricular matters, not just in how bilingual instruction was delivered, what will proceed in the pages that follow will be very general. This study does not imply that all the bilingual instruction the nineteenth century is the same or similar to the bilingual education programs of today. On the other hand, some, perhaps many, were. Regardless, any such similarities between the classroom bilingualism in that period and the current day will be explained in the following chapters.

This book could not have been written without an outpouring of support from family, friends, and colleagues. I owe a number of intellectual debts. Randal Hall, Charles Israel, Nancy Lopez, and Steven Wilson, fellow graduate students at Rice University, offered stimulating and important criticism of this intellectual enterprise. Their expertise in different fields of history broadened my intellectual horizons. Tom Biolsi, Marc Feldesman, Lisa Flores, David Johnson, and Friedrich Schuler of Portland State University read my work and cheerfully aided in its evolution. My new colleagues at Texas A&M University in College Station have been incredibly welcoming and supportive. Several of them—Armando Alonzo, Julia Kirk Blackwelder, Walter Buenger, Tom Dunlap, Walter Kamphoefner, Lora Wildenthal—read chapters of this book and pointed to important issues needing clarification. For their sage advice, I am very grateful. My students, first at Texas A&M University—Kingsville, then Portland State University, and now at Texas A&M University, probably never realize what an inspiration they are to me. Archivists and librarians at Rice University, the University of Texas, Texas A&M University, Portland State University, Texas A&M University—Kingsville, the Institute for Texan Cultures in San Antonio, the Texas State Library in Austin, and the Lyndon Baines Johnson Presidential Library, the Center for American History, and Nettie Lee Benson Center, all at the University of Texas, have greatly aided in the research for this book. Gracious development and start-up grants from Dean Marvin Kaiser at Portland State University and Charles Johnson of Texas A&M University helped get this project off the ground. My mentors, Allen Matusow of Rice University, and Emilio Zamora and Angela Valenzuela, now at the University of Texas, deserve great thanks for having consistently nurtured my growth as an intellectual and a scholar. I hope that they will detect their significant intellectual contributions, each in their own way, to my historical imagination. John B. Boles of Rice University, my dissertation advisor, is a model of intellectual daring, scholarly passion, and gracious humility. He realized the importance of this topic long before I. It is my hope that everyone mentioned above understands that any deficiencies of the book are entirely my own while they must share in any possible success.

Numerous friends and family helped me maintain a modicum of sanity from the consuming, self-absorption of researching and writing a book. It is impossible to thank everyone in the space provided. A few friends needing special mention are Rene Alvarez, Teresa Blivens, Serena Cruz, Randal and Naomi Hall, Charles and Kathryn Israel, Joaquin Jasso, Erica Moodie, "J. J." Julian Jose and Angela Saenz, Ricardo "Rick" Vasquez, Bill and Stephanie Willis, and Steven Wilson and Cheryl Matherly. My family has also sustained me. Juan, Gloria, and John Michael Bazan, Joe, Becky, Laurie, Linda, and Joey Blanton, Jim, Virginia, James "Jimmy" Dean and Lori, and Stephanie Stinebaugh, and Heather and Rich Davis, deserve thanks for their support and continued encouragement. Upon my long-time girlfriend, Kristine Renée Broglio, whom I managed to convince to become my fiancée as this book went to press, I am totally dependent. More than anyone, Kristine listened to me endlessly discuss the matters of this book and has given me nothing but boundless love and patience. To her I profess all my thanks and all my love.

The Strange Career of Bilingual Education in Texas, 1836–1981 is lovingly dedicated to my parents, Horace Lee and Belia Bazan Blanton, my siblings, Celina Kay and Lucas Scott Blanton, and to the memory of my grandparents, Herschel and Annie Blanton, and Emilio and Juanita Bazan. My childhood memories of their stories of bilingual schools, Spanish and German, became the genesis for this book. They have my eternal love and gratitude.

PART ONE
The Bilingual Tradition

CHAPTER ONE

Legal and Policy Aspects
of the Bilingual Tradition,
1821–84

The state of Texas fostered a vibrant bilingual tradition of classroom instruction in its public schools. This tradition first appeared early in the
state's history. This loose, informal, nineteenth century tradition more
often than not fell in between the letter of the law; it was neither specifically sanctioned nor explicitly outlawed. The lack of legal and even
administrative specificity regarding school languages meant that the
bilingual tradition in Texas, in addition to being informal, was, due to
the relatively undeveloped state of public education in Texas, completely dependent upon local circumstance. Classroom bilingualism,
whether used in the Mexican period of governance or later when Texas
was a state, was attempted in an effort to bring immigrant or ethnic
children into the dominant culture. Arguably, this is at least the partial
intent of bilingual education today.

Texas' experience with the bilingual tradition begins with the Spanish missionaries. Historian Carlos Castañeda notes that eighteenth-
century Spanish missionaries in Texas were ordered by the colonial
viceroy of New Spain "to incline and direct the Indians, through the
gentlest and kindest means, to the study of the Spanish language." The
ultimate purpose was to displace competing languages and customs.
Spanish was seen as the prime mechanism for proper Christian con-
version.[1] This was, however, neither a new development nor unique to
Texas. The Spanish crown in 1503 decreed that all indigenous peoples
of the New World be taught in Spanish as a means of culturally consol-
idating the empire.[2]

What is important is not why the Spanish sought to propagate their
language but rather how they chose to do so. Both the church and the
colonial bureaucracy viewed bilingual teaching as an effective means
of Christianizing Native Americans. In 1724 an order from the viceroy
for New Spain directed "all missionaries to learn the various dialects of
the tribes that were congregated in the different missions," because this
was "always the first step in the great work of evangelization and con-
version." Castañeda argues that the missionaries were already doing

this. In attempting to "reduce to writing and to try to systematize the primitive dialects spoken by the natives," the fathers took native languages seriously. One missionary noted that simply overcoming the language barrier was their first and foremost problem.[3]

It is difficult to determine the ultimate effectiveness of this language instruction designed to impart Spanish Christianity mostly because of the absence of full records. However, extant evidence suggests some measure of success. Castañeda uses one clergyman's account in 1760 to demonstrate the missionaries' success in mastering the native dialects and the use of them to Hispanicize Native Americans at the missions. Another scholar noted that by 1777 the indigenous population of the San Antonio missions had assimilated into Hispanic cultural life and spoke fluent Spanish.[4]

However, the Spanish experiment with bilingual instruction in Texas did not survive the mission system. Upon secularizing missions during the latter half of the eighteenth century in an attempt to modernize their medieval colonial administrative system—a series of actions known as the Bourbon Reforms—crown authorities intensified Spanish at the expense of the previously tolerated and utilized native languages. The crown decreed that all schools throughout the whole of the American empire completely abolish any official role for native languages. In some places this royal decree was silently ignored, although missions in Texas seem to have followed royal directives.[5] The Franciscan fathers in San Antonio wrote in the 1790s to the viceroy in support of this abandonment, saying that the Hispanicization of the indigenous tribes over several decades had succeeded so completely that there were hardly any non-Christianized indigenous people within a 150-mile radius of San Antonio. The San Antonio population consisted of a racially mixed people who were for the most part racially *mestizo* (half Indian, half Spanish) and Spanish frontier in culture.[6]

Like their Spanish predecessors, Mexicans were not indifferent to education. Indeed, the scarcity of education on the frontier made it that much more valued. Unfortunately, it was difficult to attain. For decades the historical consensus, based largely on the published recollections of early Anglo travelers and settlers, was mired in stereotypes of lazy, corrupt, and uncultured Mexicans as the cause for the lack of educational progress in Texas. The reality is quite different.[7] The poverty of the new Mexican nation, in contrast to its high expectations for education, forced educational planners to urge upon localities a variety of efforts to maximize resources such as the Lancastrian system of education, in which one teacher theoretically taught a class of 150 children with the assistance of a handful of student assistants. In 1829 the Mexican state of Coahuila and Texas enacted the Lancastrian system along with the all-important reform of compulsory attendance, which would not exist again in Texas until Reconstruction and then not again until 1915.[8] Mexican laws concerning discipline, punishment, curriculum, and teaching methods were incredibly detailed in an attempt to insulate teachers from the personal and political pressure of parents. Town charters in San Antonio for the Mexican public schools accounted for every minute of the school day: the schedule of subjects to be studied, how students were to be evaluated, how competitions functioned, even down to how students were to sit in class.[9]

The will to regulate languages in the classroom came slowly to Mexican authorities. Despite a growing number of Anglo immigrants to the Texas frontier, Mexican officials did not initially concern themselves with the subject of classroom language. Title VI of the 1827 Constitution of the State of Coahuila and Texas only vaguely mandated that "The method of teaching shall be uniform throughout the state" and that "Congress shall form a general plan of public education and regulate by means of statutes and laws all that pertains to this most important subject."[10] The fact that language is not specifically mentioned in spite of the growing number of English-speaking colonists by the late 1820s may indicate an unwillingness by the state government to dictate too strictly, an initial lack of engagement with the education of Anglo immigrants, or perhaps a lack of engagement with the whole issue of education in the farthest reaches of its borderlands.

Despite the initial imprecision of the constitution, however, the Mexican government did deal with language on a statutory and a contractual basis. The earliest *empresario* contract signed by Stephen F. Austin was clear and direct on the point of official language: "The official communications with the government, and with the authorities of the state, instruments, and other public acts, must be written in the Spanish language, and when new towns are formed he shall promote the establishment of schools in the Spanish language, in such towns."[11] The statutory definition of school languages turned up in general education bills. In a scheme to finance schools, the legislature of Coahuila and Texas decided to issue land grants for towns petitioning for money to build schools. Upon receiving its lands the town of Nacogdoches was reminded in an almost incidental manner by Vice Governor Juan Martín de Veramendi that "the Castillian language . . . shall be expressly taught."[12]

While the national and state governments may have wished to promote an all-Spanish policy, Anglo Texans such as Stephen F. Austin desired educational bilingualism to help assimilate Anglos into Mexican

life. Historians have noted that Stephen F. Austin's papers contain a
remarkable document written while he was a deputy in the Coahuila
state legislature during the early 1830s proposing a school called the
"Institute for Modern Languages" in San Felipe de Austin. This proposed school was to Mexicanize Anglo children by imparting the Spanish language along with study in English. Instructors would also teach
the French language. Austin's reverence for schools was legendary in
Texas. Historian Max Berger notes that the small settlement of San Felipe de Austin maintained between three and four schools at a time
when most comparable towns in the United States were viewed as successful if they managed to maintain just one.[13] For such efforts Austin
was damningly praised by famed biographer Eugene C. Barker as having "possessed the faculty, rare in Americans of any time, and in his
own day almost unknown, of sympathy with an alien race, and willingness and ability to adapt himself to its national mannerisms and in-
sensibilities." Even after the break with Mexico Austin remained cool
to independence.[14]

Austin's desire for an institute of languages went beyond mere loyalty toward the Mexican government. He also based his advocacy of
this language school on expediency. In his legislative bill Austin stated,
"public schools for the teaching of modern languages, and especially
that of Spanish, are of prime importance." He continued: "These col-
onies are composed of both foreigners and Mexicans; and the necessity
for disseminating the national language aming [*sic*] the former is evident." That Anglo settlers had not begun this type of school on their
own, claimed Austin, was not "because of a lack of willingness to
contribute" on their part but rather due to the "want of a legal and permanent arrangement which would give a legal existence to the institution." Austin then stipulated that Spanish, English, and French
coursework would be offered at this institute; he even planned to have
a multilingual administrative staff.[15]

Austin remained a steadfast champion of bilingual instruction in educational matters beyond his unfulfilled language institute. In letters
to various Mexican and Texan acquaintances, he sought bilingual
instructors for the colony's schools to better impart Spanish. Letters between Austin and Mexican schoolteachers regarding school supplies
such as two-way English-Spanish dictionaries and grammar books for
translation show that both languages were intended to be used in some
fashion. Austin was not the only Texan willing to support education in
both languages. A convention of Texas residents in 1832 seconded
Austin's desire for educational bilingualism. In a proclamation to the
state signed by San Felipe de Austin delegate Luke Lesassier, this

convention urged, among other things, that "the patriotic statesmen" of the Coahuila Legislature confer more leagues of land for the support of public schools as well as to create a "fund for the future encouragement of the Primary schools, in Texas, in which will be taught the English and Castillian languages."[16]

The state of Coahuila and Texas contradicted its early Spanish-Only decree through other bills that provided for some degree of bilingual instruction. In legislation reorganizing the San Felipe de Austin town government, the state articulated an educational mission contrary to its Spanish-Only pronouncements by declaring that the town "shall promote the establishment of a school in the capital of the municipality, for the purpose of teaching English and Spanish languages."[17] No clear reason for or even acknowledgment of the contradiction with the earlier Spanish-Only policy was given. The previously cited land grant for Nacogdoches schools in 1833 insisting upon "Castillian" Spanish reflected only Spanish-surnamed individuals listed on petitions and support rolls for education in that township, making Spanish-Only uncontroversial. San Felipe de Austin, on the other hand, was in a much different linguistic situation.[18] In short, the Mexican government proved itself to be flexible on school languages to the point of open contradiction.

The tangled role of Stephen F. Austin's plans for education and how the legislatures and governors in Saltillo reacted to the language dilemma in Texas ultimately provokes more questions than answers. Perhaps the state only meant to insist upon Spanish-Only when it was subject to no real controversy? Or perhaps it was only through Austin's political influence that this accommodation to bilingual education was effected at all? The real importance of Mexican policy toward bilingual education was its telling lack of decisiveness. Austin's intriguing support for bilingual (indeed trilingual) education is important but strangely ignored by most historians. Neither Austin nor his contemporaries seem to have seriously reflected on their views regarding bilingual school policy. Perhaps this is because education in more than one language seemed not to be terribly significant to many in that time and context when education was so scarce.

It is important not to overstate the possibilities for some sort of rudimentary bilingual education in Texas during this early period. There were at least some in Austin's colony who did not share his enthusiasm for being a patriotic Mexican citizen or for learning the Spanish language. There were private schools for the children of Anglo settlers, the wealthier of whom traveled to the United States for formal education. Mexican official Juan Nepomuceno Almonte in his famous report to the national government on the deteriorating position of native Tejanos in relation to the Anglo newcomers wrote that what was needed was "a good establishment for public instruction where the Spanish language may be taught, otherwise the language will be lost." Almonte concluded, "Even at present English is almost the only language spoken in this section of Texas."[19]

However, the notion of a total, complete, and inevitable culture clash between Anglos and Mexicans of Texas on the issue of language is untenable. Frontier peoples of the American West in the eighteenth and nineteenth centuries spent their early years in daily contact with such diverse people as French Canadian trappers, Spanish officials, and numerous tribes of Native Americans, truly experiencing a multicultural life. Recent Austin biographer Gregg Cantrell argues against the interpretation that Austin was especially committed to spreading Hispanic culture among his Anglo Texan immigrants, though Cantrell curiously omits the topic of education. Whatever Austin's personal motives may have been, his efforts at assimilating his Anglo settlers into the mainstream of Mexican culture through some sort of bilingual instruction was never successful.[20]

The years of the Republic of Texas produced a partial reversal of Mexican policy on school languages: there was a new official language, but the same unofficial tolerance of another language. The official language changed to English after independence, but Spanish, in and out of the classroom, met with some initial tolerance. In 1837 President of the Republic of Texas Sam Houston signed an act to incorporate the municipalities of San Antonio, Victoria, and Gonzales, providing the towns legal authority to start up their own publicly financed schools. However, the following years were chaos as Mexico militarily occupied San Antonio twice. Therefore, apart from a brief, failed attempt in Galveston in 1847, no public schools were established during this period. Town incorporation charters offer illuminating glimpses into what was possible regarding language of instruction. An early San Antonio charter stipulated that civic administrative personnel were to be conversant in both English and Spanish and mentioned only that schools should teach English in some undefined manner. It left all supervisory power over the proposed schools with the bilingual municipal officials.[21]

President Houston's approval of some sort of mandatory English instruction did not lead to the setting up of a bureaucracy to oversee its implementation. Nor did Houston's endorsement clarify how English should be taught—as a foreign language, just English grammar, or as the primary, if not the only, means of communication inside the classroom? Requiring that English simply be taught did not actually prohibit the use of other languages in the still-hypothetical schools. The 1837 incorporation charter of Nacogdoches, which initially also applied to seventeen other towns across the state, made no mention of a specific language to be taught or not taught.[22] The subject of school language was left undefined for decades to come.

In the following years there were many tentative, futile attempts to establish a system of public schools in the newly independent nation. Mirabeau B. Lamar, the second president of the Republic of Texas, is credited with being the father of public education. In 1839 and 1840 he championed two bills that created a legal and financial superstructure for the local creation of public schools. The first act reserved roughly thirteen thousand acres of land in each county for the public schools. The next legislative action spurred the passage of administrative rules granting each county the option of starting up public schools. Local county judges and their deputies were the administrators. This first school system of Texas made no provision for the language of instruction. The only stipulation mentioning language at all was the instruction to the county judges to select teachers possessing "good moral character and capacity to teach reading, writing, English grammar, arithmetic, and geography."[23] This vague directive might imply English-Only instruction; it could also be interpreted as not prohibiting Spanish instruction, for example, as long as "English grammar" was taught in some manner. Ironically, this stipulation resembled the vague dicta by previous Mexican state officials who requested that Spanish be taught but refused to indicate definitively how or in what context. No law in the Mexico or Republic of Texas years (1821–45) actually prohibited bilingual instruction. Even when the laws remarked upon the subject, they either directly favored classroom bilingualism or indirectly allowed it to exist if the local citizens so desired.

As the public school system evolved from a mere possibility to something resembling a reality, the issue of the language of instruction remained only a minor, ambiguous detail. In some instances it was worthy of direct mention in state legislation but only peripherally. The Lamar education acts, while providing the blueprint for education in Texas, did not result in the creation of many permanent schools. In essence, the reform was simply enabling legislation allowing counties to form public schools where and when they could get around to it. Many rural counties without towns large enough to have educational systems of their own simply went without schools. For example, Caldwell County was organized in 1848, almost a decade after Lamar's school laws, but it did not establish public schools until 1854 when

their establishment became mandatory.[24] In its fifteen years of operation, only forty-one counties had even completed the preliminary land
survey (the only thing they needed to do) necessary to receive public
education funds under the Lamar education acts. Education was still
viewed primarily as a home function or one of private and religious
involvement—not a proper concern of state or local government. As
historian Frederick Eby wrote in 1925 of nineteenth-century Texas attitudes pertaining to education, "'Free Schools' and compulsory attendance as we have them to-day, controlled in every particular by the
government, appeared an intolerable tyranny."[25] Given this condition,
it is reasonable for the state not to have restricted instruction only to
English when there were so few public schools in the first place and
when its regulatory presence in educational matters was nonexistent.

The school law of 1854 increased the state's burden of financing a
still largely fictional public school system and designated a statewide
supervisory role for the state treasurer, who would serve as superintendent of the common schools. This new law made no provision,
or even mention, of school language. In 1856 the legislature tried to
clarify the language muddle when it specified that English must be
included in the school curriculum of every public school and that "no
school shall be entitled to the benefits of this act unless the English language is taught therein." The new act fell short of strictly prohibiting
bilingualism in the classroom in that it failed to define the type of English to be taught. This statute allowed another language spoken or
used in the teaching of English, like teaching English as an academic
foreign language in the way Latin, Greek, or German, was taught. Also,
private schools such as the short-lived University of San Augustine, a
Presbyterian school taught in French, were completely unregulated as
to language or curriculum.[26]

The 1856 school bill did not satisfactorily address the language issue
to lawmakers, who fashioned a more specific amendment to the English requirement in February of 1858. The new 1858 requirement
stipulated: "No School shall be entitled to the benefits of this act, unless
the English language is principally taught therein."[27] Although more
specific than previous requirements, it still obscured as much as it clarified. Could "principally taught therein" disqualify all other languages?
Was there a limit to the way other languages could be taught, either
formally or informally? Ironically, language policy up to this point remained more muddled than it was before Texas independence. The
Spanish-Only regulations of the Mexican era that at times specifically
mentioned the use of both languages were clearer (though still contradictory) than any Texas policy of the three decades that followed.

After the dark, empty period of Texas education during the Civil War, the state began to assert itself more vigorously in the realm of language and vernacular education in its patchwork school system. Though it was spared the wartime destruction of other portions of the Confederacy, public education in Texas was nevertheless devastated by the state's sizable financial obligations to the Confederate cause. In 1866 the state legislature passed a new school law that made minor revisions in the 1854 bill and addressed the language issue. This new law reiterated the terse phrase "unless the English language is principally taught therein." The 1866 regulations, however, had no impact, because the federal government soon nullified the state's constitution as Reconstruction temporarily shifted power to the United States Congress.[28]

During the brief period of Republican Reconstruction, the state's traditional indecision and lack of specificity on the language question was finally resolved. Texas chose bilingualism. The Reconstruction school law of 1871, while not requiring that English be the "principal" language taught in the school, nevertheless reflected the prior concern that the schools should teach English. This 1871 law, a creation of Texas Republicans, allowed for the examination of teachers by a superintendent of public instruction appointed by the governor, compulsory attendance, a local property tax to finance public schools, and allowed the state superintendent discretion to determine the content of curriculum. The first Texas superintendent of public instruction was Jacob C. De Gress, a German immigrant who took office in May of 1871. De Gress indicated how his administration started from scratch: "No records of educational work of the past existed. No approximate estimate even, could be made of the number of children to be provided for." Under De Gress's administration the issue of bilingual classroom instruction came to figure prominently in Texas education for the first time since the era of Mexican rule. Superintendent De Gress and the State Board of Education determined in rule seven of the new state education codes that "Teachers shall be permitted to teach the German, French and Spanish languages in the Public Schools of this State, provided the time so occupied shall not exceed two hours each day."[29]

This was potentially a revolutionary development in the history of languages in Texas education![30] De Gress went further than just recounting this new rule; he also stated why the State of Texas was, for the first time, explicitly sanctioning a limited amount of bilingualism in the classroom. He stated that a bilingual climate was essential for the growth and support of the public schools. This was due to "the large proportion of citizens of German and Spanish birth and descent

Jacob C. De Gress administered the state's brief sanction of bilingual education during the Reconstruction period mostly for German- and Spanish-speaking children. He viewed classroom bilingualism as a positive agent of "Americanization." Photo courtesy of University of Texas Barker Texas History Center, Austin Texas, No. ITC-75-1230.

in our State." De Gress indicated, "This clause has met with much favor throughout the State, as it brings children of scholastic age of foreign birth or descent into the public schools." Superintendent De Gress viewed the private schools that frequently taught in a foreign language as a threat to public education. He charged that these schools "partake of a character, in which other tongues, besides that of English, is [*sic*] considered an important acquisition, and the studies pursued tend to place the language, customs and associations of that particular class in a prominence that could not possibly be tolerated in the free public schools."[31]

Caution should be maintained with interpretations holding the Reconstruction era a golden age for bilingual education in Texas. First, a precise limit of two hours was placed on foreign languages in the classroom. Second, it is not clear that the language provision meant for those languages to be taught as mere subjects or, more significantly, as a medium of instruction. Could two hours of German or Spanish be stretched over a six- or seven-hour school day as the medium of directions and general conversation while the rest of the day was spent in an all-English environment of written English grammar exercises, oral recitations, and silent reading? Or would the medium of instruction not count toward the two-hour limit? De Gress, though more specific on such matters than anyone up to that point in Texas history, perhaps intentionally never fully explained this.

De Gress did leave clues as to what he meant, however. One comment indicates that he may have meant for the non-English languages to be used in true bilingual instruction, not simply as academic subjects: "full instructions have been issued to secure the employment of the required German or Spanish teachers, and in the next scholastic term many schools *of this character* will be opened." But there were potential problems with the new language rules. De Gress at one point confided, "Great difficulty is experienced in finding teachers fully conversant with these languages, and at the same time up to the required standard in the other branches . . . or they are deficient in the knowledge of English."[32] Hiring teachers not completely proficient in English was apparently an obnoxious option but an option nonetheless. This brief experiment of allowing non-English languages a prominent role in the education of young Texans in the nineteenth century illustrates the important role that such languages played early in Texas' public school system. Bilingual classrooms were never strictly illegal; during Reconstruction they were even encouraged.

One final point to consider on school language policy during Reconstruction was the determination of the kind of English to be taught. Teaching English had been unspecified since President Sam Houston signed a town charter for San Antonio in 1837. The Republican Reconstruction regulation on this matter stipulated that no one could teach without state certification (doled out by local officials) attesting their ability to teach "reading in English" and "English grammar" with the exception that "nothing in this act shall be so construed as to prohibit instruction in the German, French, Spanish, or any other language." De Gress and his allies at the State Board of Education inferred that non-English communication in the classroom, whether utilized as a course subject or as the medium of conversation, was permissible.[33] This formal approval of bilingual education was short-lived, however.

Because of the politics of race and Reconstruction, the Republican school law of 1871 and its two-hour bilingual limit was summarily vanquished by vengeful Democrats with a new constitution in 1875 and with new legislation in 1875 and 1876. Democratic legislators gave De Gress his walking papers and abolished the state superintendency.[34] These Redeemer Democrats also abolished the approval of limited bilingualism in the classroom. But even though the Reconstruction approval of bilingual education was revoked, English-Only policy was not substituted in its place. The local county judges now had absolute authority in education. So even had there been a strong English-Only policy from what little was left of the educational bureaucracy or from the legislature, its enforcement ultimately depended upon the local county officials who may have felt political pressures from their constituents to maintain bilingual classroom instruction. Such local determinism was not a new phenomenon. The visionary Republican school laws also were largely dependent upon local enforcement.[35]

The anti-Reconstruction reaction was quick. In 1874 a new Democratic legislature, flush with excitement after having spent the years during Reconstruction out of power and having just vanquished Republican Governor Edmund J. Davis, began the process of scrapping the existing new system. Concerning language, only "English composition" was added to the preexisting requirements of "reading in English" and "English grammar." In 1876 upon creating a completely new educational infrastructure, the legislature was conspicuously silent regarding school languages, but it did require the same English mandates from 1874 in the teacher examination section.[36] Finally in 1879 the state designated English, and only English, the official medium of communication. However, it did so not as an instructional mandate but from the perspective of teacher examinations: "The examination must be conducted in the English language, and no applicant shall receive a certificate unless the board of examiners be satisfied that he or she is competent to teach . . . in the English language." This specification of exactly how and to what degree English was to be used, even if only for teacher examinations, was a harbinger of similar things to come for those practicing bilingual education in Texas.[37] By 1884 the state openly attacked the bilingual tradition.

By the 1880s the first negative statements by the state regarding the bilingual tradition were published, soon followed by the first English-Only requirements regarding school conduct. The outlook was not all negative, however. By fighting the battle against Republican centralization in the name of Democratic localism, Reconstruction-loathing Democrats unintentionally served the wishes of the state's ethnic communities who desired absolute control to ensure a dizzying array of individual bilingual practices. The explicit desire for local control and the still-vague desire for all-English instruction conflicted; consequently, the confused, informal, bilingual tradition of Texas continued. One scholar has noted that the eradication of the Reconstruction-era protections of bilingual education ended up actually expanding the bilingual tradition of Texas. The resulting irony was that even more bilingual instruction now occurred than it had with the pro-bilingual education policies under the Reconstruction-era, De Gress rules.[38]

The historical record of laws and regulations in Texas regarding languages in the classroom illustrates a few important ideas. First, the nineteenth-century tradition of bilingual education in Texas was legally obscure. Bilingual instruction was at different times allowed, disallowed, and just ignored. Second, because of the legal and administrative lack of concern for the role of non-English languages, the bilingual tradition in Texas was informal. Finally, bilingual instruction

was seen as a beneficial, if not essential, means of drawing children into the dominant society, whether it was through the Spanish language in the Mexican period or the English language in Texas' republic and statehood years. A thorough examination of the nineteenth-century tradition of bilingual instruction in Texas entails more than just legal possibilities and administrative directives. Nevertheless, such legal and policy analysis remains a crucial component of the bilingual tradition's reality. The next chapter will examine the daily practice of bilingual instruction at the local level in the public and private schools of several different ethnic groups spread over dozens of Texas counties between 1850 and 1900.

Tejanos, Germans, and Czechs in the Making of the Bilingual Tradition, 1850–1900

24   Ethnic communities loom large in the bilingual tradition of Texas. Citizens of Mexican, German, and Czech heritage chose to use their own native language in the schools at times exclusively while at other times in combination with English.[1] Local circumstance affected decisions on how language was to be used in the education of ethnic children. These schools could be private and secular, private and parochial, or public. Other factors were the particular community's size, political strength, and geographic location. While the laws and policies on bilingual instruction from the last chapter are important to the story of bilingual education in Texas, so to are the ethnic communities themselves. This chapter will examine the mostly unpublished reports of the Texas county judges and school superintendents who remarked upon local educational conditions. The unedited reports are generally handwritten and unusually personal about the daily difficulties schools faced, including problems posed by language. These reports offer an illuminating and heretofore unknown glimpse into the Texas bilingual tradition.

One of the most significant non-English-speaking groups in Texas education during the nineteenth century was Mexican Americans. The rate of growth for the Mexican American population from Texas Independence through the 1880s lagged behind that of Anglos, African Americans, and European immigrants. Nevertheless, these Tejanos represented either a dominant majority or a significant minority of the population in a number of counties in South Texas from the United States–Mexico border to San Antonio and along the Rio Grande to New Mexico. Also, at the turn of the century a mass migration of Mexicans arrived in the state, more than tripling the 1887 population of 83,000 to an estimated 300,000 native-born Tejanos and Mexican immigrants by 1910.[2] Public schooling for Mexican Americans, especially in sparsely populated areas, was not an especially pressing problem for statewide policymakers of the nineteenth century, although this was not for a lack of input from local leaders. One result of the isolated

and impoverished public schools for native-born Tejanos and newly immigrated Mexicans throughout this period often was that private education became a significant factor in the Texas bilingual tradition.[3] So before examining the bilingual tradition for Spanish speakers in the public schools, an investigation of the private schools, parochial and nonparochial, is necessary.

There were several parochial schools of long-standing success in the city of Brownsville and the surrounding countryside in Cameron County. They offered a truly bilingual and binational education in that a significant portion of the student body came from Matamoros, the corresponding city across the Rio Grande in Mexico. There were three Catholic schools in Brownsville during the 1890s, two for boys and one for girls. Public school officials viewed the Catholic institutions with animosity. Principal J. T. Cummings of the Brownsville public schools reported of the 1892–93 school year, "The Catholic clergy work systematically against us," because they allegedly resorted to "threats in endeavoring to keep the Catholic parents from patronizing us." One Catholic school was founded in the 1850s by nuns from France; upon their arrival to Texas the nuns were taught both English and Spanish in crash courses arranged for them in Galveston by the diocese.[4] Significant Protestant educational efforts also existed in Brownsville. Of two Presbyterian schools certified by both national and southern church associations, one indicated that the medium of instruction was Spanish while English was taught separately as an academic course, a modern-sounding practice.[5]

Bilingual instruction in parochial schools also flourished in other border towns for Mexican and Mexican American students. El Paso maintained three Catholic schools: two for Mexicano students and native Tejanos, and the other for Anglos. They accommodated the language needs of their students with mostly Spanish instruction; English was taught as an academic course, like a foreign language. These schools consistently enrolled hundreds of students in the 1890s and 1900s.[6] In Laredo the Holding Institute, a Methodist school consistently enrolling nearly 200 students, began advertising in the 1880s its openness to different methods of teaching English to Spanish speakers. This involved the hiring of Tejanos or Mexican immigrants as teachers. Catholic schools in Laredo were described in great detail by F. A. Parker, superintendent of the Laredo schools, who offered a reason for their popularity: "by giving them books and clothing and also free board and lodging, [the Catholic schools] offer far greater attachment than the public schools and are loyally attended."[7]

Large cities like San Antonio maintained several private schools catering to Tejanos. One of the most important Catholic schools in San Antonio was founded in 1851. The clientele of the Ursuline Convent of Saint Mary's, an average of 150 students by 1900, consisted mostly of the daughters of the Tejano upper class. Later a boy's school was introduced. One nun described the Ursuline Academy's curriculum as well as its content. The first and second groupings of students were supervised by the nuns but taught by a Spanish-speaking aide. The nun claimed, "The M.[Mexican] Assistant hears 1, & 2, classes. I have 3d class. The Mexicans learn the Spanish grammar, & some learn English lessons . . . My hours are, from 9 3/4, to 11 1/4, English class from 2 to 2 1/2 same class say French lessons. From 2 1/2, to 4 1/2, Mexicans who know English pretty well, read & say lessons, arithmetic." Even though this nun did not feel comfortable with her own ability to instruct in Spanish to Spanish speakers, she expressed no hesitancy about the principle of Spanish instruction for those who did not know English. Her description of the daily curriculum also indicates that instruction in Spanish was not only a positive thing in itself; it was also a useful bridge to mainstream successful students into her regular English and French classes. Historian Arnoldo De León records bilingual instruction in English and Spanish from the Sisters of Divine Providence at the Our Lady of Guadalupe School in Houston by 1915.[8]

There were also a number of private, nonsectarian schools. One of these schools, financed privately by the Mexican American community of Jim Hogg County, utilized solely Spanish instruction. Called Colegio Altamirano, this institution began in the 1890s and lasted until the 1930s. Historian and writer Jovita Gonzalez noted that many of the private, nonsectarian schools were called *escuelitas* (little schools) and were created by Mexican Americans frustrated with the public schools at the turn of the century. They sometimes completely ignored English instruction.[9] Examples of completely non-English schooling signify a type of cultural resistance to the growing dominance of Anglo culture.

Often these private, nonsectarian schools grew out of Mexican American cultural, political, and social organizations. As the web of labor control tightened, culminating in greater levels of social isolation and physical segregation, Mexican Americans in the 1890s and 1900s formed organizations called *mutualistas* (working class organizations offering reaffirmation of a Mexicanist identity) that provided insurance, charity, and a public forum for cultural enlightenment. Historian Emilio Zamora has found that in some instances, *escuelitas* admitted free of charge the children of the Mexican American community whose parents were unable to afford the meager tuition. Spanish instruction

was often provided by young, educated women recruited from Mexico. *Escuelitas* formed in response to exploitive economic conditions and to exclusionary and racist practices of those public schools run for and by Anglos; they were organized in large cities and small towns throughout the state. The *escuelitas* generated bitter laments from bewildered public school officials. Superintendent Parker of Laredo complained to the state about Tejano patronage of *escuelitas* as well as the language of the classroom: "many hundreds attend small schools where they are taught in the Mexican, or Spanish language." Parker argued that these *escuelitas* defeated his own schools in the battle over Mexican American patronage because their tuition, he estimated, cost only "34 cents per month." He believed that there were roughly forty of these schools in his Webb County.[10] Private schools fed the bilingual tradition and enabled it to flourish against the will of hostile public officials.

The most fascinating element to the Texas bilingual tradition of schooling, however, is the degree to which it was manifested in the public schools. In fact, public monies in Texas supported bilingual education for Tejanos from the advent of the public school system until the nativist hysteria of World War I.

It appears that Cameron County, home to the city of Brownsville, was active in supporting bilingual public schools. Shortly before Brownsville Superintendent J. T. Cummings complained about the attractiveness of the parochial schools in the 1890s, County Judge Benjamin Baker reported to the state that his schools dealt with the language issue in an accommodating manner. He valued education— even in Spanish—when many of his contemporaries did not share this open-mindedness. Baker excused the poor literacy numbers in his 1884–85 annual report by stating, "There are a larger number of pupils within this County who can read, than the number given in this report but can read only in the Spanish language. This County being populated by people of Mexican origin with but few exceptions their native language is most commonly used."[11]

In neighboring Hidalgo County, Judge J. M. De la Viña explained in his 1897–98 report that although the public schools in his county had not been patronized in previous years, they recently experienced a turnaround: "We are now gradually overcoming this prejudice by employing teachers who are thoroughly familiar with the people, and I impress it upon the teachers that not only the children but the parents must be instructed—if not in the language—in the laws of the country as far as possible, and the more intelligent Mexicans are realizing the necessity of English education for the rising generation."[12]

The public schools in West Texas around the city of El Paso not only competed with prominent and established Catholic parochial schools, but they also operated next to New Mexico, whose state constitution went so far as to guarantee language rights by protecting a limited and transitional type of bilingual education for its public schools. Also, in other parts of the American Southwest, the Treaty of Guadalupe Hidalgo's promise of respect for Mexican culture through full citizenship applied (theoretically) to bilingual instruction. As might be expected with this proximity to the proactively bilingual New Mexico, the reasons given for bilingual instruction in El Paso were the most pedagogically sophisticated of any example. In 1893–94 Principal G. W. Huffman of the schools in Ysleta (a small town outside El Paso) offered quite specific instructions to the state regarding how English and Spanish should be used to cater to a Mexican and Mexican American population. In order to best impart English, he reasoned, the schools "should use readers, first, second and third [grade level] of Spanish and English translated. This we do not have hence the teachers must supply the want by using both languages which consumes an immense amount of time."[13]

In Huffman's 1897–98 report on the El Paso schools he remarked that six-sevenths of the scholastic population (scholastics) in El Paso County were Mexicano or Tejano, and that dire poverty kept many potential pupils away. Apparently, many families could not afford to purchase books or school supplies. Huffman wrote, "In such schools teachers must be able to speak and read the Spanish language." The real difficulty, he noted, was that such teachers meeting this necessary qualification could not always pass an English examination (conducted by countywide committees appointed by the county judges). Those able to pass the English section of the state teacher certification exam were not always employable due to a deficiency in Spanish, the primary language utilized in his schools.[14]

The counties along the Rio Grande between the more settled areas near the coast and the urban area of El Paso maintained a high proportion of scholars that were Mexican and Tejano as well as strong economic and cultural ties to Mexico. The use of Spanish in the classroom was deemed essential to securing the patronage of these families and ultimately to the acquisition of English, then equated with the requisite degree of "Americanization." In his 1882–83 school report to the state, Judge L. A. G. Navarro of Zapata County wrote of the dilemma of language: "The entire population of this county are Mexican and [it] is very hard for teachers to teach the English language and make rapid progress and [it] is very hard to get teachers that speak the language in Spanish and English . . . those we have [are] the best we can do."[15]

Instruction "in Spanish and English" remained Zapata County's most prominent pedagogical innovation.

These bilingual policies of the public schools in Zapata County were continued well into the next decade. In his 1897–98 report, Judge A. P. Spohn touted his efforts to impress upon Mexican American parents the "importance of their children receiving an English education" while noting that the language obstacle, to his way of thinking, "makes it a necessity to employ teachers familiar with the Spanish language as otherwise their difficulties would be almost insurmountable."[16] Even in the twentieth century, Judge Spohn, while moving toward a more all-English instructional system in order to comply with state law, acknowledged the "prejudice" or resistance from parents who "preferred having their children educated as far as possible in Spanish."[17]

Farther up the Rio Grande other counties had much more difficulty in reconciling the two languages and did not record success in the matter. Val Verde County Judge W. K. Jones, an opponent of bilingual schools, noted that prior to the 1893–94 academic year his county employed for his Spanish-speaking students "teachers who conversed with them in Spanish," a policy he proudly announced that he had ended upon his accession to office that year. Instead, he oversaw the hiring of teachers with two central qualifications: First, they had to be well versed in English; second, they had to be entirely ignorant of the Spanish language. Home to Del Rio, a large town on the border, Val Verde County struggled with bilingualism in its schools.[18] The bilingual tradition was neither complete nor neat; it was a muddled, shifting, and at times volatile phenomenon that could be snuffed out when the political winds changed course.

One basic rule remained constant, however. Those schools choosing to educate Spanish speakers in an English-Only manner paid the price of losing Tejano patronage. Maverick County Judge J. A. Bonnet, writing from Eagle Pass in the late 1890s, complained that his schools were not advancing the Americanization of Tejano children, because it was difficult to obtain enough attendance to justify keeping the schools open. Maverick County schools were not bilingual. Mexicanos and Tejanos preferred private schools of a secular or parochial nature, or schools in Mexico that practiced totally Spanish instruction.[19]

Nueces County on the Gulf Coast southeast of San Antonio dealt with a mostly Anglo population in the port city of Corpus Christi and a predominantly Tejano population in the rural areas outside of town, which eventually came to include a separate Duval County in the far western section. From the earliest days of its public education, Nueces County listed the language difficulty of its Mexican American students as both a glaring obstacle and a glittering innovation.[20] County Judge Joseph Fitz Simmons indicated in his 1888–89 report that his county schools utilized bilingual schooling: "the majority of the Scholars being of Mexican extraction outside of the city of Corpus Christi requires that the teacher speak the Spanish language—the children, however, are rapidly acquiring a taste for our language and are being gradually evoluted [*sic*] to american ideas."[21] The idea of Americanization was not viewed as incompatible with the use of Spanish in the classroom, a cultural tolerance many in the twentieth century found difficult to fathom.

In 1889–90 Fitz Simmons claimed of Mexican American scholastics, "they are fast acquiring a knowledge of the English Language and American ideas and customs, and by the employment of competent teachers, understanding and speaking their vernacular Spanish language, gives a strong probability that the population of these frontier counties will soon become good American citizens fully understanding of their rights and duties as such." This bilingual tradition in Nueces County was publicized in the state's biennial statistical report for 1887–88: "Three-fourths of the scholastic population west of the city of Corpus Christi being of Texas-Mexican origin, and speaking or using the English language in a very few localities, necessitates the employment of teachers having a knowledge of both the English and Spanish languages."[22]

Duval County, in between Corpus Christi and Laredo, was unconcerned enough about potential illegality that they advertised the bilingual teaching philosophy of their public schools in a published state report. In the 1879–80 publication Duval County Judge James O. Luby listed as problems for the public schools "the sly digs of the clergy," hostility to the English language, and the lack of a statewide compulsory attendance law, which reduced the ability of the schools to fulfill their Americanizing potential. How did Duval County schools seek to Americanize Tejano children? Luby answered bluntly: "The children are instructed in English and in Spanish and those that have attended have made rapid progress."[23] For Luby, as for many others of his time, the concept of Americanization did not disqualify the use of native languages in most facets of daily life, including education. This vague nineteenth-century tolerance, or perhaps reticence about intruding into the personal sphere of language choice, faded after the turn of the century.

One of the few instances of academic scholarship on a part of this bilingual tradition in the Texas public schools is found in Arnoldo De Leon's groundbreaking study *The Tejano Community*. De Leon discov-

In South Texas areas like Duval County that were populated primarily by Tejanos, small, one-teacher, ranch schools utilized bilingual instruction. The Hinojoseña School pictured here in 1906 was located seven miles outside the town of San Diego, Texas. Photo courtesy of the Institute of Texan Cultures at University of Texas at San Antonio, No. 96-198.

ered that the extensive countywide schools in rural and isolated counties of South Texas (like those of Duval County in the late nineteenth century) took special pains to meet the linguistic needs of their Tejano community. These schools, in addition to using Spanish in the classroom, also utilized bilingualism outside the classroom in recitations, competitions, and theater productions for the town of San Diego (the county seat) and the outlying ranches of Duval County. These public events served to establish for the school a firm connection to the larger community and local cultural life. In the 1880s the lead teacher and director of public schools in San Diego was Luis Puebla, a former Mexican college professor educated in Washington, D.C., in the subjects of ancient and modern languages and mathematics. The bilingual tradition in Duval County endured. The Tejano ranch-life memoirs of Andrés Sáenz contain an account of a school recital of Spanish and English songs for the ranching community in Duval County as late as 1920.[24]

The bilingual tradition of schooling in Texas would be significant enough if it were simply a Mexican American phenomenon. However,

The Concepción School of Duval County, another one-teacher ranch school, was founded around 1870 on land donated by the Leal, Garcia, and Palacios families. This picture was taken at the turn of the century. Photo courtesy of the Institute of Texan Cultures at University of Texas at San Antonio, No. 96-236.

European immigrants, the most important of whom were the Germans, also participated. German immigrants came in large numbers to Texas while it was still an independent republic and continued to emigrate through the early years of the twentieth century. Accounting for roughly one-half of all European immigration to Texas in the nineteenth century, German Americans were found in significant numbers in the state's large cities like San Antonio, Houston, and Galveston. German American settlement was also rural, though, concentrated in the lush, cotton-growing counties of South Coastal Texas (Austin, Colorado, De Witt, Guadalupe, Washington, and Fayette) as well as the dry, broken, rocky hills of Central Texas ranch counties (Gillespie, Kendall, Medina, and Comal). German American immigration continued into the first decade and a half of the next century; their peak numerical, political, and cultural influence was in the 1880s—the high point of the bilingual tradition in Texas.[25]

Whereas Mexican American participation in the bilingual tradition was evenly divided between public and private schools, German American participation seems to have been mostly through the public schools, including early institutes operating as quasi-public schools before the advent of the state's system of public education. In the 1850s the German American community of Austin deplored the lack of public education and established there one of the first successful free schools in the state. In 1857 Austin's *State Gazette* editorialized that in "doing for themselves what the town ought to do for the children of the whole population," the Germans were going far to "elevate the minds of their offspring, and make them intelligent and useful American citizens." The *State Gazette* condemned the "jaundiced opposition" to the German school from the Texas Know-Nothing Party. Opposition may have been aroused by the fact that this school was to make use of three languages; it was to be "a public school in which the English, German and Spanish languages will be taught."[26] The proportion of non-English languages in the daily curriculum was never indicated directly, but the fact that it focused on German students and aroused nativist fears suggests that German and Spanish were not pursued simply as dry, academic studies. The school's charter from the state legislature was approved in 1858 without any mention of curricular content or language stipulation. This illustrates the tacit sanction that the state gave to localities and ethnic groups interested in multilingual education as well as the prominent place of the German language in the early stages of public education in Texas. A year later the *State Gazette* trumpeted the free education of the sixty or so initial students, claiming that it exemplified true vision.[27]

German Americans had older schools elsewhere. In the Hill Country region, Germans in the town of Fredericksburg attempted early to establish their own free, publicly financed school. In 1852 they levied municipal taxes for the purposes of funding such a school, but the state courts—in true antebellum, Democratic fashion—declared the novel method of using local taxation to fund public schools unconstitutional.[28] The German Americans of New Braunfels were not daunted by the setback and lobbied for a special charter from the state legislature to allow them to "levy and collect a special tax" for their schools. A twenty-year charter was finally granted in 1858, and the school was named the New Braunfels Academy. Eventually, the academy was transformed into a public school. Up to 1892 the minutes of the school's board of directors were kept in German and translated into English. German was not just reserved for board meetings. Study of the German language was mandatory for all students. In his annual accounting to the state for the 1886–87 school year, H. E. Fischer, the president of the New Braunfels Board of Trustees, dutifully reported of his school that "in addition to the English elementary branches, the German is taught."[29]

In the town of New Braunfels, a group of educators formed an organization in 1872 that met periodically to sharpen their theoretical and practical understanding of teaching methods. This teachers' institute (a form of continuing education on teaching methods and techniques) discussed the *"praxis"* (practice) of their profession in German and made available copies of their discussions in both English and German. In a small, rural Comal County school in 1868, two teachers taught a group of German Americans. One teacher, Lizzie Crawford, taught in English for two and one-half days while Clemens Conrad, Sr., the other instructor, taught in German the week's remaining two and one-half days.[30]

German bilingual schools existed in the southeastern coastal plains as well. Scholar Elvie Luetge has concisely captured what went on inside the German-English classroom. Shortly after the Civil War, a largely rural, German-speaking population in Austin County attended a common school partially dependent upon state funds. This school in the small town of Shelby was staffed by a German teacher whose method for teaching English was unique: "English instruction involved translating the reading selections into German and keeping a notebook of the English words which were not understood." English, in other words, was taught as an academic course, like a foreign language. By the 1880s the public schools of Shelby still continued to make heavy use of German; they taught it as a course and still used it as a medium of instruction alongside English.[31] In published education reports, the town of Bellville in Austin County was quite direct in describing how German was used in their schools that, by 1887–88, maintained an impressive eight grades: "German is taught in all the grades. Though instruction in the language is optional, 55 percent of the pupils pursued this study. The work of the teachers is materially increased by the addition of German to the ordinary course, but the interest manifested by the pupils in this study demands its continuance."[32]

School officials in Victoria County, home to the city of Victoria, had difficulty in administering ethnic schools with public money. Victoria County's multiethnic population rendered the English-Only wishes of County Judge J. L. Dupree quite impossible to achieve. In his 1893–94 report, Judge Dupree, after blasting the infusion of religion into the public schools, conceded, "I find much difficulty in keeping the German and Mexican language from being taught in the public free schools and now suggest that the law be amended so as that only the English language be taught."[33] Judge Dupree failed to carry out his stated English-Only plans the next school year as well. Curiously, his reports of 1894–95 only single out German as the problem, omitting his previous mention of Spanish speakers. An exasperated Dupree wrote,

"The law should be changed as to permit the German being taught in the schools or absolutely prohibited as it gives much trouble in this county."[34]

Although the bilingual instruction for German American children inflamed opposition in many places, it elicited timid public support from those who admitted to practicing it or those who wanted to practice it without saying so. In 1894–95 Judge J. T. Estill of Gillespie County containing the town of Fredericksburg, wrote that language was a huge issue in his school, "there is not one child of English-speaking parentage, and while the children can learn to read and write English, it is difficult to speak it fluently—But in all the schools English is the language used in teaching and the teacher forbid[s] the children to speak the German language on the school grounds while at play." Although this statement may infer that Gillespie County attempted an early, strict English-Only curriculum, Judge Estill later conceded, "German is taught, but only in a small way, like any other foreign language, and strictly as the law dictates." There was a place for German in Gillespie County, but not at the expense of English-language instruction. Other school systems also admitted to teaching German in a vague, unspecified manner, almost as if they did not want to indicate how it was taught.[35]

The first assumption that modern readers might make of the bilingual tradition in Texas public schools is that people then were fully aware of what they were doing in terms of the law. The bilingual tradition in Texas was an often informal and muddled phenomenon, partly because of the lack of trained, professional teachers and administrators. Most of the superintendents of public schools in nineteenth-century Texas were county judges (de facto administrators in the absence of the money or will to appoint a full-time county administrator) and amateurs in the field of education with little understanding of state regulations. Even the professionals were often in the dark as to the legality of their actions. Superintendent Charles H. Schroeder of the La Grange schools in heavily German and Czech Fayette County wrote this question to State Superintendent J. S. Kendall in his 1899–1900 report: "We have one teacher—Miss Mina Stiehl—who has no certificate and teaches German. She has a room in the school building. No extra tuition is charged for German and she is paid like the other teachers. Is it against the law for her to teach thus?" Schroeder's concern was typical of educational leaders of that day who attempted to bridge the gap between proper school regulation and the needs of their community.[36]

Readers today might also assume in regard to the nineteenth-century bilingual tradition that different Texas ethnic groups sympathized with one another and formed interethnic coalitions in light of similar language obstacles. Relations between the German American and Mexican American communities were open to as much hostility as relations between them both and the Anglo community, despite the fact that both groups chose to bridge the language issue through the use of native languages in the classroom. A 1902–1903 report from Superintendent W. T. Nobbitt of the Kerrville schools in heavily German Kerr County showed little sympathy with the educational plight of Mexican Americans: "The Mexican school is run in connection with the regular white school, but is taught in a separate building, and . . . is not very well graded." Although Mexican Americans in Kerrville schools were segregated in 1902–1903 and offered less educational benefits than were the German American children of that town, they were still classified as white in the "white school."[37] Even this meaningless whiteness disappeared after a few years. Superintendent Horace Morelock in his 1906–1907 report stated, "Our Mexicans are taught in a separate building. This school, also the colored, is not on a graded basis."[38] The Texas bilingual tradition was multicultural in the sense that it involved a diverse group of people and languages, not in that it was based on wide tolerance and sympathy on the part of the dominant culture toward the ethnic language minorities, or among the different ethnic groups themselves.

But interethnic antipathy, like the bilingual tradition, also cannot be assumed in every situation. Not all German bilingual instruction occurred in the public schools, and not all German education was hostile to Mexican Americans or Spanish. In San Antonio, for example, a bilingual private and nonsectarian school succeeded for decades as one of the state's leading educational institutions. The German-English School of San Antonio was founded in 1858, and its charter stipulated, "The German and the English language would have equal status, and instruction in all other subjects would be distributed as evenly between them as was practicable." Rote, mechanical teaching methods were disallowed. For the mostly German population that attended, the school showed remarkable flexibility in its bilingual program. After some initial experimentation, they discovered that not all students excelled in mastering a bilingual environment at the same rate. Consequently, they used these observations to form rather sophisticated pedagogical methods in which language instruction (English and German) regularly constituted one-half to two-thirds of the total academic curriculum in all grade levels. The school mixed the non-German, English-speaking students into classes with the German speakers. It was hoped that in "Learning both languages, the pupils would not be divided by

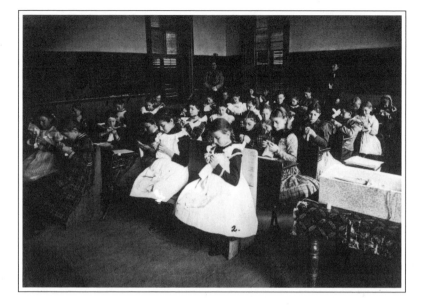

The German-English school in San Antonio was enthusiastically bilingual as well as one of the state's most prestigious educational institutions during the late nineteenth century. In this sewing class are Helena Guenther and Regina Beckmann. Photo courtesy of the Institute of Texan Cultures at University of Texas at San Antonio, No. 71-48.

arguments over nationality." It was found that non-German children picked up German rapidly in their new environment while the school still succeeded in teaching the German speakers English; it was what is called today dual-language bilingual education. After the Civil War, when it was one of the only educational institutions in San Antonio, the German-English School even succeeded in implementing a third language, Spanish, into its core curriculum.[39] This school continued until the 1890s; its decline coincided with the rise of the public schools. By the turn of the century it was shut down, and the city of San Antonio turned the building into a public school.[40]

Polish Americans in Texas, as in other parts of the United States, also sought native language instruction. In the southeastern coastal area of Texas in Karnes County, the town of Panna Maria—recognized as the oldest Polish settlement in the United States—believed that maintenance of the Polish language and Catholicism were inseparable. The Polish language was taught, and English was relegated to a lesser status in the first successful school organized in Panna Maria during the 1860s, a Catholic parochial school whose main purpose was to preserve Polish culture, religiosity, and language.[41] As late as the 1920s

St. Joseph's School existed in the small town of Panna Maria, an island of Polish immigration and culture in Karnes County. The Catholic school's stress on Polish language and culture drew the ire of statewide education officials by the 1920s. Photo courtesy of Panna Maria Museum, Panna Maria, Texas, No. ITC-72-165.

the state's education agency regarded the Polish Americans in this town a distinct educational problem due to their low attendance in the English-Only public schools and their high participation in the bilingual parochial school. In his 1896–97 report, Washington County Judge E. P. Curry wrote that unlike the Germans, the Polish community in his county failed to patronize the public schools.[42]

Whereas Polish settlers were primarily interested in maintaining Polish culture, the following example of Dutch schooling illustrates the polar opposite: rapid linguistic assimilation. Dutch settlers who in the 1890s formed the town of Nederland in Jefferson County desired that their children quickly learn English. Unfortunately, the teacher the settlers hired could not understand their language. They resolved the issue by securing for the teacher a student who knew enough English to act as an interpreter. Not as pedagogically sound as other instances in the Texas bilingual tradition, this example illustrates the more temporary and expedient nature of bilingual practices in the nineteenth-century schools.[43]

Of all linguistic minorities in Texas who participated in the nineteenth-century bilingual tradition, the largest group, after the Mexican

Dutch immigration to Nederland in Jefferson County at the turn of the century resulted in a crash course in languages for both students as well as the teacher, Miss Edith Cooke, on the right with the wide hat. Photo courtesy of the Windmill Museum, Nederland, Texas, No. ITC-72-1667.

Americans and Germans, was the Czechs. Texas has recently claimed the largest rural population of Czech Americans in the country and ranked second among states in the total number of persons claiming full or partial Czech ancestry. Most Czechs immigrated in the mid- to late-nineteenth century; their rate of immigration tapered off in the early twentieth century. They settled in heavily German-laden areas of southeastern coastal Texas such as Austin, Fayette, Colorado, Washington, and Lavaca Counties. Because of their proximity to the more numerous and powerful Germans and the historical confluence of languages in their crowded geographical location in Europe, many Czechs were fairly conversant in German and often mistaken for Germans by outsiders.[44]

Czech was utilized as the medium of instruction in both public and private schools. Language maintenance was doubly important for Czech Americans given their minority relationship to Germans in the Old Country and then once again in many parts of Texas. Indeed, some Czechs feared the possible "Germanization" of their language and thus expected the schools not only to aid in learning English but also to preserve their separate culture. One such example occurred in 1876 shortly after the creation of public schools in Lavaca County. It was rumored that local Czech Americans razed the schoolhouse due to intense dissatisfaction with the hiring of a German teacher.[45] In the 1905–1906 reports from Fayette County, Superintendent G. A. Stierling remarked on the hostility between the two linguistic groups: "The population of Fayette County is mostly Bohemian and German. As a rule they do not have much to do with one another and consequently have several schools, where one would be stronger and able to employ two teachers; but it is probably best to let them remain in separate schools."[46]

Like Tejanos, Czechs also took advantage of parochial schools when they found the public schools unwilling to accommodate their language needs. Due to the inability of the public schools of Ellis County to make lessons comprehensible for immigrant Czech-speaking students, the local Czech American community in 1911 organized a Catholic parochial school where Czech was the medium of instruction, and English was taught as a second language.[47]

In a few regions of southeastern coastal Texas where Czech Americans exercised greater local political power, the public schools were made to serve the linguistic needs and desires of their community. The 1871 Reconstruction school law required that the examinations for teaching certificates test proficiency in English. This made sense in light of the position taken by then-Superintendent De Gress regarding the allotment of non-English-language instruction up to two hours a day. Czech Americans in Fayette County, politically strong enough at that time to have elected a Czech American county judge, appealed to the state board of education to allow one of their longtime instructors to take the examination in Czech or German, in either of which he was fluent, because the teacher did not believe at that time that he had sufficient command of English. The state refused. County authorities responded by notifying the state that because the teaching assistant was fluent in English, the Czech teacher would be permitted to continue another year. The next year this teacher, after great personal application, passed the English portion of the certification exam. The instructor later relocated to another public school where he continued to teach in Czech, German, and English.[48]

Fayette Countians entertained spirited debate amongst themselves regarding the degree of bilingualism in the public schools. Ultimately the bilingualists, those who favored eventual assimilation through learning English, won out over those who desired instruction only in Czech for the purposes of cultural maintenance. Speaking for the position that bilingualism in the classroom meant a greater chance for assimilation into an English-speaking nation, County Judge August Haidusek declared, "The idea that a person who does not know the English

Some churches of immigrant populations operated summer language institutes in between the public school terms. This Czech summer school operated by Joseph Barton of the Unity of the Brethren Church in Granger, Texas, took place in the summer of 1914. Photo courtesy of the Institute of Texan Cultures at University of Texas at San Antonio, No. 76-363.

language can be as useful an American citizen as one who knows it is truly ridiculous."[49] Although his rhetorical veneration of English would later represent the position of those who wanted to eliminate all non-English languages in the schools, Judge Haidusek at this time represented the pro-bilingual assimilationist position.

These early practitioners of bilingual instruction in Texas justified their actions pedagogically. They believed that bilingualism meant greater possibilities for academic enrichment as well as "Americanization." They also believed that, in addition to its pedagogical soundness, bilingual instruction meant a greater chance of learning English while preserving the language and culture of the home. To claim that this bilingual tradition, especially in the case of Texas, was simply a defensive desire for language or cultural maintenance is incorrect. True, there was an element of cultural resistance to this tradition, but that is not the whole of the story. Such interpretations fail to acknowledge the agency displayed by these communities both in assimilating into a new national culture and tenaciously preserving some part of their ancestral identity. Texas bilingual schooling demonstrates the richness and complexity of the history of bilingual education in America.

CHAPTER THREE
The Gradual Demise
of the Bilingual Tradition,
1884–1905

42   As with the rest of the nation, the bilingual tradition of classroom instruction in Texas declined in the late nineteenth and early twentieth centuries. Bilingual schools came to be replaced by a curricular approach
to non-English-speaking children that this book refers to as English-
Only pedagogy, the subject of the fifth chapter. This was a complicated
phenomenon that has to do with two related factors: First, the growth
and development of Progressive Education in Texas; second, a shift in the
concept of Americanization. The subject of Americanization is examined in the fourth chapter, while the rise of Progressive Education and
its negative relationship to the bilingual tradition is the subject of this
chapter. The gradual but effective curtailing of the various types of locally practiced bilingual instruction was accomplished in the name of
Progressivism by statewide educational experts, political leaders, and local education officials who were unsympathetic to ethnic Americans.

Texas was certainly in the southern context of Progressivism. Southern Progressives considered themselves to be part of a fundamental
reshaping of southern society away from a dominant emphasis on pro-
vincial and agrarian values to a society more in tune with modernity
and industrialization. Concerned that public education was mired in
provinciality, Progressive Education advocates of the South desired a
fundamental transformation in the way their states offered education. The long-held, administrative disinterest for public schools characterizing the nineteenth century gave way in the twentieth century;
educational governance increasingly became the province of highly
trained, Progressive professionals. While reforms such as compulsory
attendance, the creation of teacher standards and certification, and
the centralization of education policy into a powerful state regulatory
agency seem not terribly controversial today, they were in turn-of-the-
century Texas.[1]

The Progressive Education movement began in Texas in 1884 and
dominated educational thought until 1949. The demise of the bilingual
tradition occurred as the Progressive paradigm was coming to promi-

nence in Texas. It is in the first few decades of the Progressive Education movement, when its agenda for changing the educational landscape of the state was still formative, that its adherents first attacked the bilingual tradition through several different avenues. First, the Progressive reform of school reorganization indirectly suffocated bilingual education by eliminating the general organizational schemes that allowed ethnic communities a high degree of local autonomy in which to practice it; second, English-Only pronouncements gradually infiltrated educational legislation on teacher certification and also cropped up as instructional mandates; third, there was a significant increase in nativism by the turn of the century that accompanied the Texas Progressive agenda. The earliest attacks on the bilingual tradition occurred as the Progressive Education spirit emerged during the 1880s.

Superintendent of Public Instruction Benjamin M. Baker fired the first salvo against the statewide bilingual tradition in his biennial report for the school years of 1884–85 and 1885–86. His statements best illustrate the coming statewide campaign against bilingual instruction. Regarding the allegation that bilingualism was rampant in Texas public schools, Baker noted, "Investigation disclosed the truth of some of the charges, but the superintendent in a majority of the instances found himself powerless to remedy the evil." Prior to this, state officials hardly even mentioned the subject of bilingualism in the classroom, much less referred to it as "evil." Stating his firm belief that although he did not "hold it objectionable to teach other languages than the English in the schools . . . they should be pursued as studies, while the language of the school should be English." This was as precise as any Texas official had ever been to defining English usage in the classroom specifically as the medium of instruction. After recommending that the legislature seriously consider the matter, Baker noted that administrative reform along Progressive Education principles could resolve the issue. He argued that if local "superintendents are given sufficient power, and the mode of their selection removed safely from local influences, it will not be difficult for them to establish the English as the sole language for the schools."[2] All future statewide educational leaders reasserted Baker's negativism about bilingual instruction like a mantra.

Baker's statements are a watershed marker. For decades Texas sacrificed any possible desire for all-English instruction at the altar of Jeffersonian and Democratic localism. Even the novel Reconstruction experiment that clarified the language issue ultimately failed to shape or mold local practice. Texas would come to live a lie of sorts in pronouncing with ever-increasing vigor by the turn of the century the legal necessity of total English instruction while continuing to tolerate local bilingual schools. English-Only and localism clashed throughout the nineteenth century; that is, they clashed until the reforming and centralizing tendencies of Progressive Education finally triumphed. The influence of this broad set of Progressive principles can be illustrated in Baker's hostility to "local influences." Progressive Education sought to advance the professionalization of education with the attitude that too many local liberties retarded "progress" and could only be circumvented through righteous regulation by trained experts.

The first of the Progressive-era education reforms to curtail the bilingual tradition was the issue of school reorganization. From the 1880s to the 1900s, all state superintendents vigorously supported methods of school organization that stripped local authorities of their complete hegemony over school management. Until the early twentieth century, Texas maintained three distinct methods of school organization: a community system, a district system, and a county system. County schools, also called country or common schools, were administered by county judges who acted as de facto superintendents, or they operated with a full-time superintendent of county schools appointed by the judge. This system survived well into the twentieth century. For decades this was the largest system of school organization in Texas.[3] Educational leaders disapprovingly noted that county schools were constitutionally more limited on finance matters than the system universally favored by Progressives. That other system—the district system—was favored by Progressive educators because it was under more state supervision and was not as hobbled as the other systems in the area of finance. Districts were organized in rural areas, towns, and at times within and under the supervision of cities. These district schools did have some local control in the form of the election of trustees from within the district boundaries to a local school board, but those boundaries were determined only with the state agency's assent. School districts, like their schoolhouses, were permanent and could not be dissolved without state approval. State superintendents enthusiastically approved of the district system throughout this period.[4]

Progressive educators reserved their greatest ire for the remaining method of organization: the community system. Something resembling the community system predominated in Texas before the Civil War. It was temporarily shelved during Reconstruction only to be reinstated when Democratic lawmakers, distrustful of anything from the allegedly tyrannical "Radical" Republican rule, sought a way of organizing schools to maximize local control. So Texas public schools reverted to the antebellum community system from 1876 until 1884; administrative anarchy characterized this period. If the Reconstruction school laws were too ambitious, claimed one scholar, then "the Constitution of 1876 went to the other extreme and virtually destroyed the public schools."[5]

In this primitive system of organization, minorities such as Mexican Americans, German Americans, Czech Americans, or any other group were able to create their own schools with no meaningful state regulation, providing a dizzying array of bilingual instruction. Any self-defined group of parents submitted to a figurehead superintendent (usually the county judge who already acted as de facto superintendent of the county schools) a list of children comprising the "community." The judge then appointed three trustees (who could be removed by community petition) to manage the school for one year, after which the whole process would repeat itself. There were no permanent boundaries or schoolhouses with the community system. Children were schooled in any available one-room structure: church basements, abandoned homes, stores, or public buildings. The advantage to such a method of school organization was that it shifted almost complete administrative power to local cliques of people. If the trustees appointed by the judge did not conform to parental wishes regarding the content or method of instruction, the parents easily removed them or simply dissolved the school. Also, this system put the onus of finance on the state, because the one-year community school did not have any legal authority to tax. The funding, therefore, came from the state or from parent subsidies. The only thing the parents had to do was to file the yearly paperwork with the already over-burdened county judge.[6]

The 1884 school reform bill began a decades-long process that, among other things, reorganized public schools in Texas away from the old community system and toward the district system. The act created a trajectory for future reform along the Progressive lines of enhanced state centralization of education policy and greater professionalization to curb the absolute local control of education exercised by ethnic and minority parents. Governor John Ireland signed the omnibus law, written to cover all foreseeable aspects of school governance, in February of 1884. Even though the 1884 legislation mandated the district system, it also exempted fifty-three counties, allowing them to continue temporarily with the community system. Most of these counties contained large numbers of ethnic Texans and participated in the bilingual tradition. In addition to language minorities, African Americans also desired the community system to ensure that African American parents, not white districtwide trustees, managed their children's schools.[7]

The community system sheltered bilingual schools. The lack of centralized supervision over curriculum or the employment of teachers inherent in the community system meant that language minorities were able to do what they wanted. Schools instructed students entirely in German or Spanish or bilingually if they so desired; community schools could even be used to teach religion, so long as those particular classroom hours were financed through private funds and conducted after regular school hours. German American areas were well-known for utilizing community schools and, after four or five months when the state funds ran out, retaining the teachers through private funds collected in the community for students to attend the same schools, only now as private institutions completely unregulated as to language, for an additional amount of time. T. P. Huff of Bexar County described this process in his 1897–98 school report. Mexican American counties involved in the bilingual tradition also affirmed their support of the community system as earlier illustrated by Joseph Fitz Simmons of Nueces County in 1881–82.[8]

The connection between ethnic tension and language was fodder for Progressives favoring the elimination of the community system in the 1880s and 1890s. In the late 1880s State Superintendent Oscar H. Cooper alleged that the community system fostered "local bickerings, sectarian rivalry, and even personal quarrels, [that] frequently lead to the organization of two or three weak and inefficient schools, where one good strong school would better meet the needs of the locality." For Cooper, the community schools represented an inefficient, wasteful drain of resources—too steep a price to pay for the ethnic agitation over language. Cooper allayed white racial fears by arguing that the community system was not any better at maintaining racial segregation than the more efficient district system.[9]

Nary a biennial or special report from the superintendent of public instruction went by in the quarter of a century after passage of the 1884 reform bill that did not in some way call for a final elimination of the community system. The state saw fit to hurl considerable bile at the community schools' implied ethnic empowerment. In the seventh biennial report for 1888–89 and 1889–90, Superintendent Cooper referred to the community system as "cumbrous [sic], obstructive, and inefficient."[10] In the next report J. M. Carlisle, the new state superintendent, commented that the community system offered only "constant inducement to petty quarrels and dissentions." In the eleventh biennial report for the academic years 1896–97 and 1897–98 Carlisle noted with embarrassment that a prominent national education committee, the Committee of Twelve on Rural Schools, pointed to the community system as an antiquated relic of "pioneer" society that had been eradicated everywhere in the United States except the Lone Star State. Carlisle reprinted the entire stinging rebuke.[11]

Teachers joined state superintendents and bureaucrats in calling for the elimination of the community system and its implied bilingualism. The Texas State Teachers Association (TSTA), the oldest teacher's organization in Texas, operated as a powerful statewide agent for Progressive Education. In the seventh biennial report, the TSTA recommended the uniform adoption of the district system of organization. Progressive TSTA members full of zeal to elevate the state's bottom-dwelling education statistics saw no sound pedagogical or organizational reason for continuing the community system. Progressives like R. B. Cousins of Mexia, a future state superintendent who in 1898 was president of TSTA, believed that only rank greed or crass politics led to the outrageous retention of the community system. At an 1898 TSTA conference in Galveston Cousins remarked that this system was "a relic" and would have been placed in "deserved limbo" were it not for the Republican and Populist fear of losing their counties if they abolished it, because this would, he alleged, "drive the negroes from the party" due to the fact that the school trustee position was "a lucrative office in some counties."[12]

Despite the constant pressure applied by state superintendents and other high-placed educational and political leaders, the community system did not immediately decline after 1884. It lingered on in several stubborn pockets, especially those with large numbers of non-English-speakers, well into the 1900s. State reports continued to refer to the persistent community system in unflattering terms. District system counties numbered more than one hundred by the mid-1880s and by the middle 1890s consistently numbered around two hundred. The TSTA noted that when the district system was created in 1884, the legislation allowed only fifty-three counties exemptions to continue the community system. The number of exempted counties peaked at eighty-nine in 1885, decreased to twenty-seven by 1893, and then jumped up to thirty-eight by 1895. The number rose to forty in 1897 and hovered just under there until legislation in 1905 whittled the community system down to just thirteen counties, where it would remain for several more years, like a dull, throbbing, headache for the Progressives.[13]

After three more attempts, the legislature finally succeeded in eliminating the community system. In 1897 the Twenty-Fifth Legislature decided to kill the community system by mandating that all public schools be organized under the district system. A courtesy amendment gutted the spirit of the bill by allowing individual senators and representatives to exempt counties in their own electoral districts. The state legislature did everything it could not to stir up the issue in 1899. The legislature was so cowed by potential opposition to the elimination of the community system that when it passed a modification in the law governing district systems in 1899, it added a qualifying clause promising that "nothing in this article shall be construed to affect counties that have been placed under the community system."[14]

The Twenty-ninth Legislature, encouraged by Progressives, tried to end the limping community system in 1905 by specifically outlawing it for the 1906–1907 term in the twenty-five counties in which it then existed. However, another tempering measure was included that gave community school counties a final vote on whether or not to form a district. With this referendum of sorts, the community system persisted in thirteen counties for a short while longer. Many of these thirteen counties represented areas where linguistic minorities such as Germans, Czechs, and Tejanos utilized the community system to implement bilingual schools at the local level. By the time this 1905 bill was passed, however, nearly ninety percent of the state's scholastic population attending public schools did so in counties with the district system anyway.[15]

The legislature eventually acceded to the wishes of increasingly strident educators like Superintendent Cousins in eliminating the community system once more, this time without loopholes. State Superintendent F. M. Bralley trumpeted this final end of the community system in the seventeenth biennial report for the years 1908–1909 and 1909–10. Bralley wrote that of the ten significant reforms passed by the Thirty-first Legislature, abolishing the community system was at the top. Superintendent Bralley lauded the "law abolishing forever the so-called community system of organizing public schools" in the remaining thirteen counties where it lingered.[16]

Local responses to the organization controversy varied. Many county officials in charge of educational matters who reported to the state superintendent in the 1880s and 1890s also favored the shift from community to district system. Ethnicity did not automatically mean support for the community system. In heavily German American Comal County, Judge Ernest Koebig did not display any whiff of nativism in his opposition to the community system in his report of 1881–82. His reason for favoring a shift to the district system was "to avoid the separation of communities, 1st as to religious divisions and 2nd to avoid local troubles in communities which will effectively ruin the public schools." The "religious divisions" and "local troubles" he referred to fit the pattern of ethnic schools practicing bilingual instruction that also mixed religion into part of the daily curriculum, possible only under the auspices of the community system.[17]

Religious divisions, however, were not the half of it. Another revealing statement as to the tension between educational professionalism and the local control of schools also came from Comal County. Judge A. Giesecke in his 1892–93 school report noted the deep animosity in his county toward the recently adopted district system: "The people in general are dissatisfied with the District system, and are endeavoring to subdivide the existing districts into smaller ones, which I consider a bad move." After noting the failure of district taxes to pass in his county, he conceded, "The patrons of the schools, however, willingly contribute enough money to the public fund to give their children a 9 or 10 month term." Why would German American parents of Comal County wish to vote down a districtwide tax applicable to all property holders while privately contributing, out of their own pockets, the same amount to finance the several months of schooling not paid for by the state? The answer was simple: control over who taught, what they taught, and how they taught it. Giesecke somberly noted, "One great drawback is that teachers are mostly elected by the patrons of the schools, and in consequence thereof the teachers are not near as independent as they would be if they were engaged by the trustees."[18] Parents controlled the hiring of teachers and, in large part, the curriculum to be taught in community schools; in a district the trustees controlled the hiring, and the curriculum was aggressively mandated by the state. Clearly, language was one of several intertwining issues of local versus Progressive control of the schools.

One reason for maintaining the community system, its backers claimed, was that it facilitated the separation of white children from other children, whether they be African American (for whom educational segregation was constitutionally protected), Mexican American (for whom segregation was de facto rather than de jure), or just undesirable. However, in his 1887–88 and 1888–89 reports, Val Verde County Judge W. K. Jones wrote that even though Mexican Americans in his public schools (along with a few Italian Americans) were adequately segregated under the community system, a shift to the district system would be beneficial and still would not disturb this segregationist arrangement. Cameron County Superintendent E. H. Goodrich expressed another motive for making the shift to the district system. He reported that for 1894–95 attendance was terrible and an attempted proliferation of community schools had failed to increase it.[19]

Progressive reforms of the 1880s and 1890s played a role in the destruction of the nineteenth-century bilingual tradition of Texas in two other ways: first, English-Only mandates embedded in laws governing teacher certification; second, English-Only instructional mandates in laws governing curriculum and school conduct. A significant part of the Progressive Education reform agenda went toward professionalizing the state's teaching community as much as possible. This was done not just by supporting training at the university and teachers' college level, but also through the process of teacher certification. Prior to the 1870s the concept of teacher certification did not exist in Texas and the attitude that locals could use state funds to simply hire whomever they pleased continued as one of the controversies inherent to the community system. The Republican administration of Superintendent Jacob C. De Gress during Reconstruction attempted a type of centralized, state-directed teacher examination.[20] This tentative effort was nullified when Redeemer Democrats scrapped the forward-looking Reconstruction school laws.

By 1876 the state had realized the necessity of some type of teacher certification. But the law passed that year sounded better in principle than it actually worked. Prospective teachers were to request the county judge to "direct an examination of the applicant on the following branches, viz: Orthography, reading, writing, English grammar, composition, geography, and arithmetic."[21] The law, in only requiring that certain subjects be mastered to the satisfaction of the county judge, did not specify in what language the examinations were to take place, a source of controversy in the coming years.

The legislature attempted to end any question of teacher testing in foreign languages in the 1884 school bill. In a new section of the certification law, the legislature stipulated that all certification tests were to be taken only in the English language: "The examination must be conducted in the English language, and no applicant shall receive a certificate unless the board of examiners be satisfied that he or she is competent to teach the branches named in the grade of certificate applied for, in the English language."[22] While not a true English-Only law that made mandatory all-English instruction and communication inside the classroom, the 1884 law did mark the appearance of a concrete English-Only principle in a new part of the education code.

The state logically attempted to curtail the bilingual tradition through the certification process. Reports from local education officials bore evidence of the difficulties in maintaining bilingual and ethnic schools with properly certified teachers. However, many local officials simply ignored the law—there was no punishment for hiring uncertified teachers or for violating the English-Only rules of certification exams. In fact, allegations of local education officials' ignoring teacher exams were widespread. In 1896 the *Southern Mercury,* the leading Populist newspaper in Texas, alleged that Mexican teachers in South Texas could neither pass state certification exams nor speak any English.[23] That year Superintendent J. E. Smith of San Antonio remarked in a notation to a statistical report about his teachers that "1 Spanish & 2 German teachers have no certificates." El Paso school official G. W. Huffman in his 1897–98 report admitted freely to the state that "such teachers able to pass an English examination can not always be employed."[24]

Local and state officials were disappointed in the lack of effectiveness of English-Only via teacher certification. Starr County Judge James Clarke in 1893–94 argued against the notion of long-term or permanent certificates, because education officials in neighboring counties failed to take the regulations seriously: "in many counties not the slightest regard is paid to the law in relation to examinations." He also noted, "schools are established solely with reference to some pecuniary and political advantage likely to result thereupon."[25] Hidalgo County Judge R. A. Marsh wrote in 1904–1905 that although teachers in his schools taught in English, knowledge of Spanish was necessary to "gain the confidence of the patrons of the schools in strictly Mexican communities."[26]

Superintendent Baker's 1886 shock at the mere existence of bilingual education indicates that perhaps the new English-Only additions to the teacher certification laws were thought to have taken care of the issue. The legislature continued to reinforce English-Only principles by inserting them into the teacher certification process. The legislature in 1891 expanded on the 1884 directive by stating, "Such examinations shall be conducted in the English language and in writing, and no applicant shall receive a certificate unless the board of examiners be satisfied that he is competent to teach . . . in the English language." The next clause stipulated, "The board of examiners shall examine each applicant as to his competency to teach the branches in the preceding clauses in the English language." Another clause added, "All examinations shall be conducted in the English language in writing and written in ink."[27]

Lawmakers' preoccupation with stamping out bilingual education through the teacher certification process continued. In an 1893 overhaul of the school laws, the legislature continued to hold county officials responsible for the enforcement of English-Only. They were to determine if the applicant could "speak and understand the English language sufficiently to use it easily and readily in conversation, and in giving instruction in all branches prescribed for the class of certificate for which he applies." Legislation passed in 1905 repeated the same requirements for teacher certification.[28]

Whatever the letter of the law, however, local officials who participated in the bilingual tradition conducted the exams. As of 1900 there were still no laws to punish local education officials who unintentionally or even willfully violated the English-Only requirements in the teacher certification process. County superintendents' reports during the late nineteenth century contain a score of complaints about local officials' ignoring the language stipulations of certification. Even laws to ensure that the local school trustees also demonstrate English proficiency were ignored by the local education officials. In the town of Ysleta, for example, Judge F. E. Hunter of El Paso County complained that his county superintendent went so far as to erase the section of the state trustee contract requiring that the trustees be able to "read and write the English language."[29]

Ultimately, however, English-Only mandates would move beyond the teacher certification sections of the state's education laws and into those pertaining to classroom governance and curriculum. Perhaps some lawmakers thought this a matter of common sense. Indeed, both the practice of English-Only in Texas and the bilingual tradition co-existed, without the benefit of legal specificity. Some local officials boasted to the state of the English-Only character of their schools even before the 1884 law. For example, Judge J. R. Mason of Bexar County, containing the vibrantly multicultural city of San Antonio, wrote in 1882–83: "We have a varied population in this county and difficulties are presented in some communities where the prevailing nationality desires . . . teachers who speak their language whether german, mexican, or polish, or a foreign language to be taught to the detriment of the American. Trustees however have been told that no matter what teachers may be employed, the english is the language of the public schools, and if any other is taught to the detriment of that—the teachers' vouchers would not be approved."[30]

The state first addressed the legal vagueness that tacitly allowed bilingual classrooms in 1893. The same legislature that strengthened the English-Only stipulation in the teacher certification process felt strongly enough about this principle as to mandate it as the one method of instruction in all public schools. The new Section 70 of the education code read: "It shall be the duty of every teacher in the public free schools of this State to use the English language exclusively, and to conduct all recitations and school exercises exclusively in the English language: Provided that this provision shall not prevent the teaching of any other language as a branch of study, but when any other language is so taught, the use of said language shall be limited to the recitations and exercises devoted to the teaching of said language as such branch of study."[31]

Significantly, the 1893 law was the first in Texas to stipulate the use of language in the classroom since the short-lived period of Reconstruction. The law decisively differentiated between the language of instruction and the teaching of a foreign language. The language of instruction or medium of communication was the use of "English exclusively" for "all recitations and school exercises" unless a foreign language was being taught, and then the use of that foreign language was to be "limited to the recitations and exercises devoted to the teaching of said language."[32] In theory, this 1893 law outlawed bilingual instruction in the public schools. Nevertheless, many examples of public bilingual instruction existed after 1893 simply because state officials never created a method of enforcement. This unenforceable mandate fell upon local officials to act upon at their will. Some conscientiously complied; many others, however, chose to ignore it in favor of their ethnic friends, neighbors, and constituents.

In the "Prescribed Studies" section of the state education laws of 1905, Section 100 reiterated the decades-old curricular mandate of teaching "reading in English" and "English grammar." A new addition in Section 102 repeated the 1893 English-Only directive that it was the duty of all teachers "to use the English language exclusively, and to conduct all recitations and school exercises exclusively in the English language." The distinction regarding the medium of communication and the teaching of foreign languages as courses of study was kept. As with the 1893 regulation, the 1905 English-Only law was also unenforceable. Records have yet to be discovered of any local official delinquent in such responsibilities that was either prosecuted or even threatened with punishment.[33] While the sentiment for English-Only was alive and growing in the 1890s and the 1900s, it was still a hollow endorsement.

The state finally got serious about English-Only during the heyday of nativism centered against German Americans and Mexican Americans caused by World War I and the social disruptions on the United States–Mexico border, which were influenced by the Mexican Revolution and the deteriorating economic and social position of Tejanos. It would be 1918 before English-Only arrived in Texas as a fully enforceable mandate with specific criminal punishments. The 1893 and 1905 English-Only directives, however, were important precursors, indicating educational and political Progressives' intent to eliminate bilingual instruction.

Some ethnic communities opposed English-Only by continuing with bilingualism in the public schools, if possible, or in private schools if necessary. More confrontational avenues of opposition to English-Only existed too. For example, Mexican American parents used the Spanish-language press to vent their frustration with local English-Only policies and even went so far as to organize civic groups to complain formally. One Spanish-language newspaper in Laredo, *La Cronica,* proposed in 1910 that all people in Texas of Mexican descent pull their children out of the public schools and create their own schools with imported teachers from Mexico. *La Cronica* argued that the public schools given to Tejanos were vastly inferior, racist, and culturally insensitive; the newspaper's editors supported bilingual schools that would teach an appreciation of Mexican history, culture, and the Spanish language along with English. Such demands bear a striking resemblance to Chicano-era demands in the 1960s for bilingual-bicultural education. *La Cronica's* provocative ideas galvanized enough interest for a 1911 meeting of *mutualista* delegates from twenty-seven Texas towns and cities that further debated the issue.[34]

Tejanos were correct to note a surge in official animosity from the state educational system. By the turn of the century, the highly charged and partisan political battles over Progressive Education's agenda created a context in which nativism and Progressive advocacy dovetailed. This pairing of reform-minded education advocates and nativist rhetoric simmered and stewed nearly a quarter century after Baker's 1886 statements about the necessity for Progressive reform to end bilingual education. This ideological coupling was evident in the 1906–1907 report from Superintendent W. W. Jenkins of Williamson County. He complained freely about the "foreigners" in his county who held back any hope of educational progress on consolidation or local taxes: "We have a large foreign element to out-vote." Jenkins repeated much the same sentiment the next year.[35]

State Superintendent R. B. Cousins articulated this dovetailing of Progressive Education and the rising tide of nativism in his written comments on the demolition of the community system and its incipient bilingualism. Cousins attacked the community system by alleging that it reinforced ethnic tribalism. He wrote that ethnic communities favored this system, because they believed that it best allowed for "people of different nationalities inhabiting the same neighborhoods in Texas each to have a separate school of its own." Cousins argued that this was pedagogically "suicidal," "treason," and "repulsive to every man that loves his country." He concluded, "The German children continue to be German and to speak German, and frequently grow to maturity ignorant of the language of *their* country. The same is true of the Bohemians." Cousins concluded with a rhetorical flourish: "Must Texas educate Germans, or Bohemians, or Mexicans? Are we not rather to educate Texans?—Americans?"[36] Cousins effectively identified the "enemy" by alleging of the community system's supporters that their "arguments usually set forth in favor of a continuation of this plan condemn it in *awful accents.*"[37]

The bilingual tradition of instruction in both the public and private schools of Texas continued into the early twentieth century, but it did so under a continuously darkening cloud of official suspicion, doubt, and strong intimations of illegitimacy from the state and the Progressive Education establishment. Texas education policymakers wanted the bilingual tradition eliminated as early as the 1880s and continued to support this course through the 1900s, taking decisive, but ultimately ineffective, measures through school organization policy, laws governing teacher certification, and unenforceable instructional mandates. Progressives viewed the bilingual tradition as counter to proper Americanization, a lingering anachronism of unsettled pioneer society. They believed it had outlived its previous usefulness.

PART TWO

English-Only Education

CHAPTER FOUR

The Rise of Americanization Curriculum, 1918–41

During the Progressive era a number of ideas on how to assimilate immigrants through public schooling came to prominence. Many white,
native-born Anglo Americans were fearful of the "new" immigrants,
their rate of immigration, and their ability to assimilate into what were
thought to be "traditional" American cultural boundaries associated
with the middle class, Protestantism, and speaking English.[1] Gaining
strength during the first two decades of the twentieth century was one
specific response to this fear: the Americanization Movement. The
idea of Americanization was built upon the synthesis of contradictory
and competing ideas about the meaning of immigrant assimilation.
Americanization was a diffuse, informal idea—not yet a movement—
throughout most of the nineteenth century. By the early twentieth
century, however, it came to signify a more formal, rigid process of
shedding foreign-ness learned through traditionally American institutions such as churches, the workplace, or the public schools. Hardly
anyone claims the Americanization Movement nationally to have been
a success. Rather, many view the national effort to Americanize immigrants in the early twentieth century as partially or completely misguided and ineffective. Recent scholarship maintains a generally negative view of the Americanization Movement. In the field of Texas
history, the works of several scholars stand out within this historiographical vein.[2]

The most recent work in the field, however, offers a theoretical lens
for viewing Americanization in both its positive and negative manifes-
tations. In "From the Treaty of Guadalupe Hidalgo to *Hopwood,*" an article in *Harvard Educational Review,* Guadalupe San Miguel and Richard
Valencia creatively examine two different types of Americanization.
The two types of Americanization can be classified "additive" and "subtractive."[3] Examples of "additive" Americanization would be those instances in which authorities chose not to discard the child's ethnicity,
culture, or language. English-language study, civic instruction, and
standard core academic subjects in English were added while simulta-

neously nurturing the native language and preserving some semblance of the child's culture, even if it were utilized merely as a bridge to English. The additive model leaned to the culturally pluralist perspective of Americanization advanced nationally by Jane Addams and John Dewey.[4] The "subtractive" concept of Americanization emphasized total and complete submersion—immediate linguistic and cultural conformity. Subtractive Americanization was characterized by English-Only classrooms in which ethnic children were harshly punished for speaking their native languages. In the subtractive model, children were taught that ethnicity was not only un-American but also dangerous to the very idea of democracy. The subtractive model was nativist. It expressed an irrational fear of and hostility toward immigrants, their cultures, and their languages. This form of subtractive Americanization, nationally articulated by Emory Bogardus and Ellwood Cubberley, gained momentum in Progressive-era Texas and became dominant during the passions of World War I.[5]

Additive Americanization dominated in the late nineteenth and faded early in the twentieth century. During this period, educational leaders often allowed ethnic communities to establish their own schools. To the extent that any type of Americanization was needed, the process of education was simply thought to be enough. The mere availability of schooling was itself viewed as something of a triumph. That many schools were at least partially bilingual did not seem to bother some local education leaders. Many seemed to have regarded bilingual instruction as the least the school could do for children who spoke no English. In Nueces County, Judge Joseph Fitz Simmons wrote throughout the 1880s and 1890s about the use of bilingual teachers by his county's schools to further the eventual Americanization of Tejano students. In 1887–88, for example, he wrote that the preponderance of those unable to speak English upon entering school "necessitates the employment of teachers having a knowledge of both the English and the Spanish languages."[6]

Other educational leaders agreed with these efforts. Zapata County Judge A. P. Spohn, a practitioner of bilingual schools, wrote to the state in the 1908–1909 school year of his Mexican and Tejano population, "The great majority of the parents are very poor and must make great sacrifices to send their children to school, but I am glad to state that they appreciate the necessity of their children having the English language and do all in their power to send their children to school." This fundamentally tolerant conception of Americanization regarding bilingualism in the classroom also occurred in large school systems such as San Antonio well into the twentieth century and in keeping with the national bilingual tradition as demonstrated by the St. Louis schools that sought ultimately to Americanize through bilingual instruction. New research by historian Paul Fessler indicates that bilingual schools in rural Minnesota also operated under this more positive understanding of Americanization, phasing out German after the elementary grades.[7]

This commonsense approach of Americanizing non-English-speaking children through bilingual instruction was not limited to the public schools. Numerous private schools also served the needs of language-minority children who had no access to public schooling. Some of these schools advertised their educational benefits as the teaching of English for commercial purposes. Others such as the *escuelitas*—run by Mexican Americans who believed that the segregationist practices of Anglo-run public schools excluded them—were nonparochial and, as one contemporary observer put it, "altogether Mexican in spirit and sentiment." Additive conceptions of Americanizing immigrants through language also came from teachers. B. G. Cole of Longview argued in a speech to the 1890 TSTA convention that the state should not push away ethnic students from the public schools by becoming unduly coercive in advancing English.[8]

Already contested in the late nineteenth century, this additive, tolerant conception of Americanization was in full retreat by the early twentieth century. Subtractive Americanization manifested itself in the state's educational landscape by the 1890s in a conducive political environment. For example, in 1892 the Texas legislature passed legislation barring foreign citizens from owning property. Also by the 1890s educational leaders had shifted in the way they viewed language minorities like Mexican Americans. Gone were optimistic notions that knowledge of the English language and ultimate Americanization were within reach. Educators began to regard the issue of Tejano education as a problem deserving of special state attention. The public schools of Maverick County, claimed Judge J. A. Bonnet in his 1896–97 report, had failed to Americanize in the past and would continue to, because Mexicans, in his view, were not assimilable due to their alleged ignorance and backwardness. Eagle Pass schools felt that they solved the problem of how to Americanize their Spanish speakers by retaining them in the lower grades for special English instruction. Consequently, by 1892–93 virtually no Tejanos appeared on rolls of the schools' upper primary grades or secondary grades. El Paso County Superintendent C. C. Thomas remarked that the previous efforts of El Paso's bilingual public schools were undesirable and that neither teachers nor trustees truly cared for educating Mexican Americans.[9]

The 1893 and 1905 English-Only laws exemplified this shift in

Americanization's emphasis from positive to negative. Although lacking in enforcement, this legislation spelled out the dimensions of proper and improper language use inside Texas classrooms. All lessons, instructions, recitations, songs, etc., were to be conducted in English. These early English-Only laws represented a clear break from the policies of the past. The language used to urge these changes illustrates the sharply negative tone of subtractive Americanization. In the 1909 biennial report, State Superintendent R. B. Cousins fulminated about schools still practicing bilingual instruction. Cousins argued that these ethnic schools could not inculcate true American ideals and patriotism and that "the demands of reasonable statesmanship, of patriotism, condemn such a policy as not less than suicidal" for both the state and the nation.[10]

By the second decade of the twentieth century, literature from both the State Department of Education and the university research community describing Texas school conditions greatly emphasized the need for Americanization. A 1916 report on education in rural Travis County noted that the recent arrival of Mexicans to work the cotton fields, combined with the equally substantial European immigrant population already there, diluted the Anglo population, degrading primary social institutions such as churches and schools. This particular report, only nominally about educational conditions, seemed mostly engaged with immigrant assimilation concerns. Author E. E. Davis illustrated the growing connection between Progressive politics and Americanization when he listed the enemies of education in rural Travis County as being "the selfish landlord, the restless tenant, the movement from country to town, the negro [*sic*] and the Mexican, and white foreigners of un-American spirit." Davis urged that civics in Travis County should be taught earlier than the seventh grade because in 1916 only 142 out of 2,489 eligible students were even still attending school at the seventh-grade level. That only 16 African American children got to the seventh grade and that no Mexican American children were then studying above the fifth-grade level was of particular concern for Davis, who viewed these very groups as those most needing Americanization through civics lessons.[11]

The shift from additive toward subtractive Americanization that took place in the early twentieth century culminated during World War I. Texas policymakers were not only concerned with the irredentist movement of 1915 in South Texas and the fear of spillover from the Mexican Revolution; the presence of many German Americans in the state added to preexisting distrust. Wartime hysteria targeted German Americans. In Colorado County, for example, the traditionally powerful "white man's party," principally intended to disfranchise African Americans, in 1918 purged "several men whose purposes and ideals were as foreign to America as the kaiser's."[12] Organizations formed all over the state to monitor German American loyalty. Texas newspapers carried stories on investigations of San Antonio German American groups alleged to be disloyal to the United States government. Progressive-era historian Frederick Eby remarked of the wartime crisis, "The war revealed the fact that large groups of foreign peoples living in Texas were lacking in loyalty to their adopted country. They had not been Americanized. The startling amount of illiteracy . . . and other weaknesses were a revelation of the inefficiency of our educational work." Eby also described the state response: "A new emphasis was given to patriotism, the study of history, government, American ideals, American literature, and physical training."[13] The anti-German sentiment even affected children. One rural teacher recalled a young German American student crying on the first day of class. When asked what was wrong, he sobbed, "I'm German! The big boys won't play with me because I'm a German." When asked if he would like his mother to come and walk him home from school, he replied, "She can't come because she's sick, but anyway, she's German too."[14]

In addition, state leaders feared turbulence from Mexico. One newspaper article in 1918 implied that Mexico's mobilization of soldiers along border towns for the purpose of fighting banditry was suspicious and was perhaps connected to communications between revolutionary leaders in Mexico and Germany or to the theft of rifles from a San Antonio store the week before. Officials identified Mexican economic radicalism as a threat as well. In a report on the 1916–18 school years, State Superintendent W. F. Doughty gave maximum importance to the newly perceived need of Texans to Americanize. He argued that in keeping with the "progressive movement" across the nation to invest time and resources more heavily in education, Texas should fight "bolshevikism" among immigrants through the schools. South Texas labor strife of the previous decades warranted attention from the state's leaders. Tejanos and immigrant Mexican workers in Texas during this period were becoming proletarianized; they were not averse to participating in labor unions, even turning to socialism.[15]

The period between 1918 and 1923 marked an important step for the institutionalization of Americanization in Texas. The 1918 campaign for superintendent of public instruction sealed the dominance of subtractive Americanization in the public schools. Running for reelection was Superintendent W. F. Doughty, a proven Progressive who in 1918 found himself portrayed as the enemy of Progressivism and wartime patriotism. Doughty was allied to Governor James Ferguson, who also trumpeted reform but earned the ire of many Progressives by opposing prohibition and meddling in the affairs of the University of Texas. Ferguson underwent bitter impeachment proceedings before resigning from office. Doughty's alliance with Ferguson entailed opposition to prohibition and the support of ethnic Texans. This opened Doughty to charges of disloyalty during the height of World War I paranoia. Doughty's former Progressive supporters abandoned him when he failed to sever his ties to Ferguson publicly. Texas Progressives eventually endorsed Ferguson's successor, William P. Hobby.[16]

In 1918 Annie Webb Blanton, then president of the TSTA, vice president of the National Education Association, and professor of education at North Texas State Normal College, challenged Doughty for the state superintendency. Blanton charged that Doughty's connections with Ferguson meant association with political scandal, conservative South Texas bosses who stole elections with tainted Mexican votes, insufficient patriotism, and anti-prohibition, pro-German (presumably disloyal) support. The race was particularly vicious. Blanton's campaign strategy associated her with Progressive Governor Hobby and cast aspersions on Doughty's fitness for office. She intermingled education policy with the potent issues of prohibition, wartime loyalty, anti-Germanism, and anticommunism by charging that Doughty "was on the 'Red' list of the breweries . . . [who] . . . were allied with the German-American alliance, whose declared purpose was to control the public schools and Universities in the interest of German *Kultur.*" Blanton then promised to "put the great Public School system of Texas solidly in the 'American' column," because she had "no hyphenated connections."[17] German American *Kultur* in the schools, of course, referred to bilingual instruction.

As Blanton and Doughty campaigned for the Democratic nomination, the Texas legislature addressed Blanton's particularly strident emphasis upon Americanization by passing the state's first truly effective English-Only law. In 1918 a bill was introduced into the Thirty-fifth Legislature stating that the English-speaking heritage of the founding fathers, heroes of the Texas War for Independence among others of "the great Anglo-Saxon races who speak and write the English language—our own mother tongue," should be preserved during the wartime crisis by ending what was termed "the costly and useless luxury of spending thousands of dollars teaching the language of our German foe—the language that is being used in our country in seditious propaganda to undermine the patriotic efforts of our government to secure world-wide democracy." In the ensuing debate the use of German in the schools was branded as "un-American" and yet another element of German *Kultur.* This English-Only bill proposed the total elimination of German from Texas public schools; it included not just bilingual instruction but even German as a course of study.[18]

An English-Only law passed that year, although it was watered down on several counts. The original bill targeted only the German language. A substitute amendment advanced later that sought to ban *all* foreign languages failed by a large margin. Instead, a compromise measure passed that vaguely demanded that "teachers in public free schools . . . conduct school work in the English language exclusively." Foreign languages could be taught but not in the lower grades. This was very much like older English-Only proscriptions; legislators avoided the stigma of hysterically banning all foreign languages by reinforcing existing English-Only code. But this time they included criminal penalties for violating the law.[19]

The reaction to the issue of curtailing German in the public schools was overwhelmingly favorable. One state senator of San Antonio suggested to his local Americanization board that all immigrants, citizen or not, be made to speak English to prove their Americanism and that such "Americanism should be taught in public schools the same as arithmetic or geography."[20] Seeking reelection, Superintendent Doughty lent the legislation support, defending his tenure as education chief by stating that he had always supported the singing of "patriotic songs" and class instruction "devoted at intervals to the teaching of loyalty, love of country and State."[21] In an odd twist Representative J. T. Canales of Brownsville, a maverick Tejano and Progressive who favored prohibition, opposed the Jim Wells political machine (sometimes), and even legally challenged the Texas Rangers, heartily supported English-Only targeting German. Asked sarcastically by an opponent if he would also support the prohibition of his own Spanish, Canales replied, "If we were at war with Spain, yes."[22]

Annie Webb Blanton's 1918 victory over incumbent W. F. Doughty for the state's top education job resulted partly from her open suspicion of immigrants; she based her sense of Americanization on that more than anything. This was part of a Progressive sweep of statewide offices in 1918. Blanton cast herself as the Abraham Lincoln of statewide education by stating, "the nation can [not] endure half-native and half-alien today any more than it could endure half-free and half-slave a generation ago, hence, the timeliness of the movement among public schools of the country to shape their courses in such a way as to help in a program of Americanization."[23]

The Americanization Movement died out nationally after the war.

Annie Webb Blanton, as state superintendent of public instruction, oversaw from
1919 to 1923 the governance of the Texas
public school system as it underwent a series
of Progressive reforms including English-
Only pedagogy. Photo courtesy of the Institute of Texan Cultures at University of Texas
at San Antonio, No. 76-265.

By the middle of the 1920s the nativism that had infused the national immigration restriction debate had effectively rendered the notion of structured Americanization less important. By curtailing the "new" immigration from Europe, those nativists concerned with immigrant Americanization had created a final solution to the whole issue. Contrary to these national trends, the idea of Americanization actually gained popularity in Texas in the 1920s. Americanization in Texas shifted away from European immigrants to focus intensely on Mexican immigrants, who continued to flow into the United States in large, relatively unrestricted numbers during the 1920s.[24]

Superintendent Blanton reflected this shift. She advocated a new English-Only law more stridently after the war as she sought to close a private school loophole in the 1918 English-Only law. This new English-Only proposal essentially stripped all private schools of their ability to ignore state curricular mandates, specifically those stipulating that all classes be conducted exclusively in English. Blanton, who worried of the example set by "Mexico, Russia, and . . . every other uneducated, or poorly educated nation," urged Texans to support her recommendation to Americanize through the extermination of outside languages in all elementary classrooms: "No school which educates future Texas citizens has a right to object to such requirements, and the future safety of our democratic institutions demands that they be made." The 1920 meeting of the TSTA supported this course of action. This new English-Only legislation passed in 1923 along with other "Progressive" reforms such as laws strengthening the white primary and the prevention of ballot interpreters. By then Blanton had left office; she was, however, ultimately responsible for popularizing the issue. Progressive organizations like the Texas League of Women Voters supported these new laws.[25]

For Blanton, Americanization went beyond simply outlawing all bilingual instruction through English-Only. She also wanted to institutionalize Americanization in the curriculum of each school through the creation of a permanent statewide illiteracy commission within the State Department of Education. Though this effort failed, it illustrated Blanton's subtractive concept of Americanization best articulated in a fictional conversation with an opponent: "If you desire to be one with us, stay, and we welcome you; but if you wish to preserve, in our state, the language and the customs of another land, you have no right to do this which our state will grant to you." She then scolded her fictional (and silent) adversary that unless the adversary's children spoke only English in school, then "you must go back to the country which you prize so highly, and rear your children there."[26] Others shared Blanton's sentiments. One scholar went further in defining the need for Americanization by clinically labeling ethnic enclaves in Texas to be illustrative of "social, cultural, and educational retardation."[27]

Texas' attack on foreign languages succeeded. The academic study of German dropped dramatically during and after the war. Prior to 1918, 102 public and private high schools in Texas were accredited to teach German; after the war 78 were scrapped while the remaining 24 programs had small enrollments. All the while, Blanton urged substituting Spanish for German.[28] The total number of students enrolled in Spanish classes in Texas high schools more than tripled from 13,012 in the school year 1917–18 to 44,689 in 1925–26. Between the academic years of 1917–18 and 1921–22, the total number of high school students enrolled in German decreased from 3,977 to 294.[29]

By the middle of the 1920s anti-German sentiment was no longer as prominent an issue in Texas as it had been during the war. Likewise, it ceased to be much of a dilemma for education officials as well. Some officials still accused European ethnics of un-American attitudes, but the widespread panic regarding German Americans dissipated. Bitter sentiments against German Americans in society certainly did not evaporate immediately after the war. The Houston chapter of the revitalized Ku Klux Klan marched in the 1921 German American Mayfest celebration of Brenham with banners and signs reading, "Speak English or quit speaking on the streets of Brenham." In the 1922 primary the victorious Klan candidate for United States Senate, Earle Mayfield, alleged that his opponent, former Governor Ferguson, was sullied by black and German votes. Ed R. Bentley, the anti-liquor and pro-Klan candidate for superintendent of public instruction, lost to S. L. M. Marrs, the Progressive Education establishment's candidate, by only 21,000 votes in 1922.[30]

During the 1920s anti-German nativism faded as the previously existing anti-Mexican American sentiment multiplied. A few possible explanations exist for this shift in Lone Star nativism. Historian Walter Kamphoefner writes that most German Americans before World War I maintained usage of the German language in their homes, schools, and churches. By the 1940s the second generation of German Americans, the children of those who immigrated and who themselves were often raised in the United States, maintained the German tongue to a remarkable degree even though the war decimated classroom bilingualism. Kamphoefner argues that German Americans were neither socioeconomically handicapped nor marginalized by such native language retention. German Americans had just as much social mobility and even higher rates of economic stability and home ownership than did non-German, English speakers.[31] Bilingualism worked for German Americans.

German Americans by the second generation were making the transition from the working class to the middle class. Historian Alwyn Barr in a quantitative analysis of economic mobility among blacks, Mexican Americans, and German Americans in San Antonio from 1870 to 1900 found that German immigrants rapidly and substantially gained toward the middle class while Mexican Americans—largely because of race—remained employed in exploitive manual labor. The slight economic mobility of Mexican Americans differed insignificantly from the statistical baseline of inertness provided by the African American sample. Why did German immigrants to San Antonio, as committed as Mexican Americans to the maintenance of their native tongue, advance, while Mexican Americans did not? Barr postulated, "the presence of more distinct ethnic groups such as Negroes and Mexican Americans apparently enhanced the chances for occupational advance by European immigrants and reduced the level of prejudice against them."[32] German Americans made the jump to the middle class and eventually to whiteness, whereas Mexican Americans became racialized—an "other" race with African Americans. To be sure, Tejanos had been viewed as racial others by whites long before, but their racialization increased as the proletarianization of Mexicans in Texas proceeded in the early twentieth century.

The reasons why the sharp and focused nativism directed against German Americans during the war declined after the war are complex and still not fully understood. Rarely in the educational curriculum were German Americans, or any other European ethnic groups, singled out after the war as needing special Americanization programs. The recipe for the Americanization of these white, European, ethnic groups, for the most part, consisted of not much more than speaking English—a simple Americanization. The Americanization that came after the war and targeted Mexican Americans was a scientific, sociological, and pedagogical approach so complex that it mandated that teachers of such children have special instruction in teachers' colleges with special techniques.

Segregation and Americanization for Mexican American children became synonymous with and based upon the increasing racialization of Mexican Americans in the early twentieth century. Previously, Mexican Americans had been outsiders with claim to citizenship; by the 1920s they were perceived as foreign races without. The interviews conducted during the late 1920s in South Texas by University of California—Berkeley economist Paul S. Taylor dramatically illustrated the racialization of native Tejanos and Mexican immigrants. The language and race of Mexican American children reinforced one another. One prominent businessman in a small South Texas town remarked to Taylor of the instruction given to Mexican Americans, "We provide schools which are separate for several reasons: difference in language, most of the Mexicans here are of the *pelado* type; difference of color and race; difference of locality in which each group resides. We admit some Mexicans to American schools in the higher grades, and some others who live near other schools and are of the better type."[33]

The inability of many Tejano and immigrant children from Mexico to speak English in school reinforced preexisting racist ideology. Education here perpetuated the existence of a predetermined and racially defined underclass by identifying language difference as the central focus of all schooling. One Taylor interview illustrates the aspirations and all-too-visible limitations of 1920s-style Americanization in Texas. An Anglo interviewee remarked, "When you educate a Mexican he is pretty close to the white man. The Mexican has not the bodily odor and is not so black as the Negro, so people are less favorable to the education of the Mexican than the Negroes because education removes the differences . . . The inferiority of the Negroes is biological; that of the Mexicans not so much so if any."[34] Where to start? This statement illustrates the contradictions that Mexican Americans posed to Anglo notions of racial order and hierarchy. The assumption of impermanent inferiority and hence the potential for education to elevate was the very basis of Americanization. However, when one was darker rather than lighter or smelled more like work and less like perfume, apparently Americanization could accomplish little. When the United States Congress in the 1920s held hearings on closing the hemispheric exemption in immigration law, scientists and congressmen raised serious doubts about the ability of Mexicans ever to become truly Americanized. One scientist testified that "on biological grounds, no degree of education or social action can effectively overcome the handicap" of being "an inferior or distant race."[35]

English-speaking ability was considered more important than any scholastic aptitude in Spanish; all subjects were sacrificed to the unfortunate notion that one's command of English represented the only avenue for learning. One of the state's education experts announced, "The unfortunate thing about these foreign communities in Texas is not the amount of illiteracy found in them so much as the fact that they still cling to their foreign languages and customs." The public schools were the new missions; Progressive teachers, the new missionaries; and Americanization through English-Only, the new catechism. One young and sympathetic teacher characterized her sentiments about Mexican American education: "When you see an inferior race that can't help themselves, the missionary spirit makes you want to do something to Americanize them."[36]

Mexican American education was all Americanization all the time. A Harlingen principal of a "Mexican School" in the 1930s argued "certainly Americanization and citizenship cannot be separated—therefore, it would follow that education and Americanization are working toward the same end."[37] As early as 1905 Hidalgo County Judge R. A. Marsh illustrated this reductive view of Americanization by equating the exclusion of all other forms of academic learning for English instruction as his county's general pedagogical approach. Americanizing through language meant that true academic achievement was made impossible. Superintendent D. B. Burrows of the San Diego schools in Duval County noted of his Tejano population, "more than half of the pupils are in the first and second grades." Most of the academic work at these levels was preparatory in nature—not standard.[38]

The degree of segregation was never uniform statewide and subject to debate among educators. One school superintendent argued for extended segregation and Americanization for Tejanos: "These children need five or six years of Americanization before being placed with American children."[39] One pedagogical journal printed an article in 1932 as to the degree of segregation that would be best for Tejano students, stating that in many South Texas schools, the length of segregation ranged from grades one through three to grades one through seven. Some towns allowed limited "admission to the American school" for

One of the ironies of the Americanization Movement for Mexican Americans was its rationalization of segregation and inadequate facilities. Professor Herschel T. Manuel of the University of Texas documented such discrimination in this picture from the late 1920s. Photograph courtesy of Herschel T. Manuel Photographs at the Nettie Lee Benson Latin American Center, Folder 4, Photograph 19.

those Mexican Americans meeting the necessary "residence, language ability, or social position."[40] One educator who generously argued for the segregation of Mexican American children on an individual basis remarked that "the better classes are white, both in body and spirit." Thus, they deserved, he claimed, some rough equality with whites, while the others, "the ill-clad, unclean, poverty-stricken children of peon extraction," warranted little more than a cleansing program of Americanization.[41]

One important intellectual justification to the already common practice of segregating Mexican American students in the public schools was the intelligence quotient test. The state of Texas in the early 1920s commissioned IQ research by scholars Helen Lois Koch and Rietta Simmons. Through a host of flawed, methodological practices, they argued that Mexican American children in Texas were inherently less intelligent than whites. They argued that Mexican Americans occupied a middle ground between the high scores of white students and the lowest of scores belonging to African Americans. They took their conclusions so far that, in light of their own admission of a lack of conclusive evidence, they still concluded that darker-skinned Mexican Americans scored lower and were, thus, less intelligent than those of lighter skin. Other states throughout the American Southwest also commonly used

IQ (and achievement) tests to justify educational segregation in the early twentieth century.[42]

All Americanizers deplored Mexican American poverty and often blamed it on the need for Americanization in the first place. The desire to Americanize through the schools could not be realized if the children were not in school, though. Tejano children formed a large segment of the farmworker population. This fact was not lost on local school administrators who on the one hand were charged with the enforcement of compulsory education and the Americanization of Mexican American students, and on the other hand were reluctant to interfere with the pool of cheap child labor utilized by local agricultural interests. Administrators usually sided with the growers, limiting their ability to Americanize. Explained one school superintendent of his non-enforcement of compulsory attendance, "The board . . . told me they preferred to keep the Mexicans ignorant." One Anglo reflected this attitude when he claimed, "I am for education and educating my own children, but the Mexicans, like some whites, get some education and then they can't labor. They think it is a disgrace to work. The illiterates make the best farm labor? Yes, that is exactly it."[43] Webb County Superintendent E. R. Tanner excused the lack of Tejano attendance at his schools by explaining that his pupils and their families regularly needed "to go to the interior points in Texas to pick and chop cotton." Nonenforcement of the compulsory education law was widespread enough to trigger a state investigation of South Texas counties in the early 1920s resulting in the discovery of massive school census fraud.[44]

Institutionalizing the Americanization of Tejanos through the public schools continued unabated in the 1920s and 1930s. State Superintendent S. M. N. Marrs succeeded Blanton, and he kept up the Americanization drumbeat. In 1929 he requested the creation of a specific bureaucratic arm for the State Department of Education, as had Blanton before, to specialize in using Americanization to deal with the "illiteracy" problem. His proposed "division of Americanization" sounded much like a "division of Mexican American education."[45] The prime directive of Americanization curriculum in the Texas public schools was English-Only language policy. Foreign languages were to be substituted with the English language, regardless of how many other subjects were sacrificed or how many times small Tejano and immigrant Mexican children repeated the first grade.

The Americanization Movement began as a relatively benign idea in nineteenth-century Texas in its additive form. It became a more racist and negative idea by the turn of the century in its subtractive form. It emerged as a sharp anti-immigrant, anti-German response to the crisis of World War I. By the 1920s Americanization had evolved into a whole scientific approach of teaching Mexican American inferiority through segregation and English-Only language pedagogy. Language policy was affected by Americanization when real English-Only appeared in 1918 and was dramatically expanded in 1923, officially ending the already limping bilingual tradition of classroom instruction. Though Texas briefly considered reforming Americanization curriculum during the next world war, it would not significantly alter Americanization's influence until decades later. From 1918 until the late 1960s, any form of bilingual education in Texas remained illegal and the education of Mexican Americans was based, in large part, on the attitudes of the Americanization Movement.

CHAPTER FIVE

The Theory and Practice of English-Only Pedagogy, 1893–1941

74   The confluence of the ideology of Americanization and its intellectual parent, the Progressive Education movement, created the context for the development of a new way to teach English to non-English-speaking children: English-Only pedagogy. This new method required the use of solely English instructions, directions, and drills in the education of non-English-speaking students. It was an entire system of learning for young, language-minority children. English-Only purposely disregarded use of the native language as an unnecessary hindrance to learning English. The intent of English-Only was to assimilate immigrant children rapidly by substituting an all-English environment for bilingual instruction. English-Only pedagogy in the United States has received even less attention from historians than the little-studied nineteenth-century bilingual tradition. Its historiography derives from scholars' focusing on the resurgence of English-Only in the 1980s and 1990s. Typical of the lack of reflection on the subject are the comments of one scholar who simply equates English-Only with "the crusade for Anglo conformity" that suddenly appeared in the twentieth century without referring to Progressive Education or the changing conceptions of assimilation created by the Americanization movement.[1] Others attempting to examine English-Only do so in cursory fashion from fields outside of history.[2] Scholarship on the history of bilingual education generally ignores the role of English-Only pedagogy in the destruction of early bilingual education, focusing simply on World War I–era nativism instead.[3]

   English-Only pedagogy in the United States has an even stranger career than bilingual education. English-Only was a pedagogical system consisting of assumptions about the acquisition of language that sharply diverged from traditional notions: One, it held that the act of translation hindered learning a second language; two, it maintained that children and adults learned second languages alike. Since antiquity the teaching of foreign languages involved the heavy use of reading, translating, and transcribing academic languages into vernacular form and vice versa. Verbal ability was considered less important under these long-held ideas than was written ability. Thus, bilingualism was implicit in the learning of new languages. This method of language teaching was referred to as the "grammar-translation" method and dominated as a pedagogical theory in the United States until the late nineteenth century.[4] Progressive Education's belief in non-rote, creative curriculum stimulated educators to rebel against any translation in the learning of new languages. This newer scientific pedagogy regarded the bilingualism inherent in the grammar-translation method as a hindrance in teaching English to non-English-speaking children. These pedagogical innovations on language acquisition were recently imported from France, which at that time was attempting to spread French throughout its rural countryside.[5]

French scholar François Gouin provided most of the ideas on language acquisition that influenced the shift away from grammar-translation. In the 1880s and 1890s Gouin revolutionized educators' concept of languages and how they were learned. Gouin began his research on language acquisition out of his own personal frustration at being unable to learn German through the old, grammar-translation method for his doctoral studies. He developed what he called the "natural method" by which adults could learn a second language the way a child would learn a primary language, orally and without any bilingual reference. Americans picked up on Gouin's methods, created a more descriptive terminology, and then transplanted it to the United States public school system as the answer to educating immigrant children without resorting to the politically uncomfortable practice of bilingual instruction. American linguists used the terminology "direct method" to describe Gouin's use of oral word association without native language reference and "indirect method" to refer to the old bilingual methods of instruction. The former abstained from any native language reference while the later involved the translation of a word from one language to another through written or oral transmission.[6]

Most American linguists at that time believed the bilingual or indirect method to be deeply flawed. This notion became the dominant position of educators and researchers between the turn of the century and World War I. One of Gouin's American supporters argued against any kind of bilingualism in teaching language-minority children English with the claim that such methods involved a complicated "triple association of idea, native expression, [and] English expression" that would retard ultimate English-speaking ability. Another pedagogue warned teachers in possession of bilingual capabilities: "Every time the teacher resorts to translation in making clear a word or sentence, she is making it easier for herself at the expense of the pupil's progress. The more English the pupil hears the sooner he will be able to speak."[7]

Texas' desire to introduce English-Only was pronounced by the turn of the century. Attempts both in 1893 and again in 1905, though significant as portents of change, failed to completely eliminate the Texas bilingual tradition. The 1893 and 1905 laws suffered from a lack of enforcement. Some schools in this period, such as those of Gillespie County for German Americans and Hidalgo County for Mexican Americans, belied their boasting about teaching English with admissions of lingering bilingualism in their schools. Others, as documented earlier, simply ignored the English-Only directives, secure in the knowledge that the state had neither the will nor the bureaucratic machinery to fulfill its English-Only desires. Both will and ability soon arrived, however.[8]

The 1918 English-Only law took the state's unenforceable English-Only sentiments from partially fulfilled wish to concrete reality. Legislators argued that they were defending the culture of those who died at the Alamo from German—"the language that is being used in our country in seditious propaganda to undermine the patriotic efforts of our government to secure world-wide democracy."[9] The 1918 law stipulated that officials would charge violators of this policy with a criminal misdemeanor. Conviction carried with it several possible punishments that could be handed down separately or together: a $25–$100 fine, revocation of state teaching certification, and automatic dismissal. The offense was not considered cumulative; it began anew each day a non-English word of instruction was uttered. The 1918 English-Only law was totalitarian in its scope and finality. On the criminal law books as article 288 of the Texas Penal Code, English-Only remained in force, albeit with a few minor modifications, until the late 1960s.[10]

The war against foreign languages in the classroom continued after World War I—focused on Spanish instead of German. As the war hysteria died out, Superintendent Annie Webb Blanton justified the need for a tremendous expansion of state control over education to target new immigrants to Texas (primarily Mexicans). Blanton remarked in 1920, "The need for Americanization was brought forcibly before the American people by the Great War. The draft and other war activities revealed many unassimilated and unamalgamated groups of nationalities who had not caught the vision of America, who knew nothing of its institutions, and who could not even understand its language."[11]

Superintendent Blanton sought expansion of the English-Only requirement to private schools. Trading on residual wartime patriotism, Blanton talked of the necessity of remembering "the stalwart khaki-clad youths of America whom American mothers and fathers bravely sent forth as sacrifices" when considering the necessity of another English-Only law. Blanton also evoked the red scare. The Russian and Mexican Revolutions made particularly good boogeymen: "The history of Mexico, of Russia, and of every other uneducated, or poorly educated nation or state, gives evidence that a people without education, or with insufficient education, soon lose possession of their most valuable natural resources, to better educated or more skilled leaders from without." Blanton clearly intended the new legislation to apply to Mexican Americans: "In certain counties along our borders are many men and women, born and reared in the Lone Star State, who speak a foreign tongue and cherish the habits and ways of another country."[12] Blanton claimed, "There are many communities in Texas in which the children are trained in private or parochial schools in which the medium of instruction is a foreign tongue. Many of these children become adults without having learned to read or write the English language." Although Superintendent Blanton popularized the issue, it was actually enacted under her successor, S. M. N. Marrs, in 1923 as an amendment to the state's compulsory attendance regulations.[13]

Unlike their 1893 and 1905 ancestors, the 1918 and 1923 English-Only laws proved effective. They were so successful that they soon had to be revised to correct their excessiveness. The 1918 and 1923 laws prohibited the study of other languages as academic subjects in the lower grades, allowing it at the high school level only. In trying to tackle the German- and Spanish-oriented bilingual tradition, these draconian laws unintentionally dampened the study of those languages even as academic courses. Shortly after an important United States Supreme Court decision, the state legislature quietly passed piecemeal revisions to rectify the collateral damage that English-Only had inflicted upon the study of foreign languages.

The state first backtracked in 1927. The legislature decided that its earlier wisdom of outlawing all foreign languages and foreign language texts in the lower grades was flawed. The 1927 correction allowed for "the Spanish language in elementary grades in the public free schools in counties bordering on the boundary line between the United States and the Republic of Mexico and having a city or cities of five thousand or more inhabitants according to the United States census for the year 1920."[14] This correction did not much alter the way English-Only functioned. The law's enforcement went generally unchanged as did the stipulation that all other languages be taught only at the high school level. The legislature explained that "under the present law it is unlawful to teach Spanish in the elementary grades in the public free schools of the state." The meaning of this statement was purposely vague. Though the legislature would never openly backtrack on the prohibition of bilingual instruction, they were more aware of English-Only's negative effects. They claimed that it was of "inestimable value" that citizens so geographically situated near the border be schooled in Spanish, concluding it was "imperative that instruction in such a language be begun at the earliest possible period."[15]

The next backtracking from the English-Only laws came in 1933. The 1933 modification extended the previous exemption of Spanish in the border counties to the rest of the state but broadened it to include all modern languages, including German. The 1933 revision stated that "it shall be lawful to provide text books, as now provided by law, for and to teach any modern language in the elementary grades of the public free schools above the second grade." It further remarked, "the present law greatly hinders the teaching of foreign language by restricting it to high school grades."[16]

English-Only pedagogy was not solely an ideological or racist subterfuge. Behind its application from local and state education officials was a locally derived body of academic research and theory in addition to the national literature. It is true that English-Only in the hands of state and local educators quickly became used for racist and nativist ends. However, the science behind the pedagogy was not hollow. Well-intentioned citizens and those of lesser motives accepted English-Only's pedagogical background as incontrovertible and fundamentally Progressive. The pedagogy of English-Only was capable of nuance and sophistication, making it much more than a crude excuse to segregate Mexican Americans and label them inferior, to which end it was undoubtedly applied.

The Texas education establishment couched the content of English-Only lessons and its manner of application as supportive of the principles of John Dewey, the national symbol for Progressive curricular reform. One instructor echoed Dewey by writing that English-Only be flexibly applied with regard to the individual student's capabilities: "By giving each child individual attention and by shifting him from one group to another as often as is necessary we feel that he has a chance to advance as rapidly as he can without any serious drawback." A teaching manual published by the State Department of Education quoted Progressive pedagogue G. Stanley Hall's plea for flexibility and for teachers to "resist the extremists who insist there is only one best and exclusive method."[17] Ironically, this Progressive plea for pedagogical flexibility that reformers originally utilized in championing English-Only soon gave way to rigidity once they embedded English-Only in law and curriculum.

English-Only in Texas had been a Progressive trend well before the wartime crisis. Progressive State Superintendent R. B. Cousins wrote in 1909, "It was the writer's pleasure to visit schools in a great seaport city and watch a teacher teach children that had been in this country only four weeks, and others a little longer. In the same room were Russians, Italians, Germans and Jews from many parts of the world. The children did not speak the same language and could not understand one another. The teacher could not speak the language of a single child in that room, and yet in two years all those children learn to speak English and are then sent to their respective schools about the city, the question of speaking English forever settled." Cousins noted that this effort was duplicated in El Paso, which, he claimed, "will not allow the teachers to speak Spanish in teaching little Mexicans." He went on to write, "Pedagogically there is nothing in the argument that the teacher must speak the language of the child to teach him." Similar classrooms of that era in which linguistic minorities were grouped together for an extended length of time in remedial, preparatory environments to learn English were given the moniker "steamer schools" or "soup schools" in places like Cleveland, New York, and Boston.[18]

Texas teachers were encouraged to make the direct method of English-Only more Progressive by ensuring that lessons were relevant to the individual child's everyday life concerns. Elma A. Neal, a teacher in San Antonio, developed a Progressive pedagogical system for teaching young Mexican American children how to speak through English-Only. Neal realized that many practitioners of English-Only did not utilize the method properly due to reliance upon old, sterile recitations that were "largely literary in content and foreign to the child's experience," instead of the more Progressive lessons based on "a practical vocabulary" that was in turn "based on the everyday experiences of the child." She believed the direct method of English-Only followed Progressive Education theory, seconding national commentators that bilingualism entailed a triple or "three track association which retards the language process and accounts for the hesitation noted in the speech of those who learn a new language by this method."[19]

However, the totality of English-Only pedagogy, its insistence upon being the beginning and end point of all education for non-English-speaking children, inherently contradicted those very same Progressive principles abhorrent of staid, rote, and tiresome drills. The State Department of Education exemplified this contradiction when it claimed, "The teacher must keep in mind that she is to make English function in

English-Only pedagogy made every minute of the day an exercise in language instruction. Note the absence of translation on the board. By linking language to everyday activities, English-Only pedagogy intended to supplant, not complement, native languages. Photo courtesy of Herschel T. Manuel Photographs at the Nettie Lee Benson Latin American Center, Folder 4, Photograph 24.

every activity of the day." Every activity became an English lesson. The most important principle to consider in the instruction of the non-English-speaking child was that "Drill, drill, and *more drill* is an absolute essential here." Lessons were ambitiously all-encompassing: "Teach the children English by the direct method and not by translation of their language into the English. Train them to *think* in English. This is absolutely essential if they are to acquire any facility in the use of English."[20]

The administration of English-Only pedagogy eventually became a functionary branch of all Tejano education; this was especially so in the 1920s when Tejanos officially became a "problem" in the state educational community, garnering specialized deliberation from the State Department of Education in pedagogical handbooks. An example of this occurred in 1924 with publication of the *Texas Educational Survey Report,* a multivolume series of studies on Texas education commissioned by the legislature. Mexican Americans occupied a prominent place in several reports; several sample lessons of English-Only were reprinted.[21] This was significant, for, even during World War I, German American children were never singled out in special state publications. Although the state claimed of its statewide curriculum that "no special interest shall be given undue privilege in the organization and manipulation of its courses of study," the direct method was practiced with specific regard to Mexican American children. This intimate connecting of English-Only language pedagogy to Mexican American education existed even before World War I.[22]

South Texas schools teaching Mexican Americans were regarded as pedagogical laboratories upon which to base the statewide curriculum. The aforementioned Texas Survey Commission found that "much good work was being done in various communities of the state in handling the non-English speaking children." Administrators and teachers of Mexican Americans had already organized local pedagogical associations to keep abreast of and share new instructional innovations as the state was just getting involved in developing a standardized English-Only curriculum. The Valley Superintendents' Association was formed in 1924. In 1926 came the Lower Rio Grande Valley Elementary Principals' Association. This organization centered upon implementing an English-Only curriculum for Mexican Americans. A participant wrote, "One of the major problems confronting the Valley Schools is that of the proper instruction of the foreign-speaking child."[23]

This pedagogical ferment in South Texas created the models for statewide English-Only policy during the 1920s and 1930s. In 1930 the Valley Superintendents' Association, after a few years of planning and experiments, published with the State Department of Education a special curriculum for Spanish-speaking children in the first three grades. This was adopted as the official English-Only curriculum of Texas. The Rio Grande valley educators started with the familiar direct method justifications of using the child's foreign language, English, as the sole medium of expression. They warned of using Spanish in the classroom, "Such methods are entirely unsuited for teaching foreigners English . . . the method should be one which emphasizes the spoken word, not the written word. Understanding and speaking the language should come first."[24]

English-Only for Tejanos was a direct method application that demanded almost as much from the teacher as it did from the pupil. The teaching of object nouns was made easier by pictures, but teaching verbs, or "action words," must have been exhausting. The instructor pantomimed the verb she or he taught, all the while slowly repeating it with emphasis on enunciation, over and over until the children learned, osmosis-like, the desired verb: "In teaching the action words the teacher first performs the act several times herself, at the same time telling what she does." The teacher was then taught to call upon the students to mimic her own pantomime while repeating the sound.[25] Other pedagogical treatises for implementing English-Only to Tejanos echoed the same techniques. W. J. Knox of the San Antonio schools recommended to TSTA participants in a 1915 convention using a version of the direct method "richly supplemented with pictures, objects, actions, games, songs, and excursions." Knox emphasized that a knowledge of Spanish on the part of the teacher was—unlike in past, bilingual years—now unnecessary. In addition, Knox urged teachers, "Be sure to make haste slowly. Repeat, repeat, drill, drill, drill."[26] Brownsville Superintendent Lizzie M. Barbour urged that in addition to using pictures, dramatization, and "phonics," teachers should also adopt the direct method of English-Only: "The very fact that it is easier to translate than to develop would show that great restraint and much discretion is needed to avoid giving too much help."[27]

It was not enough that Tejano children learn to speak in English; they would have to learn to "think" in English as well. Thus, the full application of English-Only's more extreme theoretical principles involved the policing of thought as much as the policing of speech. One teacher from San Marcos wrote that inability to think in English would always render Mexican Americans mentally handicapped. English-Only was applied ruthlessly to Spanish-speaking children to the exclusion of other subjects and in a manner that suggested that knowledge in Spanish was unimportant. Another teacher put it succinctly: "Never give the Spanish word first for we do not wish the children to translate from Spanish to English, but to think in English."[28]

The total application of the direct method of English-Only to such young pupils had unduly harsh effects. A superintendent from El Paso illustrated one common outgrowth of such an English-Only policy, "English must be used not only in the classrooms but also in the corridors and on the premises." He remarked that any Mexican American "who is habitually neglectful or is willfully indifferent or is defiant in the observation of this rule . . . should be suspended from school until he is willing to return with the assurance of abiding by the rules of the school." Such expulsions were to help the "Spanish-speaking pupils become acquainted with English."[29] Teachers and administrators even monitored the playgrounds. One guidebook argued that school authorities outlaw the use of Spanish in the playground through "supervised play." Actions of even well-intentioned teachers applying English-Only pedagogy appear harsh by today's standards of acceptable behavior. In the school year of 1928–29 in the small, segregated Mexi-

One of the early practitioners of English-Only pedagogy was a young Lyndon Baines Johnson during his first teaching job in Cotulla, Texas. Fittingly, Johnson, the only United States president with experience teaching non-English-speaking children, signed into law the 1967–68 Bilingual Education Act. Photo courtesy of the LBJ Library, No. 28-13-4.

Though at times a stern practitioner of English-Only pedagogy, young Lyndon B. Johnson was not without compassion. For example, LBJ donated a portion of his first paycheck to purchase a set of permanent athletic equipment for the school pictured here. Photo courtesy of the LBJ Library, No. 28-13-8.

can school of Cotulla in La Salle County, a young teacher whose compassion and sympathy some students later credited with turning around their lives, practiced the Progressive methods of physical punishments (ear pinchings and spankings) for English-Only violations. That teacher was Lyndon Baines Johnson on his first teaching job.[30]

Learning new ways in which the mouth must be contorted and the tongue positioned was and still is an important part of learning foreign languages. In the teaching of foreign languages in high schools, teachers simply explained how the tongue, lips, and teeth worked in order to produce difficult or exotic sounds. However, such moderation was lost on smaller Mexican Americans learning English as a foreign language. For Spanish-speaking children in the first three grades, teachers were encouraged to grab students' tongues, lips, or jaws to demonstrate pronunciation. The manual advised, "the teacher should have him come close to her while she shows him just how to place his teeth, tongue, and lips in order to utter the sound correctly." If this method proved unsuccessful, the teacher was to "Have the child then repeat the sound again and again, endeavoring to place the organs of speech as they should be, until he is able to give the sound correctly."[31]

The direct method of English-Only to Mexican Americans was not only demeaning but unfair, especially considering that it was never applied so stringently to native English-speakers at the high school level. Shortly before World War I, the state educational leadership considered the pedagogical options that could be used to teach high school pupils foreign languages. By 1915 teaching guides already advocated teaching foreign languages using "the direct method of presentation." In 1918 Superintendent W. F. Doughty went further and dismissed the use of the "Grammar-Translation Method" and advocated use of the "Direct Method."[32] But this direct method in teaching foreign languages to white high schoolers was applied differently to them than it was to six- and seven-year-old Tejanos. For high school language classes, Doughty argued that even though recent pedagogical conventions pushed for the direct method, "extremes" were to be avoided with a moderate approach utilizing some native language translation. He identified this approach the "semi-direct" method.[33] English-Only's application to Mexican American children was extreme, less flexible, and less fair— nothing "semi" about it. Educators were not to make any distinction between the adult English-speaking student of foreign languages and the six-year-old student learning English. One scholar observed that, ideally, "English should be taught to foreigners as a foreign language; foreign-speaking children, learning English, should be looked upon by instructors as being in the same position as American children who are

learning French or German." This was a mistake. One far-sighted pedagogue lamented this notion when he argued that the defects of the direct method lay "in attempts to apply the method in unmodified form
to the teaching of English at the primary level on the assumption that
the problem at this point is essentially identical with the problem of
teaching a foreign-language at a more advanced level."[34]

The coexistence of official direct method, English-Only, and its un-
fairly selective application continued unchallenged through the 1920s
and 1930s.[35] This contradiction served to ease high schoolers' discom-
fort and embarrassment at uttering alien sounds around their peers.
Superintendent Marrs formulated a curriculum guide on the assumption that for high school students, spoken foreign language fluency
would never be attainable. To ease the language teacher's load, Marrs
stated that even though "the direct method is the preferable plan" for
high schools, it also was unrealistic, and that in reality "Very few teachers . . . use the so-called modern or pure direct method." He added,
"Occasionally, when acceptable methods break down, the teacher resorts to translation, and so substitutes English for Spanish in the classroom."[36]

State curriculum was tailored to do all it could for high school students in de-emphasizing the spoken word for the written one. The
value or soundness of this policy is not the issue here; it is how the same
pedagogy was applied to the unbending detriment of much younger,
native Spanish speakers. Texas wielded two separate policies on languages: Older white students were allowed indirect methods (bilingual
instruction), and the youngest, most vulnerable of Mexican American
children had to learn in a purely direct method of instruction originally
popularized by a middle-aged, nineteenth-century French scholar's efforts to pass his German exams.

Because few records of the English-Only era critically evaluated it,
the question of its effectiveness proves difficult to assess. Were small
children able to keep up with a fast-talking teacher speaking an alien
language? A cursory examination of the data on Mexican American
age-to-grade ratios, dropout rates, and failure rates indicates overwhelmingly that the educational achievement of this group of students
was exceptionally poor when compared to that of all others. Mexican
American enrollment in the Texas public schools by the 1940s was dis-
proportionately concentrated in the first grade. The first grade population across the state for the Mexican Americans was roughly twice that
of the second grade, a staggering statistical anomaly that can only suggest a shocking failure or dropout rate. Most Tejano children were not
getting past the first grade in one year. This was not an insignificant

number of failures as the Mexican American student population between 1922 and 1928, for example, grew as a percentage of the total
scholastic population at a rate five times that of all other whites and
more than nine times that of African Americans.[37]

Its most ardent practitioners implicitly acknowledged that English-Only resulted in a certain level of academic failure. Failure was
expected in the English-Only system of education; most Mexican
Americans were expected to fail anyway. The teachers' pantomime
performances must have left many blank stares, downcast eyes, and
empty faces if the staggering failure rates are to be properly understood.
A teacher from El Paso stated the failure of English-Only pedagogy
quite bluntly: "In schools which follow a more or less formal type of
procedure Mexican children sometimes spend four years or more be-
low the second grade without mastering enough English and reading
to attempt a more advanced type of work. Eventually these children
become discouraged and bored with endless repetition of incompre-
hensible stories and meaningless routine. Apathy and indifference follow, if not behavior problems, until teachers consider them slow or
mentally incapable of progress."[38]

The disastrous consequences for Tejanos under English-Only did not
go unnoticed. A Del Rio teacher in the 1930s noted the cruel unfairness
of asking a Spanish-speaking child to learn as many as 3,000 English
words (then taken as the usual number of words known by the average English-speaking student upon completion of grade one) by the
end of the first grade if he or she entered school with only 500 words
and the English-speaker started off with some 2,000 words. She argued
that the lack of success in school meant that "Personal egotism has been
crushed under the unnecessarily severe burden and instead are engen-
dered anti-social feelings of inferiority and the inescapable psychic
consequences of hopeless comparisons under such unequal circumstances . . . leading to suicide, whether partial or complete, to the in-
stinct for self improvement—the only really indispensable factor in the
educating process."[39]

English-Only application sacrificed all other learning to the unfortunate notion that non-English-speaking children's grasp of English
represented the sum of all learning. D. B. Burrows, superintendent of
San Diego schools, noted as early as the 1910–11 school year that more
than half of his school's pupils, most of them Tejanos, were in the first
and second grade and that the first year was entirely preparatory to the
regular, state-mandated first grade curriculum. Of academic subjects
beyond English for his Spanish speakers, Superintendent B. Richard-

son of Webb County wrote in 1902–1903 that he "directed the teachers to make everything subsidiary to teaching English."[40]

The state's educational leaders knew that English-Only was a failure yet continued to base the entire statewide curriculum around it. Cheering on the practitioners of English-Only, one teacher opined that in many cases the *diligent* and *talented* Mexican American first-year students might "make good second grade pupils by mid-term of the following year instead of staying in the first grade two or three years." This teacher's argument that the successful Spanish-speaking child be retained (failed) only one semester is by far the most optimistic of expert prognostications. For example, in the public schools of Laredo during the late 1920s—over a decade after the imposition of the English-Only law—the percentage of the total student population (overwhelmingly Tejano or Mexican) classified as overage (academic failures) was 81 percent. In Eagle Pass, Brownsville, and El Paso corresponding rates were mired at 78, 70, and 52 percent.[41] That the schools were cavalierly and routinely failing this many Spanish-speaking students is shocking and reprehensible. Such was the toll of English-Only.

The evidence seems so overwhelming today that one wonders how such failure could be possibly rationalized in any society claiming any kind of democratic ideals. Educators often relied on intelligence testing to justify this massive school failure. Intelligence test administrators held throughout the 1910s and 1920s that Mexican Americans, like African Americans and other ethnic groups, were of flawed intellectual heredity. By the 1930s and 1940s throughout the American Southwest school failure and low test scores came to be regarded a cultural deficiency of "language handicap."[42]

Other observers were less generous in the degree of failure to be expected from Mexican Americans. One teacher from Rio Grande City succinctly characterized as the main tenets of educating such students: "the welfare of the child, the mastery of the English language, and the mastery of specified academic subject matter." He went on to claim, "These objectives are not necessarily incompatible; however, a disastrous situation results if the latter proposition becomes the dominant aim of the school." English-Only in this border town did not gain students access to any real academic enrichment or greater opportunity. If anything, it precluded even the remotest possibility of academic achievement; real academic achievement was written off as inherently unattainable. The teacher summarized the practice of his school: "we have substituted in the place of an absolute academic program a wider and more significant concept of education."[43]

One of the ways in which the institutionalized failure of English-Only was transmitted to new teachers was through their training in teachers' colleges. Important for the curricular development of English-Only was the opening in 1925 of the South Texas State Teachers' College in Kingsville, later renamed Texas A&I University. The state depended upon this college to lead the way in teaching Mexican Americans. Recruiting Dr. L. F. Heinmiller, an education professor from New York University, the school built its education department on a solid experimental footing with its laboratory schools, which were conducted in the direct method of English-Only. The laboratory schools were able, in controlled conditions, to create such a learning environment that their subjects, potentially the brightest Mexican American children in town, took no more than two years to complete first grade level work. The University of Texas offered similar coursework in its education department in the 1930s and 1940s under Professors George I. Sánchez and Herschel T. Manuel.[44]

Educators conflated English-Only for Mexican Americans and the notion of Americanization. Teaching manuals on the daily lessons of English-Only exercises also served as texts in Americanization. Indeed, for many educators of Mexican Americans, English-Only pedagogy was most valuable because its focus was really on Americanization. One teacher commented, "In launching an Americanization program for such a group first place has been given to the substitution of English for Spanish in school life." More succinct was a principal in the 1930s who claimed of her attempts to teach English to Tejanos, "education and Americanization are working toward the same ends."[45]

However, the most significant ramification of English-Only pedagogy was that it served as a convenient tool for maintaining segregated schools for Tejanos. Language was racialized; "special" language instruction was one of many excuses made for segregated schools. One author, for example, justified the pedagogical segregation of Mexican Americans on the basis that they needed specialized curricula, among other reasons. In some respects, the Mexican American's racial distinctiveness in the eyes of many Texans made the language barrier an additional hurdle for respectability, a double racial marker. One educator observed, "While the negro's standard of living is equally as low as that of the Mexican, the negro is not such a serious social problem . . . (1) The negroes speak the English language while the Mexicans do not; (2) the negroes have a separate school system while the Mexicans are legally classed as white and are entitled to school privileges along with other whites."[46] The existence of the above point two was a problem for whites desiring to segregate Mexican Americans racially until point one, language difference, helped solve the Mexican American's elusive racial classification. This utilization of pedagogy for the maintenance of segregated schools was legally protected in Texas throughout the 1930s and 1940s, established by the *Salvatierra* decision.[47]

The practice of segregation justified by special language pedagogy was widespread. Basil Armour, a principal in the Rio Grande valley, conducted a study of neighboring school districts and found varying levels of segregation. Two towns in the sample segregated only through the first three grades; two towns segregated grades one through four; eight schools were segregated in the first five grades; and one segregated all the way to the seventh grade. Many towns maintained separate junior highs and high schools. Armour plainly stated the pedagogical reasons for such widespread segregation: "It seems that segregation in the first few grades is best for the Mexican child in order to enable him to become adjusted to and to aid him in overcoming his language handicap."[48] Other school systems in Brownsville and Eagle Pass also admitted to segregating on the basis of linguistic difference and the need for specialized curriculum. Corpus Christi's Tejano children were only allowed a half day of school in the 1896–97 school term "so as not to interfere too much with the other grades."[49]

Mexican Americans both accommodated English-Only and resisted it. Bilingual private schools were surreptitiously continued when Mexican American parents believed that local public schools were too discriminatory or failed to prepare their children adequately. Again, however, Tejanos did not respond by completely rejecting English. Mexican American parents still viewed English as the crucial component of education but in most instances sought to preserve some level of Spanish either as a bridge to English or in its own right. This practice persisted with assistance from the United States Supreme Court. The bilingual tradition in Texas private schools (indeed, throughout the nation) continued due to the ultimate unconstitutionality of its 1923 English-Only law. In 1924 the U.S. Supreme Court overturned a Nebraska English-Only law that was similar to Texas'; they both mandated total English instruction in all private schools in their states. *Meyer* v. *Nebraska* held that this was a violation of parents' fourteenth amendment rights to choose the language in which their children were schooled. The ruling preserved the right of public schools to continue with English-Only, however, and affirmed the intent of forcing Americanization through English-Only pedagogy.[50]

Texas education officials soon came to disdain the continuing practice of Tejano parents' pulling their children out of the public schools and sending them to small private schools. In 1930 Superintendent

Marrs outlined his concern that Mexican American students were avoiding the public schools and attending temporary private schools that taught entirely in Spanish. "As late as the current year we have signs of the determination of some to have Spanish schools. An administrator in a small town in the Valley discovered one morning that a group of his grade pupils had been sent to a school organized overnight in which Spanish was to be used exclusively."[51] A San Antonio woman wrote of her own school experiences during the 1930s in a private, nonparochial institution called Colegio Altamirano, located in the town of Hebbronville in Jim Wells County. Her teacher was *"La Señorita"* Emilia Davila of Saltillo, Mexico, who taught all subject matter in Spanish. While this person did not learn adequate grade-level English at Colegio Altamirano, she kept up in all other academic subjects for her grade level, and, when she eventually transferred to the public schools, she had confidence stemming from academic accomplishment; she learned enough English to jump three grades in her first semester. National literature holds that Mexican American nonattendance of the public schools in favor of participation in private, Spanish-language ones in the nineteenth and early twentieth centuries was a form of resistance to English-Only.[52]

Mexican Americans generally wanted both English and Spanish for their children. The story of the Alice chapter of the Order of the Sons of America in the 1920s illustrates this. The Sons of America was a forerunner to the League of United Latin American Citizens. On March 13, 1927, thirteen members of the Alice Sons met to debate the subject of language in their children's education. Two members disagreed on whether or not the temporary school that their organization planned to create in the summer months should be run in Spanish or English. One of the vice presidents desired that it be run in English to help the members' children remember what had been taught in the public schools. The president sought Spanish instruction to best maintain the language and culture that the public schools taught their children to forget. The potential conflict was settled with the suggestion that the school be bilingual, so as not to lose the home culture or get behind in the public school's English-Only curriculum.[53]

The emergence of English-Only pedagogy in Texas was shaped by acceptance of the direct method of English-Only. However, in Texas, English-Only intensified for Mexican Americans after World War I. The pedagogical makeup of English-Only centered on assumptions regarding language acquisition that, in addition to being flawed, were not even fully applied to older, white students in the ruthless manner that they were applied to young, Tejano children. Sadly, Spanish-speaking children were taught under an unbending version of English-Only language pedagogy that went to such extremes as to favor expulsion for the utterance of a single Spanish word on school grounds, wildly gesticulating teacher pantomimes, and hands and fingers stuck in their faces. That young Tejanos performed miserably under English-Only and that it was not at all unexpected establishes direct evidence for condemning English-Only as grossly ineffective and ultimately racist. Despite this well-documented and commonly understood history of failure, English-Only remained Texas' official pedagogical approach for non-English speakers until the 1960s.

CHAPTER SIX

The Promise and Limits
of the Politics of Accommodation
and Wartime Opportunity,
1930–47

92   From the 1930s until the 1960s Mexican American leaders utilized the strategies of patriotism, middle-class acceptance, integration, and accommodation. This Mexican American Generation formed a consensus of leadership to battle for better schools.[1] Already galvanized by repatriation and the Great Depression in the 1930s, the Mexican American community perceived an unparalleled political opportunity in the nation's battle against racism and fascism during World War II. However, efforts during the 1940s bore only bitter disappointment.[2] This failed opportunity resulted in increasing militancy among Mexican American activists across the nation by the late 1940s and 1950s. Ultimately, the inability to alter the way schools functioned for their children, especially how language reinforced segregation, added to the pent-up frustration that would explode in the 1960s with a new generation of activists: The Chicano Generation.

The Mexican American community's response to English-Only during the 1930s and 1940s is quite impossible to separate from its response to segregated schools. Historian of the Mexican American Generation in San Antonio Richard Garcia notes of this interrelationship, "LULAC councils in San Antonio and throughout Texas . . . lectured and organized around the themes of education, citizenship, the English language, economic opportunities, and civil rights."[3] English-Only was discrimination, it had become segregation, and it reflected a lack of confidence in the educability of Mexican Americans.

By the late 1920s Tejanos were already ideologically prepared to take advantage of the strategies of patriotism and accommodation to middle-class Anglo aspirations as well as to important cultural norms such as the elevation of speaking English to sacrosanct status. This ideological preparation formed over three experiences: (1) the horrors of the violence of 1915 and El Plan de San Diego; (2) discrimination against Tejano veterans of World War I; and (3) the failure of *mutualistas* and the mutualist ethic to solve the ingrained racism of society. These three negative experiences taught Mexican Americans that discrimination hinged upon the presumption of foreign-ness and disloyalty. The Great Depression and repatriation in the 1930s greatly reinforced these notions. Therefore, a newer generation of Mexican American activists across the nation, and especially in Texas, stressed a hyphenated Americanism. Unlike some Chicano-era scholarship, this study interprets the Mexican American Generation as a positive and unique group of like-minded individuals pursuing logical political strategies. The Mexican American Generation was proud of and responsive to its community, not blindly assimilationist or self-loathing.[4] This new ideological framework—a significant shift from the mutualist ethic of the preceding Mexicanist Generation—represented the community's best chance at defeating societal prejudice.

By the late 1920s the subject of language in the schools began shifting in the Tejano community from an emphasis upon reinforcing Spanish to a more exclusive emphasis upon English. A 1927 meeting of the Order of the Sons of America of Alice, Texas, debated this issue. The OSA was a transitional organization for Mexican Americans of this era, bridging the older *mutualistas* and future patriotic, middle-class organizations. Manuel Saenz Escobar, the second vice president, proposed a motion recommending that they utilize the summer months for English instruction of their children: "what made Brother Saenz Escobar to write this artical is that he knows better what little benefit of education our children gets in the 9 months of school, in the three months of vacation they forget everything they learn and with 2 months of Summer School will be a great thing for our boys and girls and we believe everyone of the members of the order Sons of America will help this course to get to the top."[5]

President Frank Perez responded affirmatively to Saenz Escobar's proposal. But he also gave a short speech in Spanish to demonstrate the point that although English instruction was important, Spanish was equally important, and that the proposed summer school should instead be run in Spanish, in keeping with tradition. Summarizing President Perez's remarks, the OSA secretary wrote, "when he was a boy his father and other good citizens from San Diego made the same identical thing, they had a Professor paid by them and they gave us a better education and had use of the sunny days." The first vice president realized the conflict and moved to combine the original proposal of teaching English in the summer with the counterproposal of teaching Spanish: "First Vice President had a little trouble he didn't understand, he say this that in the motion made by the Second Vice President, wants a English School and the President wants a Spanish School, and wish that children would learn the Spanish correctly and the use of

English was easy for them. I would be glad if they learn the two languages." The issue thus settled, they congratulated one another on
reaching the same goal: bettering the education of their children in
both Spanish and in English. The Alice OSA's attitude regarding language was still bilingual, but it inched toward a greater emphasis upon
English.[6]

Male movement

The OSA was a patriotic organization of younger men and one of
the original parent groups for what eventually became the League of
United Latin American Citizens. LULAC's beginnings are important. In
1921 a group of eight Mexican American friends in their twenties and
early thirties, three of them World War I veterans, spent time at a small
ranch outside of San Antonio camping, barbecuing, and discussing the
discrimination facing their community. This resulted in the creation of
the OSA, chartered in October, 1921, in San Antonio. The OSA did not
cater to incoming Mexican immigrants or have a Mexicanist cultural
predisposition; rather, it was exclusively composed of Tejanos who
were born U.S. citizens or naturalized. It rejected the cultural nationalism of the Mexicanist *mutualistas.*[7]

The Alice OSA minutes illustrate that the Tejano middle class
still considered Spanish to be important. This represented a thread of
continuity between Mexicanist *mutualistas* and middle-class organizations. The OSA did not simply or completely represent blind, sub-
servient assimilation or middle-class warfare against the poor. Nevertheless, whatever this new generation of community leaders thought
of Spanish, it was relegated of secondary importance to knowledge of
English and some limited conformity to American cultural norms. Of
the breaks with the Mexicanist Generation illustrated by OSA and
LULAC—one being the exclusion of noncitizens from participation—
most important was the one related to language. LULAC projected
Americanism by adopting English as its official language in its meetings as did the OSA. LULAC mandated in its 1929 constitution that
only English be used in all meetings and official correspondence.
However, in a comic thread of continuity, the original LULAC discussions of the English-Only constitutional provision were conducted in
Spanish. Indeed, the measure itself was originally written in Spanish![8]
Spanish remained a central element to the Mexican American Generation's identity. Of this historian Mario Garcia writes, "On the question
of the use of English, Lulacers reemphasized that this did not imply an
abandonment of Spanish." He also argues of LULAC, "It chastised
those Mexican Americans who remained skeptical that they could accommodate to the use of Spanish and English as well as adjust to dual
cultures." Historian Richard Garcia notes of Alonso Perales, a LULAC

founder, that he wrote three books, *El mexicano-americano y la política del sur de Texas* (1931), *En defensa de mi raza* (1937), and *Are We Good Neighbors?* (1948), the last two with Artes Gráficas, a San Antonio bilingual publisher.[9]

By officially choosing English, however, the Mexican American Generation pursued a type of political and cultural accommodation. This strategy was designed to effect reciprocity from the Anglo power structure. By showing what good Americans they could be, the Mexican American Generation fought racial discrimination; by eliciting white sympathy and working within the existing political system, they sought to end discrimination. However, white sympathy, at times it seemed, differed little from white animosity. In 1930 University of Texas political scientist O. Douglas Weeks favorably concluded of LULAC, "In order, therefore, that these people may be able to stand their ground, they must correct their own deficiencies, resulting from ignorance, docility, and prejudice against the Anglo-Saxon and his ways. And doing such, they must show him that they can meet his standards and hence can demand his rights."[10]

From its birth LULAC and the Mexican American Generation dealt significantly with the language issue in a legal challenge to racial segregation in the Texas public schools. Although their primary strategy was not to challenge radically the entire educational system, early actions by LULAC belied this professed conservatism. Litigated by LULAC attorneys, the *Salvatierra* case first challenged the segregation of Mexican American children in Texas and the American Southwest. In 1930 a group of Mexican American parents sued the Del Rio Independent School District for illegal segregation. The school district won the lawsuit by claiming that although segregation did exist, it was not racially motivated—a necessary distinction because Mexican Americans were legally classified as Caucasians. Rather, Del Rio claimed that segregation served pedagogical needs. Its superintendent testified, "I find it advisable to devote twice as much time to teaching English to the Spanish speaking child in the first three grades in order to develop in him the necessary facilities and use of the language so that he can cope on equal terms with *American* language." The San Antonio state judge hearing the case dismissed the charge of race-based segregation, contending that the court had no business meddling in the administrative and pedagogical decisions of school professionals. In effect, the judge claimed that the pedagogical experts knew best and that, provided the existing pedagogical segregation was limited to the first three grades, it was not inherent race discrimination.[11] A victory for Mexican Americans on paper as de jure racial segregation was declared illegal, *Salvatierra* was actually hollow in that the court ordained English-Only pedagogy, already a common subterfuge for racial segregation, as a legal loophole to continue de facto racial segregation.

This 1930 decision was the most significant legal challenge to the educational status quo by any Tejano organization prior to World War II. LULAC confronted local officials with demands to allocate more resources to schools serving their children as with the San Antonio based organization (originally a LULAC effort), Liga Pro Defensa Escolar in the 1930s. LULAC stressed consultation and mediation with local school districts, urging them to end their segregatory policies. They also spurred creation of parent-teacher organizations. However, when such gradualist, mediation-oriented strategies failed, LULAC aided with parent protests and boycotts of the public schools through the establishment of alternative temporary schools that were sometimes bilingual, remnants of the Mexicanist Generation's pre–World War I strategies.[12] The Mexican American Generation in the 1930s, therefore, preached the politics of accommodation, yet accommodation was never servilism, nor was it anti-Spanish.

World War II offered Mexican Americans an incredible opportunity to challenge the educational status quo. The Good Neighbor policy of the national government during World War II provided the perfect context. In Texas, as in the rest of the country, educating on the home front was regarded one of the most important of domestic weapons in the American war arsenal.[13] The Good Neighbor policy became a central component of national wartime diplomacy. It was originally a casual, ad hoc effort by the Hoover administration to repair relationships in Latin America frayed by decades of U.S. intervention and interference. The United States under Franklin D. Roosevelt sought hemispheric support for its war aims in return for aid and promises of autonomy. The treatment of Mexican Americans at home became an important component of the Good Neighbor policy, a sort of domestic wartime diplomacy.[14]

The Good Neighbor policy had an effect upon the American people. For some, Good Neighborism was clearly connected to wartime aims. For example, one teacher, citing statements by Mussolini on the bitterness between the United States and Mexico, pronounced of the "150,000 Mexicans in Texas" that "The invasion of Germany by way of the fifth column has shown clearly that we should have acted more wisely long ago in educating and protecting and strengthening the bonds of friendship. Good neighbor tours may impress national leaders, but the real need is to impress every individual." Although this San Antonio teacher mixed her Italian and German threats, her other message was clear, "The duty of Texas and the United States toward Mexicans should be one of mercy and intelligence."[15]

Publicly expressed sympathy for Mexican Americans increased. Recounting the squalid and overcrowded conditions in which she labored, one teacher noted, "I strive to find the best way to do my job with sixty squirming little Mexicans." The fault lay not on fellow educators, she insisted, but on a society that allowed such conditions to be acceptable in the first place. She claimed, "Our progressive superintendent is earnestly trying to do all he can to help solve this problem." The cotton county teacher then alleged, "The board has a deeper interest in the school for the white children. If they would only realize that in the Mexican school lies a fertile field for richer and united community living! . . . I say give these Mexican people an equal educational advantage and in ten years this community's Good Neighbor Policy would be a fact and not something that the government has crammed into our minds."[16]

Administrative connections between the Good Neighbor Policy's domestic efforts and that of local areas were organized through the coordinator of inter-American affairs, situated in the State Department and reporting directly to President Franklin Roosevelt. Nelson Aldrich Rockefeller accepted leadership of this office in 1940. The national agency oversaw and supported Good Neighborism in the public schools. Domestic Good Neighbor education policy was important enough to be distinguished from international education efforts with the creation in 1943 of a Division of Education and Teacher's Aid within the Department of Inter-American Affairs. This division had three mandates: teacher training, the distribution of educational material, and assistance to states and localities in the implementation of Spanish programs. A number of "Inter-American Workshops" were established, teaching materials distributed through a clearinghouse in the Office of Education, and state educational agencies aided in the creation of Good Neighbor curricula and language programs. Texas was regarded the most involved and cooperative state in the union in implementing such inter-American education initiatives. The Division of Education and Teacher's Aid, in conjunction with the statewide Good Neighbor Commission of Texas, produced a number of documents relating to the experience of Tejanos.[17]

Historians have generally ignored this domestic diplomacy directed toward Mexican Americans. Mexican American leader J. Luz Saenz expressed this theme forcefully by distinguishing foreign policy to Latin Americans abroad from domestic policy to Latin Americans at home. Domestically, Good Neighborism meant treating Mexican Americans better. Saenz, a World War I veteran and LULAC founder, wrote, "The urgent need of more closely knit understanding and solidarity between the Latin-American and Anglo-American nations touches both Americas, but we must not neglect the same need toward Latin Americans born and raised within the confines of the United States."[18]

Institutionalization of the Good Neighbor policy by the Texas State Department of Education actually began before the inception of the statewide Good Neighbor Commission in 1943. One Texas official claimed, "Since November of 1942, the State Department of Education in Texas has, with the very active cooperation of the Office of Inter-American Affairs . . . been making some effort to bring about a greater interest in our neighbor republics."[19] After receiving a grant from Washington, the Texas State Department of Education created a new sublayer of bureaucracy within itself called the Inter-American Relations Education Division, the administrative apparatus for the injection of Good Neighborism to Texas schools. It was an ambitious undertaking. Pauline Kibbe, member of the State Department of Education's Good Neighbor division, labeled this shift the "movement" of inter-American education in Texas. Though the description is overstated, it nevertheless captures an honest belief in the monumental possibilities ushered by war.[20]

Good Neighborism's injection into state education policy resulted in three short-term accomplishments: (1) the undertaking of a massive study on the educational conditions of Mexican Americans; (2) the creation of workshops to promote better instructional techniques, especially regarding Mexican Americans; (3) the revision of statewide curriculum pertaining to the teaching of Spanish to promote more tolerance, acceptance, and understanding of Mexican Americans.[21] These efforts sought reform of the state's language policies, demonstrating a lack of confidence in English-Only's traditional practice.

Texans were heavily involved in formulating and administering the Good Neighbor policy at all levels. The most important participant was Dr. George I. Sánchez of the University of Texas. Professor Sánchez served as chair of the Committee on Inter-American Relations at the University of Texas, thrusting him forward as the university's spokesperson on the subject. He temporarily left this and State Department of Education committee assignments to serve as an educational consultant to the federal Inter-American Affairs effort. Sánchez also coauthored a bibliography of material on the education of Mexican Americans. Austin schoolteacher Connie Garza Brockette, initially a member of several committees for the State Department of

Education, moved to the federal level in 1943 to head the Division of Education and Teacher Aids for Inter-American Affairs in Washington. Dr. Herschel T. Manuel of the University of Texas was involved with its efforts; so was Myrtle Tanner, head of the Inter-American Relations Education committee of the Texas State Department of Education. Historian Guadalupe San Miguel has noted that several Mexican American schoolteachers—Sophia Lozano of Corpus Christi, Estella Canales of Falfurrias, and Consuelo Méndez of Austin—participated in policy committees for the State Department of Education.[22]

William Little, the project director for the University of Texas Good Neighbor Committee, authored a groundbreaking study of the Mexican American child, *Spanish-Speaking Children in Texas*. Little turned his attention to examining all that took place in the name of English-Only, including segregation. Professor Little noted that all of this "special" instruction took place in vastly inferior buildings staffed by teachers often untrained in the very "special" instruction they gave. His closing questions indicate a growing dissatisfaction with English-Only: "Is it not obvious that present practices in the education of these children need honest appraisal in terms of generally accepted purposes of education in American democracy? Do not present practices suggest tremendous waste, both of human resources and of money?"[23]

Little's ambivalence about the effect of Texas' English-Only policies broke from the unquestioning attitudes of previous pedagogues. Within the State Department of Education the war had unleashed a certain institutionalized skepticism about English-Only that bordered on cynicism. The possibility for a change in the education of Mexican Americans finally existed. Educators of the previous two decades had planned on a high level of failure from English-Only but—under the then-prevalent attitudes of supposed racial, cultural, intellectual, and physical inferiority—pinned the blame for failure upon the Mexican American children themselves. In the 1940s educators at the top decisionmaking levels, stripped of much of this racial and ideological baggage, faced the failures of English-Only.

The second benefit of all the coordinated effort by state, university, and federal agencies was the holding of several conferences and workshops to promote the education of Mexican Americans and the teaching of the Spanish language. After Texas College of Arts and Industries in Kingsville, Southwest Texas State Teachers College in San Marcos, and Sul Ross State Teachers College in Alpine contacted the Department of Education about furthering Pan-Americanism (an oft-used phrase for Good Neighborism), the federal Office of Inter-American

Affairs convened a statewide conference in January, 1944. Ten Texas higher education institutions attended the event, held in Austin. Numerous other conferences followed.[24]

Another Austin conference that April involved a number of prominent Inter-American educators. Attending were university professors, State Department of Education staff, nationally prominent pedagogue Lloyd Tireman of New Mexico, and college presidents E. N. Jones of Texas College of Arts and Industries (also a member of the State Department of Education's Inter-American Relations Education committee) and John McMahon of Our Lady of the Lake College in San Antonio. Workshop recommendations were to upgrade the teaching of Spanish in the elementary grades, to increase the number of Pan-American clubs, and to eliminate as much as possible the amount of pedagogical segregation justified by language. Not willing to question English-Only as cynically as did Little's report, the participants in this workshop still implicitly and cautiously indicated the ineffectiveness of pedagogical segregation through existing English-Only pedagogy.[25]

Another workshop featured Professor Tireman as speaker. He discussed the affinity that the educational currents of Good Neighborism had with philosopher John Dewey's educational theories: "Sociologists have a term which will help our thinking, 'cultural pluralism.' This refers to the fact that in every culture something of special merit or value can be found."[26] A 1945 Inter-American Relations Education workshop at Texas State College for Women in Denton enrolled their participants, mostly Spanish teachers or English teachers of Mexican Americans, in seminars on instructional technique. The second half of the workshop took place in Saltillo, Mexico, to immerse the teachers in an all-Spanish environment. Another summer workshop at the Texas College of Mines in El Paso in 1945 highlighted the production of new teaching methods and stressed constant experimentation, new language exercises, and better vocabulary lists.[27]

The combined inter-agency efforts at promoting the Good Neighbor ethic also significantly revised curriculum away from the harsh Americanization of previous decades. In fact, the first changes in the curriculum transpired before the State Department of Education could organize its own Inter-American Relations Education division. In early 1943 it developed a comprehensive course of study for the teaching of Spanish to all Texas schoolchildren from the third to the eighth grade. A mere decade before, the teaching of foreign language in the primary schools had been against the law. Pedagogically, the state backed off its earlier double standard of teaching English to non-English-speakers in English-Only while allowing for liberal translation techniques for

English-speaking children learning Spanish as a second language. By 1943, curriculum with regard to Spanish stated, "Conversation should be the basis of all classroom activity."[28] Ironically, just as the direct method approach of English-Only pedagogy began to erode in the eyes of some pedagogues, it finally came to be completely and uniformly applied to Mexican American and non-Mexican alike.

The most obvious experience of teaching Spanish in the elementary grades was with monolingual, white, English-speaking children. Reiterating the obvious, two university professors in 1941 sought to reform teaching Spanish as a foreign language in Texas schools by introducing "The so-called natural method . . . to develop these skills." Educators debated the use of all-Spanish textbooks in elementary grade courses: *Spanish-Only* pedagogy to English-speaking children. This required more than usual from the teacher: "An elementary school teacher of Spanish should have a good accent; she should speak the language fluently; she should be acquainted with, and sympathetic toward, the Spanish Americans; [and] she should have had special training in the problems of elementary teaching and in methods of teaching Spanish."[29]

Instructions for teaching white English speakers Spanish in Spanish-Only classrooms were accompanied by details to implement the novel idea of teaching Spanish to Spanish speakers. One Austin observer noted, "For over a century Texas tried to forget her Spanish and Mexican past. She looked upon with contempt, fought against and tried to stamp out every thing Spanish or Mexican." The commentator noted with irony that "Stop-Speaking-Spanish clubs" were at that moment being displaced by elementary-level instruction in Spanish. Both communities viewed Texans' desire to make Texas "a bi-lingual state" as a tremendous opportunity to build bridges. Declaring that instruction in Spanish at a tender age would not hurt the capacity of Mexican Americans to speak English, the observer then hinted that bilingual instruction could be a positive factor for all children.[30]

Statewide policymakers considered implementing the pioneering curriculum of an elementary Spanish program initiated in Corpus Christi under teacher and administrator E. E. Mireles, who was married to historian, folklorist, teacher, and literary figure Jovita González. Mireles's Spanish program was unique; it came into existence when teaching Spanish in grade schools not located on the border was still prohibited by law. After receiving a special dispensation from the state before the start of the 1940–41 school year, the Corpus Christi Spanish program was successful enough to influence the Texas Legislature to pass a bill in March, 1941, to allow other elementary schools the right

In one of E. E. Mireles's Spanish classrooms, children recite the simple Spanish sentences on the board to the teacher, a Mrs. Young, in the front of the class. Mireles observes in the background. Photo courtesy of the Edmundo E. Mireles Papers at the Nettie Lee Benson Latin American Center, Box 1, Folder 12, XII-129.

to adopt such a Spanish program. Mireles had the support of conservative U.S. Congressman Richard "Dick" Kleberg of Kingsville who wrote of the still-nascent program, "Present world crisis accentuates importance of neighborly and friendly relationships between North and South America. For these and many other reasons I am for your fine program." Statewide Good Neighbor organizations also endorsed the Mireles curriculum.[31]

Corpus Christi maintained active Spanish programs in all nine of its public elementary schools beginning in 1940. The courses were made mandatory for all students. Each school had a head Spanish teacher who submitted lesson plans to Mireles. The courses, while billed as grade-school Spanish, actually extended into what would today be considered junior high or middle school—six years of instruction from grades three to eight. Not all primary teachers believed that they were capable of teaching Spanish, even though Mireles swore that "it is unnecessary to know much Spanish to teach a little." The most confident teachers often took the classes of others. Even these teachers did not spring from Mireles's head fully formed. Texas had not previously taken the care to develop skillful Spanish instruction. Therefore, many elementary teachers attended weekly Spanish seminars that Mireles conducted. Supplemental night courses, over a couple of years, enrolled more than six hundred adult learners.[32]

Mireles required that the grade-school classes use the direct method of Spanish-Only. There was to be absolutely no spoken English during Spanish lessons, which lasted anywhere between twenty to fifty-five minutes a day. In an outline of suggestions for his teachers, Mireles articulated several tips on conducting a Spanish-Only class: "(1) Answer roll in Spanish; (2) Use common expressions repeatedly; (3) Let children answer questions normally rather than in complete sentences."[33] In 1945 the state finalized guidelines mirroring Mireles's program in that "All Spanish in the elementary grades should be of an oral and conversational type." However, aware of the limitations of many schools, the state also qualified that if no Spanish teachers were found, then the amount and type of instruction could be eased—"a period of at least ten minutes per day [should] be set aside and called the Spanish period. The teachers should be instructed to use this period to present materials in Social Science in the Latin American field intended to implement the Good Neighbor Policy."[34]

Through his Spanish program Mireles sought no less than the rehabilitation of Spanish as a civilized and cultured tongue. He also set out to rehabilitate the perception of Spanish-speaking children as uneducable by instilling pride and accomplishment at their being bilingual. For Mireles, language was only partially about bilingualism. It was also about biculturalism: "Bilingual competence is an integral part of developing a knowledge of the cultural aspects of the Spanish and the English languages and the fostering of an appreciation of the reflection of these peoples and their contributions to our American heritage."[35] In many ways, Mireles's desire for bilingual-bicultural education in the 1940s foreshadowed the bilingual education movement's goals of linguistic competence and cultural affirmation of the late 1960s and 1970s.

Many, like Mireles, pointed out that all of this language instruction ultimately aimed to teach cultural tolerance and diversity. This was 1940s-style multicultural curriculum, a bicultural corollary to bilingualism. One teacher noted this emphasis on language instruction when she claimed, "More emphasis is being placed upon the spoken language." She followed, however, with a counterclaim: "In connection with the learning of the language, information about the people and their country is given in belief that a true understanding may make

This photograph of Mexican American and Anglo boys and girls represents an ideal of the Good Neighbor movement. This Corpus Christi school implemented E. E. Mireles's experimental Spanish program during the 1940s and 1950s. Photo courtesy of the Edmundo E. Mireles Papers at the Nettie Lee Benson Latin American Center, Box 1, Folder 12, XII-130.

way for better appreciation of one another." The organization of Pan-American clubs, theatrical productions, banquets, socials, and field trips to Mexico were advised to stimulate more interest in Latin America.[36] One school in West Texas under their "Attitudes to be developed" criteria of Pan-Americanism listed: "1. Understanding of our Mexican neighbor. 2. Friendliness toward Mexican people. 3. More tolerant attitude toward Mexico and Mexican people."[37]

However, the more things changed, the more they stayed the same. The new Inter-American Relations Education branch within the Texas State Department of Education maintained several old pedagogical assumptions and instructional dead ends of English-Only. In his study Professor Little was willing to label English-Only a failure; however, few others questioned it so severely. Even Sánchez expressed renewed hope in English-Only once the institutional culture of schools changed. After stating the evils of segregation, Professors Sánchez and Henry Otto of the University of Texas extolled the virtues of English-Only taught by caring teachers in good facilities. In such ideal environments, they reasoned, Mexican American children could easily pick up the necessary English in a year.[38]

Although the potential was great for doing away with English-Only during the war, it was not fully taken advantage of either by the pedagogical theorists or by local educators. One El Paso educator gave several tips for the teaching of Spanish. He assumed that Mexican Americans in the early grades were not to be in the same class as Anglos and so did not bother to discuss them. He recommended the direct method of Spanish-Only but for no more than a few minutes a day. This educator revealed his distrust of the direct method for Spanish by assuring his readers that many students would not learn Spanish due to natural disinterest and that little could be done to alleviate such circumstances. This same double standard of the 1920s and 1930s now proved much more hypocritical, as it was shrouded in the rhetorical ethos of Pan-Americanism.[39]

Also, sympathetic educators such as Sánchez effectively ignored the larger problems of English-Only. Sanchez went so far in his stress on socioeconomic and racial discrimination as factors in explaining away Mexican American school failure that he let English-Only pedagogy off the hook. Sanchez believed that segregation was the true evil and wanted no pedagogical excuses. In doing so, he and others put their heads in the sand. In 1943 Sánchez was directly involved with the experimentation of new variations of English-Only at the University of Texas. These experiments involved getting foreign exchange students to speak rudimentary English or preparing future English teachers in Latin American countries. The goal was to apply the experience directly to "Anglo-Americans interested in the teaching of English to Latin Americans, or in the allied field of teaching English to children of Spanish-speaking communities in the United States." Sánchez did not fundamentally question the theoretical underpinnings of English-Only; he assumed that language techniques for college students could be readily applied to five-year-old Tejanos.[40]

Sánchez supported the teaching of Spanish as a means of aiding Spanish-speaking children's self-confidence. He qualified this support, however. In an article soon after the end of Good Neighborism in Texas schools, Sánchez attempted to move beyond the issue of language by arguing that a "teacher's concern would be less with 'teaching English' than with helping children learn how to think—helping them to acquire the tools for thought and to utilize those tools in the construction of ideas, in the solution of problems, in communication. In brief, she would be concerned with the *education* of the child rather than with English—and the two are not synonymous!"[41] How else would higher level "concepts" be taught when the child's still-developing cognitive framework was already in Spanish? The obvious answer Sánchez was leading up to was vernacular instruction—bilingual education. This is the theoretical wall that Professor Sánchez hit as early as the 1930s and continued to butt against well into the 1950s. His theoretical understanding of language was still formed by English-Only concepts and would remain so until the revolutions in language theory of the 1960s.

At war's end Professor Herschel T. Manuel wrote an article stressing the need to continue with Good Neighborism. The momentum, he pleaded, must not be lost. Though he applauded teaching about Central and South American nations, Manuel emphasized the policy's real importance: "Finally, we are coming to grips to a greater extent than ever before with the problem of molding the Spanish-speaking and English-speaking people of our own country into an effective democracy." Of the goals of "inter-American education in the Southwest," he recommended "that we make the improvement of the education of Spanish-speaking children a matter of immediate urgency."[42]

Manuel recommended the use of kindergarten education (not yet mandatory in Texas) especially designed for Spanish-speaking children. These special kindergartens would focus intensely on imparting enough English vocabulary to allow Mexican Americans to survive in a regular (integrated) first-grade class. Sánchez made similar recommendations in the 1930s. The innovations sought to remove the excuse for pedagogical segregation by alleviating the need for "special" segregation. The State Department of Education and influential Mexican American leaders in the 1950s eventually implemented such recommendations. These proposals, like the Good Neighborism of World War II, would not be lasting solutions for segregated, English-Only schools. The Mexican American Generation was bent upon changing the child but not so much the school. The Chicano Generation would recognize this failure in the 1960s.[43]

The strategy of accommodation by the Mexican American Generation did elicit some sympathy and support from parts of the Anglo community during World War II. Nevertheless, the overall effort did not pay off. After almost two decades of accommodating to flagrantly discriminatory school systems, many Mexican American leaders felt their patience running out. After almost two decades of working from within the system and overwhelmingly supporting the war effort during World War II, the education of Mexican American children remained as poor as ever. In the South Texas town of Three Rivers, for example, the segregated "Mexican Ward School" was housed in three wood, frame buildings with leaky roofs, neither indoor plumbing nor water fountains, hardly any windows, and no insulation; the Anglo schools, meanwhile, had all these amenities. Sixteen teachers taught the 800 children in attendance (out of 1,400 potential Mexican American school age students), averaging 50 students per class.[44]

The writings of J. Luz Saenz highlight this growing sense of frustration, this rage. In a 1946 article Saenz hewed to standard LULAC rhetoric by disassociating Mexican American citizens from immigrant workers: "They are victims to inevitable circumstances prevailing at their homes or in their country. Let us thank our God for our advantages." But Saenz soon warmed to the subject of discrimination in decisively less accommodationist language: "Poor attendance on the part of these children and selfishness and narrow-mindedness on the part of other children and parents have created the well known and much disgusting racial problem known in Texas as the 'Mexican Child Problem in Texas Schools.'" Saenz waxed indignant that "very little credit has been rendered us for fighting for flag and country. We have done this. We are doing it. We shall keep doing it. Till when? . . . Do not take our loyalty for servilism." Saenz concluded this article with a patriotic plea couched in wartime rhetoric: "We have destroyed or are trying to destroy Hitler's racial theory. Why not do the same thing with Bilbo and his imitators here in Texas, or in any other part of our union? This is the right thing to do if Christian civilization and democratic principles mean anything to us."[45]

This righteous indignation resulted from missed opportunities to alter the education of Mexican Americans in the Texas public schools. Anger would manifest itself in a series of court battles in the late 1940s and 1950s, foreshadowing the civil rights activism of the Chicano Generation of the following decades. Groups like LULAC still attempted accommodation but with a more urgent, confrontational tone. Disappointment stemmed in part from a failure to agree that *all* English-Only pedagogy served the racist ends of segregation. English-Only pedagogy would topple in the 1960s, though the Good Neighbor years had certainly begun to crack that edifice.

PART THREE

Modern Bilingual Education

Mexican American Activism and Language Theory in the Gradual Demise of English-Only, 1947–65

The English-Only paradigm—an entire way of teaching with its own rules, assumptions, and scientific language—gradually crumbled during the 1950s and the early 1960s. Educators and language minorities came to regard this dominant way of thinking about the education of non-English-speaking children since the turn of the century as a relic of a distant and shameful past. Two largely unrelated factors spurred this change: (1) the increasingly successful challenges to educational segregation by the Mexican American Generation; and (2) the evolution of language theory—how and when children and adults acquired language—as well as a reevaluation of bilingualism's link to mental and educational retardation. Mexican American activists created the political context, and academicians contributed to the intellectual context that discredited English-Only Pedagogy. The two crosscurrents approached English-Only from different perspectives with completely different aims, a fact that few scholars have noted.[1]

Although the strategy of accommodation by the gradualist Mexican American Generation did achieve some support, it ultimately failed. After almost two decades of filing occasional lawsuits against flagrantly discriminatory school systems and supporting local efforts at improving education, many Mexican American activists, especially World War II veterans, were growing impatient. Their work from within the system had not improved the education of Mexican American children. George I. Sánchez wrote of the disappointment of the immediate postwar years after the hope of the brief Good Neighbor movement. Sánchez estimated that during the 1950s about eighty percent of non-English-speaking Tejanos spent two years in the first grade due to supposed language handicap. He noted that roughly twenty-five percent reached the eighth grade while less than ten percent reached the twelfth grade. In the 1955–56 academic year, dropouts measured over eleven percent of the entire Mexican American scholastic population.[2]

During the late 1940s and 1950s, LULAC and other middle-class, patriotic groups intensified their challenges to the educational segregation justified by English-Only pedagogy. The American GI Forum, created in 1948 by Dr. Hector P. Garcia, a Corpus Christi physician, represented a more spirited and activist entity. As World War II grew further distant, the Mexican American Generation of leadership inched progressively closer to the militancy, confrontation, and immediacy of the future Chicano Generation.[3]

Alonso S. Perales—a World War I veteran, U.S. diplomat in Central America, attorney, and founding LULAC member from San Antonio—expressed the growing frustration of the Mexican American Generation in a 1948 book that included congressional testimony on discrimination, speeches from legislators, clergy, and educators, and letters submitted to Perales from ordinary citizens detailing their own experiences with discrimination. The mocking title *Are We Good Neighbors?* intended to shame well-meaning Texans into realizing the discrepancy between Good Neighbor rhetoric and reality.[4]

No one exhibited more strongly than Professor Sánchez this attitude of futile, impotent disgust at how little had changed since the war. Sánchez rhetorically asked what would have happened if Poles or Italians met with the same level of school segregation on the basis of language. He even cast aspersions on the intelligence of segregationists: "Communities practicing the segregation of Spanish-speaking children are, in my conception, educationally backward and misguided." Sánchez concluded, "The practice of segregation does not square up to good pedagogy, to the best learning of English, or to good Americanism." Maintaining the momentum gained during the Good Neighbor era was difficult, however. The Texas State Department of Education was overhauled in 1949 by the Gilmer-Aiken reform laws, becoming the Texas Education Agency. Eliminated was the Good Neighbor bureaucratic niche from which Mexican Americans were influential. Governor Allen Shivers in 1950 created the Texas Council for the Study of Human Relations to report to the state legislature on matters regarding Mexican Americans. Professor Sánchez and Gus Garcia, a highly successful attorney for LULAC and the GI Forum, both served on the council, which proved purely cosmetic and was disbanded in 1952.[5]

As the 1950s progressed, Mexican Americans shifted in tone away from the gradualist and overly patriotic attitudes characterizing LULAC in the 1930s. Legal challenges to pedagogical segregation in Texas became more numerous after receiving a push by judicial rulings elsewhere in the Southwest. In 1947 a federal court in California ruled in *Westminster School District* v. *Mendez* that schools could segregate among different races, but that whites and Mexican Americans were not legally classified as such. The judge then ruled that the California school did in fact illegally segregate by race. The pedagogical excuses for segregation were found unjustified. This was the first time Mexican Americans were concluded to be "racially" segregated in public schools; this was also the first time English-Only pedagogy failed a legal test as a justification for segregation. The judge declared of the standard legal defense of limited segregation on the basis of pedagogical necessity that "Omnibus segregation of children of Mexican ancestry from the rest of the student body in the elementary grades in the schools involved in this action because of language handicaps is not warranted by the record before us."[6]

In response to this stunning decision, as well as pressure from LULAC, Texas Attorney General Price Daniel wrote a binding legal opinion on *Mendez* for Texas schools. Daniel's ruling in turn caused Mexican Americans to spring into action, successfully challenging the legality of pedagogical segregation in the courts almost a decade before the universally recognized *Brown* v. *Board* case outlawed all racial discrimination in the schools. In Opinion Number V-128 Daniel agreed that *Mendez* established precedent for challenging the practice of pedagogical segregation in Texas. Daniel claimed, "It is our opinion, therefore, that based solely on language deficiencies and other individual needs and aptitudes, the school district may maintain separate classes, in separate buildings, if necessary, for any pupils with such deficiencies, needs, or aptitudes through the first three grades." This partially upheld the 1930 *Salvatierra* decision. Although Daniel allowed some possible pedagogical segregation, he made two important and significant changes to the legal status quo: (1) he declared that while individual pedagogical segregation was permissible, group pedagogical segregation was not; (2) he mandated that scientific, objective testing must establish the designation of those individual children needing "special instruction." Daniel went on, "But as emphasized in the *Salvatierra* and *Mendez* cases above, the classification under consideration must be based on the language deficiency, or individual need or aptitude, after examinations, and other properly conducted tests, equally applied to all pupils who come within the classification."[7]

Professor Sánchez sent a stinging rebuke to Joe R. Greenhill, Daniel's legal assistant who had shaped the published opinion. Sánchez argued that there was no reason for *any* type of segregation—that it made *no* pedagogical sense. Asking if other children (Italian, Polish, etc.) could be segregated on this basis, he then queried, "why can't they be segregated on the basis of deficiencies in arithmetic, or ability to draw, or muscular reaction speed, or any other arbitrarily selected subject matter, accomplishment, etc.?" Sánchez claimed that there was no pedagogical justification for arbitrarily setting the cutoff point at grade three. He prophesied (correctly) that Daniel's position "will boomerang on the very first instance that the matter is brought to the attention of the federal courts."[8]

LULAC, now joined by the American GI Forum, directly challenged this decades-old legal justification for racial segregation in *Bastrop v. Delgado*. The *Delgado* case was based upon the pedagogical segregation practiced by the public schools in the towns of Bastrop, Elgin, and Martindale, and of Travis County. Twenty-one Mexican Americans obtained LULAC's Gus Garcia, the experienced civil rights litigator who had solicited the potentially useful, but limited, legal opinion from the state attorney general's office, as their legal representation. A legal fund chaired by Professor Sánchez and representatives of LULAC and the GI Forum financially supported Garcia's efforts. Armed with the fresh *Mendez* precedent, the attorney general's recent opinion, and the statewide Mexican American leadership, Garcia proceeded with the case in 1948 in federal district court.[9]

The federal court in *Delgado* ruled similarly to the *Mendez* case: Segregating Mexican Americans on different campuses and separate buildings was on its face illegal discrimination, and the Texas schools in question, like those in California, were indeed guilty of this. These offending districts were judged to have illegally segregated, yet the court upheld the legality of segregating some Mexican Americans for instructional reasons, so long as such decisions were scientifically derived through testing. The foundational decision concerning pedagogical segregation, the 1930 *Salvatierra* ruling, did not go so far as to stipulate many specific conditions upon which pedagogical segregation might exist. *Delgado* preserved the existence of English-Only and pedagogical segregation—but at a price. Objective criteria were to establish whether individual children needed special, segregated instruction; the special instruction was not to be conducted on separate campuses or for extended periods of time. More important symbolically was that the school districts in question were found guilty of rampant, long-term, de facto, racial segregation. *Delgado* represented a significant moral victory that encouraged further challenges.[10]

The state scurried to comply with the federal ruling's stipulation to provide some sort of standardized testing for the classification of children needing "special" language instruction. Dr. L. A. Woods—head of the Texas State Department of Education since the Good Neighbor days of the 1940s—communicated to teachers, administrators, and school boards the gist of *Delgado* by stating that segregation based on race or national origin was illegal; separate classes were permissible in the first grade; and also that his agency did have the authority to enforce these new regulations.[11] Woods made available to schools a state-approved test—the "Inter-American Test in Oral English"—developed by Dr. Herschel T. Manuel of the University of Texas. This test was intended to fulfill the requirements of *Delgado* by offering objective criteria to determine the necessity and degree of pedagogical separation. The state provided instructions on when and under what conditions schools could administer the exam, including a disclaimer that "no certain *score* or *grade* will be fixed to be used as the dividing line between the pupils who show ability to take instruction in English, and those who are found to have a decided language handicap. Each district or school will be allowed to fix its own standards for such dividing line. After one year of experimentation and adjustment, then we may be ready to fix a state-wide standard, based on the data which we secure during the year 1948–49." Woods reminded Texas educators, "There must be no discrimination at any time in the testing program."[12]

Unfortunately for Mexican Americans, certain schools did not take Superintendent Woods's test, or his authority, seriously. In early 1949 the Del Rio Independent School District, the site of the *Salvatierra* decision two decades earlier, was investigated for noncompliance of the *Delgado* rules based upon the complaints of a Mexican American student group at the University of Texas. The state investigator determined that Del Rio was guilty of illegally segregating Mexican Americans. Superintendent Woods thus canceled the school's certification. However, the state legislature shortly thereafter passed the sweeping Gilmer-Aiken laws that completely reorganized the public school system and its bureaucracy. In the overhaul, Woods's position as superintendent of public instruction was replaced by a new office of commissioner of education. The new head of the revamped agency, J. W. Edgar, promptly recertified Del Rio.[13]

Also, Woods's approved tests were particularly unsuccessful because not all schools with Mexican American youngsters even bothered to use them, choosing to derive their objective criteria in other ways or not at all. Also, these tests were not free; cost may have deterred some districts. While not every school district provided "special" or segregated education for Mexican Americans, those that did mostly did so without the use of standardized tests.[14]

The 1957 case of *Hernandez* v. *Driscoll* finally punctured the balloon of pedagogical segregation in Texas. Between 1949 and 1955, LULAC and the GI Forum monitored the public schools of Driscoll, a small farming community near Corpus Christi where almost three-quarters of the student population were the children of Mexican American farmworkers, many of them migrant. Upon entering school these children had little command of English. Legal action was threatened after 1949 because the school had retained all Mexican American children in the first two grades for four years without any testing, contrary to the *Delgado* and Daniel mandates.[15] The *Hernandez* case was filed in federal district court in 1955, with the decision coming in January, 1957—hot on the heels of the landmark *Brown* v. *Board* case in which the U.S. Supreme Court overturned the legal principle of "separate but equal." Driscoll school officials claimed their actions were fully justified on the pedagogical grounds of language deficiency. However accurate those claims may have been, wrote Judge James V. Allred, a former governor of Texas in the 1930s, they were made immaterial, because "This is not a line drawn in good faith, based upon individual ability to speak and understand English." Allred continued: "It is the very opposite. It is unreasonable race discrimination against all Mexican children as a group throughout the first two grades. That it has this *effect* cannot be disputed. If scientific or good faith tests were given the *result* might not weigh so heavily. But where, as here, no such tests have been given, it is unreasonable on its face; and, when considered along with the other facts and circumstances enumerated, it compels the conclusion that the grouping is purposeful, intentional, and unreasonably discriminatory."[16]

The Driscoll schools were using the pedagogical argument in such an unsophisticated manner apparently because it achieved the segregation of all Mexican Americans by race. Allred concluded: "Judgment will be entered declaring the District's separate grouping of students of Mexican extraction is arbitrary and unreasonable because it is directed at them as a class and is not based upon individual capacities; (2) that any grouping, whether in the beginning or subsequent years, must not be based upon racial extraction but upon individual ability to speak, understand and to be instructed in the English language; (3) that individual capacities and abilities in this respect must be determined in good faith by scientific tests recognized in the field of education." Though a political liberal by Texas standards, Allred was not a particularly activist jurist. He simply applied the *Delgado* test in *Hernandez* and found the separation arbitrary.[17]

However, not all judges adjudicated as did Allred, and not all school districts that improperly segregated did so as flagrantly as Driscoll. The activism of the Mexican American Generation changed the legalities while not really altering the fundamental reality of pedagogical segregation. Educational conditions for most Mexican American schoolchildren were still very poor. One study of the 1950s said that over eighty percent of one border city's total student population (including high school) were still enrolled in segregated schools. Punishment for speaking Spanish on school grounds, an element of English-Only dating to the 1910s, continued in everyday practice. One blank detention form labeled, "VIOLATION SLIP—SPANISH DETENTION," from the El Paso public schools read, "_____ was speaking Spanish during school hours. This pupil must report to Spanish Detention in the Cafeteria . . . on the assigned day." The slip was dated September, 1966.[18] The everyday practice of English-Only pedagogy and segregation in Texas persisted, despite the legal victories of *Delgado* and *Hernandez.*

The behaviorist perspective of the social sciences emanating from the intellectual milieu of the 1930s and 1940s eventually influenced language policy. Two specific intellectual trends had an impact on English-Only and bilingual education: (1) a gradual reevaluation of the innate intelligence of non-English-speaking children as well as the previously held belief (stemming from IQ studies of the 1910–30 period) in the link between bilingualism and intellectual retardation; (2) a gradual reevaluation of how children learned languages. These two academic influences came to view English-Only attitudes more negatively and bilingualism more positively.

From 1945 to 1965 the correlation between bilingualism and low IQ turned almost 180 degrees. By the early 1960s bilingualism came to be associated with higher than average intelligence rather than labeled a handicap as it had been since the work of early IQ scientists. Most historians have ignored these developments.[19] The shift took place in three phases. First, the old guard or traditionalists, represented in the literature from the 1940s to the middle of the 1950s, still held (although in a more qualified manner) that bilingual children, especially Mexican Americans, were either intellectually or educationally handicapped—that they were inevitable school failures. Next, a transitional group, best represented in the literature during the middle and late 1950s, believed that the earlier research linking cognitive defect to bilingualism was either greatly overstated or methodologically flawed. Finally, the new guard, the bilingualists, by the 1960s conducted studies that accounted for many more socioeconomic and behavioral factors than their academic predecessors. They concluded that in some situations, bilingual children actually scored higher in cognitive measurements than monolingual children.

The traditionalists of the 1940s and early 1950s had taken University of Texas Professors George I. Sánchez and Herschel T. Manuel's critique of early IQ racial science to heart. They still concluded that bilingualism resulted in educational retardation but arrived at such conclusions in a more cautious manner. For example, by the 1940s schools had scrapped the exclusive use of verbal tests in determining the amount of language handicap, long a target of Manuel's criticism. Also, this old guard functioned in an academic environment less permissive of race-based explanations than that of the 1920s. Therefore, they arrived at conclusions of bilingual inferiority by methodological techniques that at least made the pretense of taking into account environmental factors. Two traditionalists noted of their evolving field, "Renewed effort is being directed toward the analysis of socio-economic factors in relation to intelligence and achievement."[20]

These traditionalists were less sure of potentially racist assessments than were previous researchers and accordingly attached numerous qualifications to their conclusions. Advising the use of nonverbal tests, researcher Natalie Darcy indicated that both verbal and nonverbal varieties were so unreliable on their own that she urged they be used only in conjunction with one another. Selma Herr evaluated mandatory kindergarten classes of preschool language instruction offered to Mexican Americans for the alleviation of alleged language handicap. Herr found that the control group, Mexican Americans receiving no special instruction, all failed the first grade. Forty-seven percent of the group undergoing this special training failed. So the pre–first grade language instruction, while measurably effective, was not a complete success. Darcy's review of the literature of bilingualism and intelligence in 1953 cited many studies equating mental handicap with bilingualism.[21]

A transitional group of scholars on the subject of bilingualism and intelligence emerged in the 1950s. In her 1953 article Darcy also referred to a growing number of these studies concluding that bilingualism had neither a positive nor a negative correlation to intelligence. One transitional study by Seth Arsenian best stated this middle position: "bilingualism neither retards nor accelerates mental development." A Texas State Department of Education researcher argued that the social attendants of segregation such as "Poor housing, inadequate teaching materials, poorly trained teachers, and improper attention to the needs and interests of the children involved" really caused educational failure, not inferior intellectual capacity wrought by bilingualism.[22]

These transitionalists pointed to gaps in the old guard's methodological handling of environmental factors. One researcher at Our Lady of the Lake College in San Antonio, Sister Mary Arthur Carrow, conducted an impressive study of the relationship between bilingualism and intelligence. When picking the bilingual group, Carrow, unlike other academic researchers, chose only those who were *truly* bilingual (fluent and literate in both languages), not those classified as bilingual simply because they were Mexican American. She discounted those children who tested at exceedingly low IQ scores in both bilingual and monolingual groups. She then tested for any hearing, learning, or other psychological disabilities as well as grouped all according to socioeconomic background. Carrow found no meaningful connection between bilingualism and intelligence. Later studies reaffirmed the notion that IQ alone was not a reliable enough factor to correlate bilingual handicap to school failure.[23]

By the 1960s, leading psychologists, linguists, and educators increasingly reasoned that bilingualism actually benefited intelligence. These bilingualists paid even more attention to isolating environmental factors. Yet this seeming sophistication is a matter of some relativism. Scholars in the field of intelligence measurement today view their own methods at isolating and studying such factors as open to improvement. Few existing studies in the early 1950s held that bilingualism was a positive factor in intelligence. One study published in 1953 on Puerto Ricans in New York City's Spanish Harlem argued that bilingualism in certain contexts resulted in increased intellectual capacity. The authors noted that Puerto Rican children reacted negatively to the nonverbal tests: "Verbal refusals, crying, and other significant emotional disturbance were likewise observed. No such general resistance was encountered among the Negro or white children." They found that verbal tests translated into Spanish with simple vocabulary and instructions administered by a Puerto Rican adult resulted in better scores.[24]

Others noted similar findings, particularly when class and socioeconomic factors were more tightly controlled. One article in the middle 1960s vaguely hinted at this by remarking, "it is likely that bilingual students may have somewhat higher potentialities than monolingual students from a similar environment." These studies in the 1960s inferred that language-minority students learned better in all subjects when trained early in their native tongue. One study found that bilingual Chinese American students were not adversely affected by dual-language ability: "less confusion results when Chinese is known well."[25] These newer studies also went so far as to question English-Only pedagogy. Two such bilingualists in 1961 concluded that "it would seem reasonable that a teacher or clinician conversant with a student's verbal or gestural language would facilitate the learning process. By utilizing the repertoire of associations available to the student, the instructor may be able to elevate the student's functional language more efficiently." Implicitly, perhaps even unwittingly, these authors were advocating bilingual education.[26]

This scholarly reconceptualization simmered until 1962 when Canadian researchers Elizabeth Peal and Wallace E. Lambert published a groundbreaking study on bilingual instruction in English and French for ten-year-old French speakers in Montreal. After a devastating review of the literature that pointed out numerous methodological and interpretational inaccuracies in older studies, Peal and Lambert then studied bilingual students who had full mastery of both languages. They found that the fully bilingual students of the same socioeconomic status invariably scored higher than their monolingual counterparts in IQ tests. In explaining the divergence of their work from earlier studies, Peal and Lambert argued that "the structure of intellect of the bilinguals appears to be more diversified than that of the monolinguals," in part, they hypothesized, because "People who learn to use two languages have two symbols for every object." Peal and Lambert boldly characterized the superior scores for bilinguals: "From an early age, bilinguals may be forced to conceptualize environmental events in terms of their general properties without reliance on their linguistic symbols." Conversely, "The monolinguals may never have been forced to form concepts or abstract ideas of things and may be more likely to think mainly in terms of concretes."[27] This revolutionary study was the product of a gradual evolution over many years of the academic community's understanding of the meaning of bilingualism and the nature of testing. Peal and Lambert's work, along with the other psychometric research of the late 1950s and '60s, capsized English-Only's scientific base, which by then consisted mostly of traditional assumptions. New research in mental testing paved the way for linguists to dispel English-Only pedagogy. The newer scientific understanding of primary and secondary language acquisition and its relationship to cognitive ability undermined the English-Only paradigm.

World War II brought renewed attention to the teaching of language, even altering the way scholars practiced English-Only. Schools employed a modified version of the old direct method called the audio-lingual method (also the oral method or oral bombardment). The armed forces experimented with audio-lingual approaches during World War II with some success in rapidly teaching adults a second language. Maximilian Berlitz advertised a similar audio-lingual method shortly after the war. The theoretical rationale for the audio-lingual method came from the behaviorist theories of B. F. Skinner—habit created fluency. This approach resembled the old-style, direct method inherent in English-Only; only now, it had behaviorist theory behind it and stressed even more the repetition and rote learning that had been despised by the Progressives, in theory. Also, the global position of the United States as a cold war superpower compelled educators to renew an emphasis on the study of language, especially after 1957 when the Soviets launched the *Sputnik* satellite, and the federal government responded with the National Defense Education Act.[28]

The audio-lingual method taught older students in high schools, colleges, and the armed services how to speak modern languages such as French, German, or Russian. This approach differed from the direct method of English-Only by occasionally utilizing the native tongue. Unlike the older methods of infusing reading and grammatical translation, audio-lingual study was almost totally oral. Adult learners saved time by dispensing with reading and writing foreign languages through pure repetition to drill the symbols and meanings of language. This conversational method was soon implemented for non-English-speaking children with the hope of alleviating the direct method failures of English-Only pedagogy.[29]

Despite the new behaviorist influence, scholars began to question the absence of some degree of native-language instruction in the education of non-English-speaking children. Social psychologist Joshua Fishman in his 1950 research on a bilingual Yiddish school, argued that not utilizing the native tongue in the teaching of the smallest of students was a monumental waste of time, energy, and potential. Fishman's later work in the 1960s reinforced this thesis. Theodore Andersson, one of the leaders of the Foreign Languages in the Elementary Schools (FLES) movement, maintained the drumbeat for elementary grade, foreign language instruction in the 1950s. In doing so, Andersson, who himself was traumatized as a six-year-old upon arriving to America from Sweden speaking no English, inched closer to the realization of how wastefully the nation was squandering its foreign language capital, especially regarding Mexican Americans educated in a language they did not understand.[30]

While the brief era of audio-lingual techniques partially altered how educators thought of English-Only, it was the contributions to the field of theoretical linguistics and cognitive formation by the young Noam Chomsky in the late 1950s and early 1960s that delivered the final blow to the behaviorist rationale for the direct method. The direct method of English-Only rested upon the behaviorist theoretical argument that language represented a finite set of symbols mastered through repetition. Chomsky postulated that language was not a closed, limited process. Instead, language was an open-ended and limitless activity formed not through constant drill but by adherence to basic principles of language and cognition, or how the brain processes the symbols of language into meaning.[31] The Chomskian revolution in language theory allowed younger pedagogues such as Theodore Andersson and Joshua Fishman—unlike their elders in Herschel Manuel, Lloyd Tireman, and George Sánchez who had no alternative to the direct method of English-Only—to break free from reconciling the contradictions they perceived. They now had the theoretical cover to fully explore bilingual education.

The State of Texas struggled to incorporate these academic influences. The FLES movement, spearheaded by Theodore Andersson at the University of Texas, made but a limited impact by the 1950s. Many Texas school districts (29 out of 216 polled) in 1957 chose not to take advantage of the state's permissiveness regarding Spanish instruction in the elementary grades. The majority of participating schools did so through administrative action, not local school board policy.[32] Texas also labored to adapt the direct method of English-Only to the behaviorist, audio-lingual method. A 1962 state document on newer methods of language instruction for non-English speakers cited World War II and the cold war as reasons for its increased emphasis. Although this pedagogical manual adopted the audio-lingual technique over the direct method, the actual lessons still resembled the old, English-Only methods.[33]

Texas attempted to reach out to the Mexican American community while still working within the increasingly strained confines of English-Only pedagogy. This was the duty of the Hale-Aiken Committee of Twenty-Four, a body of public leaders, educators, and citizens who were authorized in the late 1950s to make recommendations for the improvement of the schools. One of the twenty-four was Felix Tijerina of Houston, a national president of LULAC. Tijerina was involved with the creation of a successful pilot program of teaching English to preschool Mexican Americans through a radio program called the "Little Schools of the 400."[34] The Hale-Aiken Committee recommended a program similar to Tijerina's. The LULAC-approved effort was called the "Little Schools of the 400," because it sought to impart a base vocabulary of 400 English words to non-English-speaking Mexican Americans. The committee, however, still supported English-Only law (article 288 of the Penal Code of Texas), apparently viewing the preschool program's limited use of Spanish instruction as a harmless compromise. The program lasted three months in the summer for youngsters entering the first grade that fall term. State and local schools shared the burden of financially supporting the program. Administrators hoped to alleviate the still large number of Tejano students failing the first grade because they had not mastered enough English to keep up with their peers. Theoretically, such instruction would have also eliminated the pedagogical justification for segregation.[35]

Similar programs coincided with LULAC's radio instructional effort, including a 1957 preschool program for Mexican American children in West Texas. The Odessa public schools used the audio-lingual techniques of "oral bombardment" of English vocabulary through a rigorous and systematic drill of "high frequency words" by specially trained teachers. This was simply a more intense application of English-Only. Despite the new audio-lingualism in school curricula, an Odessa principal listed goals for his program that were not too dissimilar to old English-Only practices. Corpus Christi schools under the direction of E. E. Mireles had begun their own pilot program for preschool English instruction for non-English-speaking children in 1956. Similar to the "Little Schools of the 400," Mireles's program hoped to teach a vocabulary of approximately 500 English words and 50 to 60 common expressions to aid in successful mainstreaming. Mireles actively promoted the preschool program well into the 1960s and advised policymakers of his suggestions for improvements.[36]

By the late 1950s and early 1960s cognitive development scientists had identified the aptitude of non-English-speaking children, in their own language, as no more or less retarded than their English-speaking peers'. This was as far as English-Only pedagogy would stretch to accommodate the Mexican American child. The State of Texas forced cultural, linguistic, and curricular concessions upon the old English-Only pedagogy. These concessions were embedded in the statewide Good Neighborism of the 1940s, the postwar emphasis on foreign language instruction in elementaries, and also by established Tejano leaders' support of preschool programs to bring some Spanish instruction to their children without technically violating the state's 1918 English-Only statute. The preschool program fulfilled Manuel and Sánchez's recommendations of the 1930s, but the 1960s illustrated that it was too little, too late. Sincere and significant efforts to temper the harsh English-Only educational experience of Mexican American children failed simply because they were too limited. Neither educators nor activists could *reform* English-Only. The federal government, language theorists, and the Chicano Generation of leadership would soon supply the drastic action necessary to eradicate this failed pedagogy.

CHAPTER EIGHT

The Birth of the Modern Bilingual Education Movement, 1965–68

124 The 1967–68 Bilingual Education Act signaled the triumphant return of bilingual instruction. The act's champions conceived it not just as a linguistic tool in the education of non-English speakers but also as a mechanism of empowerment and integration for language minorities, mostly Hispanic, into the mainstream of American life. Meanwhile, English-Only became officially discredited. Since World War I the English-Only paradigm had dominated opinions among the nation's linguists, teachers, scientists, attorneys, judges, and public leaders on how to educate non-English-speaking children. The acceptability of the all-encompassing system of English-Only pedagogy, interlaced as it was with racist assumptions on assimilation and intelligence, eroded with help from the academic community, Chicano activists, and (not least) the federal government under President Lyndon Baines Johnson. During the Kennedy and Johnson administrations, the federal government carried out studies and experimental programs; these studies borrowed from the changing conceptions of language in the scientific community and ushered new ways of teaching non-English-speaking children English through a greater use of the native language. Johnson as a young man had inadvertently—or perhaps commonsensically—employed some Spanish in his own English-language instruction in the late 1920s while teaching at a "Mexican" school in Cotulla, Texas. The Office of Education within the Department of Health, Education, and Welfare experimented with bilingual instruction in the early 1960s before its official legalization.

Rapidly evolving intellectual perceptions of citizenship, assimilation, and ethnicity affected major cultural changes in the United States during the 1960s. The nation was becoming less white; immigration from Asian and Latin American nations increased dramatically, causing long-forgotten language problems for the public schools. Much of this new increase in immigration was spurred by the country's abandonment of the restrictionist quotas inherent in the National Origins Act of the 1920s. The concept of assimilation was in a similar process of revision. Intellectuals like Milton Gordon in *Assimilation in American Life* reevaluated the differing patterns of assimilation in the American past, sophisticatedly moving beyond the "Melting Pot" construct. Others found lingering ethnicity and discrimination to be the most significant, unexamined phenomena of the United States.[1]

The federal government translated these broad trends into national policy. The Office of Education busied itself throughout the early 1960s with experiments and studies on language. From 1959 to 1963 the number of National Defense Education Act (NDEA) language learning centers increased from nineteen to fifty-five, modern language fellowship awards increased from 171 to 902, and the number of federally funded language research projects increased from twenty to twenty-nine. The total expenditure on such NDEA foreign language activities rose from $3,415,847 in 1959 to $7,999,999 in 1963. Part of this increasing largesse supported language experiments on bilingualism and native language instruction. For example, a 1963 amendment to the NDEA allowed the Office of Education "to support institutes for advanced training of public school teachers in teaching English as a second language to non-English-speaking students." Government linguist James E. Alatis explained of such experimentation that the science of language acquisition was evolving, and that other factors such as cultural clash and reinforcement were now considered central to the acquisition of languages. In addition, Alatis claimed, the child's culture was important. Alatis provided a vivid analogy to explain that a certain nod to the student's ethnicity was granted in newer versions of the audio-lingual approach: "the modern linguist does not reject outright the native tongue or dialect of the various students. He believes, rather, that we should leave the student's language alone (and teach him a second idiom as if it were a foreign tongue). His native language or dialect is vitally important to him in maintaining social acceptability in his own immediate environment. Certain of our young men, to put it in down-to-earth terms, need to be able to communicate properly in the employment office without losing their status in the poolroom."[2]

One specific research project in San Antonio sponsored by the Office of Education and the University of Texas in 1964–65 articulated the failures of English-Only and the partial successes of some kind of native language instruction. Dr. Annie Stemmler published a preliminary report on the project's research goals and methodologies in which she scathingly noted of the curricular status quo in Texas that eighty percent of non-English-speaking children in public schools failed the first grade due to language. Stemmler sampled a number of San Antonio elementary schools with an almost exclusively Spanish-speaking population. She found that after intensive instruction in Spanish, the attitudes of Mexican American children toward school and themselves dramatically improved. This was unexpected. Stemmler had been initially interested in a form of all-English instruction and had only used the all-Spanish instruction as a type of control in order to isolate the degree of what was expected to be the native language's hindrance of English acquisition. Instead, she wrote, "we became aware of the tremendous positive impact of according Spanish an accepted role in the traditionally English-speaking classroom. Spanish all too often is considered a second-rate language in Texas and other border states, and to speak Spanish is a mark of low social status. The benefits of true bilingualism have generally been overlooked. In fact, a tacit and nearly general policy has been to punish children for using Spanish at any time in school."[3]

The federal government still favored the post–World War II modification of the direct method of English-Only: the audio-lingual approach. The modern technique of English as a Second Language (ESL) came about in the 1960s due to the increased presence of non-English speakers in the schools. The Teachers of English to Speakers of Other Languages organization was formed in 1966, a year before the Bilingual Education Act was passed. The Office of Education reflected a growing shift away from English-Only and toward ESL, a newer pedagogical approach less dismissive of native languages.[4] This was not yet a pro-bilingual attitude, but neither was it the old, inflexible English-Only attitude.

Even FLES warhorses like Theodore Andersson, a onetime director of the foreign language program of the Modern Language Association, approved of some native language instruction. He came to believe that foreign language instruction to foreign-speaking children (native language instruction) would aid in their eventual assimilation into mainstream society and further the acquisition of English. Andersson shifted in his original academic interest; initially, his focus was with English-speaking children learning foreign languages. But by the late 1950s Andersson came to advocate such courses for native speakers. Citing a groundbreaking UNESCO study on language instruction in the Philippines, Andersson as early as 1957 was convinced that a two-year program of two-way bilingual education consisting of both English speakers and non-English speakers could effectively mainstream language-minority students to an all-English classroom.[5]

New York conducted impressive pilot programs on native language instruction during the early 1960s. Studies had already documented the inadequacy of English-Only instruction to Spanish-speaking

Puerto Rican children in New York City schools by the 1940s. One federal report exposed of English-Only in New York City during the 1950s that "Many classroom teachers were forbidden by their supervisors to use Spanish and have stated how they had to close the door so the principal could not hear them and see that this rule was being broken." By the early 1960s school officials had caught on to the dissatisfaction with English-Only. In 1963 the superintendent of citywide schools Dr. Calvin Gross advocated that "Puerto Rican children and other new arrivals to the city be able to develop biculturally and bilinguistically" and that "bilingualism and biculturalism will be encouraged for all pupils, particularly Spanish-speaking ones, as an aspect of excellence which will benefit our community and nation in their relationship to a multi-cultural world."⁶

Federal officials and the public schools in South Florida matched New York's activity. As a flood of Cuban refugees in the early 1960s concentrated in Miami, the federal government encouraged unique educational opportunities. One scholar characterized the federal government's unprecedented efforts to aid in the immigration, settlement, and assimilation of Cuban refugees: "Special visa waivers and resettlement programs for the post-revolutionary immigration were part of the strategy to use Cuban immigrants to discredit the Cuban revolution. In 1961, the United States brought more than 15,000 Cuban children to this country through the State Department–sponsored 'Peter Pan Operation.'" Federal authorities allowed Dade County public schools to engage in bilingual instruction to demonstrate to the world the creativity and flexibility of American schools to political refugees. Memos between the directors of the Dade County Cuban Refugee Program and federal education officials indicate that preschool bilingual programs for Cuban children were initially financed through the Office of Economic Opportunity and were offered to all low-income children in Miami—including African Americans and whites—but with special regard to Cuban children.⁷

While the federal government involved itself in the plight of language minorities on the East Coast, conditions for Tejanos remained abysmal. In 1970 Dr. Joseph Cardenas—director of migrant education for Professor Andersson's research agency at the University of Texas, the Southwest Educational Development Laboratory—estimated that the dropout rate for migrant children was ninety percent. As shocking as it seems today, this statistic did not faze officials; rather, the real surprise was the age of the dropouts. Cardenas calculated that "one-fifth of migrants are school dropouts at the preschool age. That is, one-fifth of all migrant children never enroll in any school in spite of the State's compulsory attendance laws. So by the time they start the first grade, or they are 6 years old, you have already lost 20 percent of your population." Professor George I. Sánchez estimated that all seventeen-year-old Texans (whites, African Americans, and Mexican Americans) attended a total average of more than 10 years of school. However, for just the African American group that average dipped to 8.1 years, and for Mexican Americans it bottomed out at 4.7 years.[8]

Throughout the 1960s teachers and administrators continued to punish students for speaking Spanish on school grounds. These disciplinary measures were intended to demean the language and its speaker—to shame a student into speaking English at all times. A civil rights report published in 1972 contained the writing exercises of a group of seventh-grade Mexican Americans assigned to relate their own grade-school experiences with English-Only. One wrote, "In the first through the fourth grade, if the teacher caught us talking Spanish we would have to stand on the 'black square' for an hour or so." Other students repeated similar punishments such as paying fines of a penny to a nickel, staying after school for detention, or getting extra homework.[9]

Meanwhile, Tejanos were becoming more adamant about the role Spanish should play in the public schools. Even older members of the Mexican American leadership establishment, including George Sánchez, lent support to this new emphasis: "I would also teach part of the curriculum in the home language of the students, in Spanish, so that they would attain language development in the language that is easiest for them."[10] Superintendent Homero Sigala of the "Mexican" school district of San Felipe (ninety-seven percent Tejano, two percent African American, and one percent Anglo) in the border town of Del Rio, Texas, testified in 1968: "Now, one more thing, one more thing that we have in San Felipe that as soon as I got there I put a stop to it—we have always spoken our language very softly because of the fact that people have said: 'Don't speak Spanish in the classroom. Don't speak Spanish.' So, consequently, the Chicano residing in Texas, whenever you hear him speak Spanish he will whisper Spanish to his comrade in there. And I am asking that Spanish be spoken correct, loud and clear. Y que no se dejen. *Don't be intimidated.*"[11]

Sigala's defiant words suggested the cultural and political shift taking place in the late 1960s. Younger Mexican Americans experienced a greater sense of ethnic pride, racial distinctiveness, and cultural recognition. The leaders of this generational and cultural shift preferred to identify themselves as Chicano, not Mexican American. Chicanos rejected the liberal rhetoric, accommodationist style, and professed patience of the preceding generation for the radicalism, confrontation, and immediacy that grew out of the 1960s civil rights and antiwar movements. More than their predecessors, they strove to include Spanish not only in their daily lives but also as an officially recognized language of instruction. In the late 1960s the "Chicano Generation" of cultural and political leadership challenged the older "Mexican American Generation." But Chicanismo of the late 1960s and 1970s did not stem simply from the young. The older generation's hopes of working within the system to effect gradual, meaningful change had been dashed by the mid-1960s. The roots of this frustration came from having witnessed a national civil rights movement and a war on poverty, little of which seemed geared to them. In Texas, Mexican Americans held a heightened sense expectation from the "Viva Kennedy" clubs that resulted in the formation of the Political Association of Spanish-Speaking Organizations (PASSO), consisting of a cross section of GI Forum and LULAC members. The failure of the Kennedy and Johnson administrations to follow through on their promises of greater influence and participation was a bitter pill for Mexican American activists.[12]

Scholars date the Chicano Generation's political origins to a series of botched conferences between 1966 and 1967 in which the Johnson administration demonstrated a lack of political tact regarding its Mexican American supporters. The established Mexican American leadership loudly and publicly broke with the administration on substantive policy issues, and younger, more radical Chicanos first organized themselves politically. The Chicanos completely broke not just with Johnson, but also with traditional politics, including the community's established leadership. The first sign of trouble occurred at a March, 1966, conference of the Equal Employment Opportunity Commission (EEOC) in Albuquerque, New Mexico. The EEOC had promised Mexican American leaders of LULAC, GI Forum, and PASSO an opportunity in Albuquerque to air grievances over the lack of action taken on discrimination against Mexican Americans. All but one of the commission members, including EEOC head Franklin Roosevelt, Jr., failed to attend, prompting some fifty Mexican American leaders to walk out of the meeting to protest what they termed a fundamental lack of respect. In response, the EEOC offered to convene another meeting to listen to Mexican American demands seriously and professionally. The walkout leaders organized a committee to petition Johnson directly to intervene. Johnson legitimized the walkout by creating a cabinet-level committee solely for Mexican American issues, the Inter-Agency Committee on Mexican American Affairs. Never before had leaders of the Mexican American Generation been so confrontational, or successful.[13]

Johnson named Vicente Ximenes to head the new cabinet-level agency. Ximenes was a GI Forum member from New Mexico and director of the 1964 "Viva Johnson" campaign. He was indisputably loyal to Johnson and functioned, next to GI Forum founder Dr. Hector P. Garcia of Corpus Christi, as LBJ's line of communication to a Mexican American community whose leadership was rapidly changing in makeup and tone. Johnson wanted Ximenes to moderate the confrontation emanating from the activist youth of the community, the Chicanos. After some delay due to his suspicion of a political ambush, Ximenes eventually did coordinate another conference the next year in El Paso specifically to address Mexican American issues.[14]

Many scholars identify the El Paso conference as the point from which the Chicano movement and the Chicano Generation of leadership emerged. Mexican American participants presented papers advocating the elevation of Hispanic culture and language in the schools to an equal status with Anglo culture. Mainstream social scientists argued that it was just such lingering whiffs of ethnicity that prevented Mexican Americans from more fully participating in American life, leaving them open to discrimination in the first place. Many of the younger and more radical conference delegates suspected the conference as nothing more than a ploy by Johnson to co-opt the growing unrest in the Chicano community with words, not action. In addition, organizers had omitted many young and more radical leaders from the list of those invited to the conference, while other prominent young Chicanos chose not to participate. These disaffected Chicanos responded by meeting in the El Paso barrio for a rump conference, organized chiefly by Stanford professor and labor organizer Ernesto Galaraza, an early mentor to César Chávez. These efforts eventually coalesced into La Raza Unida Party, which existed for several years in Texas and fielded credible candidates for statewide office in the 1970s.[15]

Students represented the vanguard of the Chicano movement. Several student organizations took part in the walkout at El Paso; one of them was the Mexican American Youth Organization (MAYO). The MAYO-lead student protests in the late 1960s at several South Texas public high schools commonly demanded the immediate institution of bilingual-bicultural education. These boycotts, referred to as "blowouts" by high school students, occurred at the public schools of Edcouch Elsa in 1968 and in Kingsville and Crystal City in 1969. Many Chicanos at the university level in the late 1960s desired a more institutionalized and activist student movement to unite various youth groups in the common cause of furthering the goals of the Chicano movement. They articulated their ideas for higher education in the document "El Plan de Santa Barbara" and formed a university student group named Movimiento Estudiantil Chicano de Aztlán (MECHA).[16] The Plan de Santa Barbara discussed the ways in which Chicano studies programs could connect the university and university-educated Chicano student body to the larger Chicano community and its issues. Plan authors believed that synergy of research, knowledge, and activism benefited both the university and the community. Chicano studies, it was argued, would support the necessary research for teachers implementing bilingual-bicultural education in the community.[17]

Bilingual education even garnered support from the older generation of leaders like Professor Sánchez, who had previously championed English-Only pedagogy. Sánchez supported bilingual education mostly due to its "lingual" part, however, and not out of any sense of Chicanismo. For Sánchez, bilingual education was needed to assimilate Mexican American youngsters, not to reinforce elements of their identity that he believed unbecoming. For example, Sánchez defended bilingual education by lamenting, "How many times have I seen a child cringe and crouch, physically and emotionally, because the language of the home was taboo at school and the language of the school was nonfunctional at home. Here is the genesis of the *pachuco,* the delinquent."[18] Young Chicanos then taking part in the formation of bilingual education programs celebrated this very same *pachuquismo;* it was a matter of racial pride rather than shame.

The younger generation saw bilingual education as equally bicultural. Unlike Sánchez, they were not as interested in the use of bilingual education for assimilation. Chicano activists in the early days of bilingual education viewed its purpose as one of strengthening ethnic pride and distinctiveness. Many viewed bilingual education's contribution to English acquisition as admirable, yet ultimately secondary to the cultural power of Spanish instruction in the early grades and the empowerment that it would bring. The cultural realm of Chicanismo associated speaking Spanish at school with cultural authenticity and solidarity, especially because schools were considered a key institutional tool of Anglo domination throughout history. Chicanos without Spanish-speaking ability had no cultural authenticity; those who could speak Spanish most colloquially best established such authenticity and had greater influence. Scholar José Limón took note of these cultural symbols at the meetings of Chicano student organizations at the University of Texas. Students participating in searches for positions in the Mexican American studies program judged candidates partly on their ability to converse in Spanish. Those who used working-class colloquialisms or "folk" Spanish proved themselves more influential than those who employed textbook Spanish or no Spanish at all. This very sense of *pachuquismo* that Sánchez saw as regrettable, Chicano activists viewed as genuine.[19]

Given their view of Spanish in such private settings, it is no wonder that Chicano activists viewed bilingual-bicultural education in grade schools as an important element in empowering the Chicano community. Some observers might easily regard bilingual education as a reflexive attendant to the rise of the Chicano Generation. This would be false. The history of bilingual education is more complex than such a simple causation. Although these academic and cultural trends took part in the coming of bilingual education, the federal government ultimately birthed it.

One of the central ironies in the history of the Bilingual Education Act and the modern bilingual education movement is that both were officially legitimized by President Lyndon Baines Johnson, the only United States president to have had actual experience in teaching non-English-speaking children. In fact, the very man who signed into law the Bilingual Education Act in January, 1968, practiced English-Only pedagogy in his first job six decades earlier at a poverty-stricken, segregated, Mexican American school in Cotulla, Texas, called Welhausen Elementary. In 1928 while teaching at Cotulla, the young Johnson awoke in the morning to "the hum of motors before daylight hauling the kids off in a truck to work on the neighboring farms." It was not Johnson's first experience with poverty, as one childhood friend put it, for he had seen plenty of that in the Hill Country region of his upbringing, but it was an altogether different type of poverty. The blatant exploitation of and prejudice against Mexican Americans affected Johnson; he wanted to "spark something inside them, to fill their souls with ambition and interest and belief in the future."[20]

As was his way, Johnson energetically (or frenetically) threw himself into his work. He sacrificed and worked tirelessly for his young Mexican American charges. In one instance, the future chief executive asked his mother to procure a crate of toothpaste for his students, because many of them were so poor that they did without: "I want 200 pkg. [*sic*] of toothpaste. We soon will have over 250 in school. They are all rather small and I think that they would appreciate it very much." In the same letter Johnson asked his mother for twenty to twenty-five short speech selections for his students.[21] Dan Garcia, a former Johnson student who became a furniture store owner and the first Mexican American city alderman of Cotulla, claimed that the gangly teacher pushed for extracurricular activities and purchased the school's first athletic equipment out of his own salary.[22]

Although these Mexican American children considered Johnson a kind and beloved teacher, his former students several decades later recounted Johnson's sometimes harsh application of the day's most Progressive techniques: English-Only pedagogy. Young Johnson administered corporal punishment for Spanish spoken on school grounds. One former student, Ed Gonzalez, a teletype operator for the *Durham Morning Herald* in North Carolina, remarked of Johnson, "He was a pretty good teacher . . . We had him for a foreign language, English. It was foreign to us since the whole school was Spanish or Mexican kids." If those English lessons were incomplete or lacking in effort, claimed Gonzalez, older children could anticipate spankings; the younger ones, ear-pinchings. Remembered Gonzalez, "I'll say this for him, he could pinch ears harder than anybody I ever knew." Juan Rodriquez, an ironworker in Chicago, recalled a Johnson spanking such that he "could hardly sit the rest of the day."[23]

Lyndon Johnson sternly applied English-Only pedagogy neither to be dogmatic nor cruel but with a sincere desire to help. Of the many students who remembered some form of corporal punishment from the future president they uniformly followed those statements with recollections of how they never had a teacher who cared so much or made them feel such a powerful sense of self-worth. Their parents were proud of the effort that the young Johnson made on their behalf. Ed Gonzalez claimed that Johnson was not completely insensitive to the young children's language difficulties, "People don't understand how hard it is to learn English, and Mr. Johnson was very patient with us. He was a good teacher and he had the advantage of knowing Spanish so when we came to an English word we couldn't understand, he would tell us what it was in our language."[24] Also complimentary were the comments of Dan Garcia, who recalled, "This may sound strange but a lot of us felt he was too good for us. . . . We wanted to take advantage of his being here. It was like a blessing from the clear sky." Juanita Ortiz remembered, "He also made us compete with other schools in the area in debate and declamation. . . . This helped our self-respect a lot."[25] Young Lyndon Johnson, perhaps the best teacher these disadvantaged students ever had, bent and contorted the rules of English-Only pedagogy to serve them best.

By the time LBJ became president the federal government already supported the concept of bilingual education in a variety of contexts. Officials supported it as an experimental program, a useful tool for what they termed "culturally handicapped" students, and a political bone to throw to Mexican Americans clamoring for more legislation geared to their communities. The administration qualified its approval. On the other hand, legislators supported bilingual education more broadly and enthusiastically. Both branches commonly regarded the idea of bilingual education as generally good but only in a vague, unsettled manner. The program was impressive enough to be enacted yet mysterious enough to be open to future changes and adaptations as it grew and obtained institutional support. The political establishment was stepping into a darkened room with bilingual education and was initially content to feel its way around slowly.

The overwhelming approval for the Bilingual Education Act indicates something of the opportunistic climate for innovation in education. The iron was hot, and Lyndon Johnson struck hard and often. Johnson initiated and signed the Higher Education Facilities Act and the Vocational Education Act in 1963, the Elementary and Secondary Education Act in 1964, the Higher Education Act in 1965, and numerous other initiatives. In early 1967 Johnson announced to Congress several additional legislative goals on education including more aid to the poor, the policy category into which the administration designated bilingual education. Bilingual education was thus a component of the Great Society's antipoverty efforts through education. There was little precedent for such actions, however. Johnson cautioned, "This has been an ambitious venture, for no textbook offers precise methods for dealing with the disadvantaged."[26]

The genesis for this policy direction had come a year earlier as LBJ reflected upon his own English-Only experiences. On a visit to Cotulla late in 1966, only a few months before U.S. Senator Ralph Yarborough of Texas proposed a bilingual education bill, Johnson spoke informally and eloquently to "his" Texas people. Johnson's speech was vague on specific policy, but the passionate intonation of the distinctively Mexican American educational experience hinted at some future—as of yet unformed—action: "Thirty-eight years have passed, but I still see the faces of the children who sat in my class. I still hear their eager voices speaking Spanish as I came in." Warming to the subject, Johnson offered an awkwardly phrased promise: "the conscience of America has slept long enough while the children of Mexican Americans have been taught that the end of life is a beet row, a spinach field, or a cotton patch. . . . I intend to have all of our educational experts explore practical programs that will encourage these children to stay in school and improve their chances of learning, to prepare themselves, and to equip themselves, to become lifelong taxpayers instead of tax eaters."[27] Into this dewy atmosphere of personal nostalgia and urgency, President

Professor George I. Sánchez of the University of Texas shaped the Bilingual Education Act. He was a national president of LULAC, a cofounder of PASSO, a civil rights advocate, and the most important Mexican American intellectual of his era. Nevertheless, he abandoned a lifetime of working within the English-Only intellectual paradigm to support bilingual education near the end of his life. Photo courtesy of the Institute of Texan Cultures at University of Texas at San Antonio, No. 68-561.

Johnson ushered the emergence of modern bilingual education in the United States.

One of the central fallacies of historical scholarship is the notion that the Bilingual Education Act aberrantly squeaked through unknowledgeable, uninterested legislative and executive branches and grew as a federal policy due to pressure from radical, militant ethnics.[28] Many congressional supporters were actively aware of bilingual education. It represented the rare instance of a bill's achieving wide popularity even though participants supported it for different reasons and held paradoxically different conceptions of it. This condition does not indicate a dearth of interest or the result of a campaign of purposeful misinformation but an exuberance based on the wide possibilities of the legislation.

Ralph Yarborough of Texas fueled interest in the subject in January, 1967, by introducing a bilingual education bill in the U.S. Senate. This proposed legislation only intended to better the quality of education for Spanish speakers of the Southwest. Yarborough had contemplated such an initiative for some time with Mexican American leaders and educators like Professor George I. Sánchez. Senator Yarborough originally limited the "Bilingual American Education Act" to Spanish speakers: "In recognition of the special educational needs of the large number of students in the United States whose mother tongue is Spanish and to whom English is a foreign language, Congress hereby declares it to be the policy of the United States to provide and carry out new and imaginative elementary and secondary school programs to meet those special educational needs." Several of Yarborough's Senate colleagues in both parties—including Senators Jacob Javits and Robert Kennedy of New York, Joseph Montoya of New Mexico, Thomas Kuchel of California, and John Tower of Texas—attached themselves as cosponsors of this legislation during its initial reading.[29] Other coauthors soon followed. The House of Representatives began deliberation that February, and individual representatives issued their own versions of bilingual education. By the month of May, thirty different congressmen had introduced no fewer than thirty-three separate bills to promote bilingual education of some kind, widening Senator Yarborough's original focus on Spanish speakers. The House initiatives eventually coalesced into a bill by Congressmen Edward Roybal and James Scheuer, Democrats from California and New York. Scheuer's idea, accepted by most bilingual education proponents in the House, held that the research behind bilingual education was ultimately too promising to limit to just Spanish speakers.[30]

Historian Hugh Davis Graham, an important commentator on the history and politics of bilingual education, alleges of bilingual education's eventual popularization that "the militant Hispanic lobby won" and that it was nothing more than a "Hispanic job corps."[31] Aside from an interview with Commissioner of Education Harold Howe II and the memoirs of LBJ aide Joseph Califano, Graham cites no persuasive evidence to explain this charge; he fails to identify these "militants" or the name of the "lobby." Possibly Graham incorrectly refers to older, established Mexican American groups like LULAC, the GI Forum, or PASSO. Does Graham seriously allege that these supposedly influential "militants" were members of the Chicano movement, a movement that would only catalyze *after* the El Paso conference in October, 1967, *after* legislators had already passed two separate bilingual education bills that August? Did these "militants" force more than thirty separate congressmen (some in states with no significant Spanish-speaking population like West Virginia) to try to broaden the scope of bilingual education? Was Professor George I. Sánchez an alleged Brown Power "militant"? Did the testimony of Professors Joshua Fishman of Yeshiva University and Theodore Andersson of the University of Texas constitute the prospective heads of a conspiratorial "Hispanic job corps" searching for federal plums? Graham most likely, and unfortunately, conflated his interview subjects' political views toward bilingual education that were a decade or so removed from the historical action with historical reality rather than examining the actual administrative record.

Graham's claims are difficult to entertain seriously. Theodore Andersson's testimony at the subcommittee hearings on bilingual education illustrates that many in the academic community regarded the concept of bilingual education to be worthy of consideration. Evidence refutes Graham's assertion that bilingual education was not scientifically or pedagogically justified, or that it was an unknown quantity in 1967. Its proponents may not have been correct in every contention, but Graham could hardly claim to dismiss their testimony and support so completely as to imply that pedagogical justification was nonexistent, unless, of course, *they* were ethnic militants. Indeed, Andersson was Swedish.[32]

The Mexican Americans in the Johnson Administration—Californians Lupe Anguiano of Los Angeles and Armondo Rodriguez of San Diego, both at HEW—lobbied for passage of bilingual education and opposed attempts to weaken it with too much of an emphasis on English. They feared that bilingual education within the rubric of compensatory education would lead to stigmatization.[33]

The rest of the Johnson administration did not seem to know what to do with bilingual education. It was, after all, not strictly their initiative but was incredibly popular in the Congress. Secretary John Gardner of the Department of Health, Education, and Welfare (HEW) articulated his agency's mixed feelings to the House Committee on Education: "We already have a number of programs which support bilingual education. With the assistance of Titles I and III of the Elementary and Secondary Education Act, a number of schools are carrying out bilingual education programs at this time." Gardner enumerated other existing structures that could just as easily be used to provide for experimental bilingual programs, such as the National Defense Education Act and legislation like the Cooperative Research Act, the Higher Education Act, and the Education Professions Development Act.[34]

Commissioner Harold Howe II of the Office of Education exhibited mixed responses to bilingual education, the majority of them hostile. The issue of bureaucratic turf concerned him about the Senate and House bills that passed and awaited a conference resolution in August, 1967. In an internal memorandum to Johnson domestic policy aide Douglass Cater, Howe remarked that he might possibly support the idea of a bilingual education law and specifically Yarborough's proposal, "only if it is viewed as a short-term demonstration program designed to spotlight an area which urgently needs attention. I would base my support on the assumption that, after a few years, other education programs (particularly Title I of ESEA) would have picked up the most effective bilingual education techniques."[35]

HEW Secretary Gardner and Commissioner Howe agreed that the legislation should not entitle any one group of non-English speakers above another. In a memo to Cater, Commissioner Howe flatly proclaimed, "Entitlements should not be determined by the number of persons of Mexican and Puerto Rican descent or who have Spanish surnames. The program should instead be directed to persons who come from non-English-speaking backgrounds . . . it is offensive to use ethnic or national origin (or surname) as a basis for an educational program."[36] Howe did not share Johnson's or Yarborough's intensely personal interest in bilingual education or Mexican Americans. Howe supported bilingual education in limited, experimental form; he did not support it as an institutionalized, mandated, and protected pedagogical technique.

Howe apparently feared that Yarborough's bill targeting Spanish speakers was an ethnic giveaway. This judgment makes some sense in light of the Office of Education's desire to limit the Bilingual Education Act to little more than an enabler of experimental programs. But Johnson's aides on education policy dared not openly oppose the legislation. Jim Gaither, one such aide, wrote to Joe Califano, Johnson's chief aid on domestic policy, "Because of these political and legal reasons, plus the likelihood that the committee will pass the bill regardless of what position we take, Budget and HEW now agree that the Administration should support Senator Yarborough's bill." Gaithers indicated of the desired modifications of Yarborough's bill, "These changes will give the bill more of a pilot project, demonstration and teacher training orientation."[37]

No memo between the Office of Education and Johnson's domestic policy staff actually debated bilingual education on the basis of pedagogical science. Correspondence dealt exclusively with how to couch objections in such a way as not to oppose the *idea* of bilingual education, a popular subject for Congress in 1967, so that it would appear as if they had problems with only its bureaucratic fit or its funding. There were reasons to support the bill beyond its pedagogical merits. Howe's aggressive enforcement of Titles I and III of the 1965 ESEA regarding African Americans had created a firestorm of difficulty for the administration, not to mention threats to his person. Therefore, one reason for supporting the Bilingual Education Act was to take pressure off Howe. If bilingual education were defeated, he would be forced to continue funding bilingual programs under Titles I and III at a time, remarked one aide, "when we are fighting to preserve the Commissioner's approval authority in the Congress."[38]

The flood of bilingual education bills in the House and the number of coauthors for Yarborough's legislation in the Senate convinced Howe and the White House that going along with a partially objectionable bill was preferable to being stuck with an entirely objectionable one. For example, Ralph Huitt, a White House legislative aide, wrote to aides Douglass Cater and Barefoot Sanders that "There is considerable unhappiness on the Committee that the Administration is not supporting the Bilingual Education bill; it is likened to our earlier opposition to Senator Yarborough's 'cold war G.I. bill.'" The next day Sanders wrote to Califano, "Joe: Are we on solid ground in opposing this bill? I understand the Latinos are upset with our position." Califano forwarded the memo with a scribbled reply the next day to Jim Gaithers, "Let's get in this—shouldn't we support it?"[39] The administration scrambled to get on board the bilingual education bandwagon.

President Lyndon Baines Johnson signed the Bilingual Education Act into law on January 2, 1968. In his public statement about signing several ESEA amendments passed in late 1967, of which the Bilingual Education Act had become one, Johnson mentioned bilingual education specifically. He claimed that the amendments contained "a special provision establishing bilingual education programs for children whose first language is not English. Thousands of children of Latin descent, young Indians, and others will get a better start—a better chance—in school."[40] The Bilingual Education Act became Title VII of the ESEA. Local entities applied for grants to conduct experiments and pilot programs in bilingual education. In the first year of its existence in 1968, the expenditure limit authorized by law was $15 million. That limit for 1969 rose to $30 million, and by 1970 it was to be appropriated up to $40 million. However, even though such amounts were authorized, nothing could force the administration to spend that much. Bilingual education remained severely underfunded for some time as it developed grassroots constituencies capable of lobbying for funds.[41]

In the Great Society rhetoric concerning educational matters, bilingual education was not simply for Spanish speakers. No full-fledged effort existed to bring it to every school with non-English-speaking children. It was intended to fall under the rubric of "compensatory education." Aid to the handicapped, rural school aid, direct federal grants for minority institutions, and bilingual education allowed local schools to improve the overall level of education to poor people and minorities in addition to erasing the effects of Jim Crow segregation. The National Advisory Council on the Education of Disadvantaged Children reiterated this theme to the White House: "The Council, therefore, continued to place its hope in efforts that combine desegregation and compensatory improvement of the schools—not one without the other.[42]

For one so hostile to the Bilingual Education Act, Commissioner Howe quickly embraced it once it came under his bailiwick. In a 1968 speech Howe boasted of fifteen projects at that time being funded by his agency that "have shown promise of redeeming Mexican American children from the near-certainty of educational failure." These programs, he stated, "emphasize a bicultural, bilingual approach which says, in essence, that Mexican American children must learn the English language and Anglo ways—but that they can do so without having to reject their knowledge of the Spanish language and of Mexican American ways." Howe hoped to champion the idea of "cultural diversity" through bilingual education.[43]

As his presidency in 1968 came to a close and the Vietnam War became his own personal albatross, Lyndon Johnson probably paid little attention to the small, inexpensive law that officially sanctioned bilingual education after decades of its official repression. It was only one law among sixty dealing with education enacted during his tenure. Two recent studies of Johnson's relationship to Mexican Americans and his use of English-Only as a young teacher implicitly demonstrate the high irony of Johnson's signing of the Bilingual Education Act.[44] Johnson's action stood the Progressive pedagogical techniques of his own teaching days on their head. The scientific shift in the pedagogy of language instruction and the growing political presence of Spanish speakers throughout the country demanded some sort of federal legislation by the late 1960s. The reemergence of bilingual education in this vital decade represented the opening of an educational door long closed to Mexican Americans and other immigrant peoples of the United States. After the signing of this enabling legislation in 1968, however, it would be up to bilingual education's supporters and local activists to force individual states and communities to act. In this sense, the Bilingual Education Act marked the first of many battles to come.

CHAPTER NINE

The Return
of Bilingual Education to Texas,
1964–81

The State of Texas pioneered the modern bilingual education movement. After the passage of the national Bilingual Education Act late in
1967 and Johnson's signing of it into law in early 1968, Texas soon legitimized bilingual education through legislative action and local initiative. Although there was no immediate match to the federal government's passage of the Bilingual Education Act, experiments in Texas
concerning bilingualism in the classroom for Mexican Americans
had already been initiated by the mid-1960s at the insistence of concerned and sympathetic teachers, school administrators, and university
professors. In addition, bilingual education in Texas quickly became a
charged political issue for Chicano student activists during the school
walkouts of the late 1960s and early 1970s. It was also politicized as a
key mechanism for the enforcement of desegregation efforts. Bilingual
education's role in the integration of Texas schools heightened during
the 1970s as a response to federal court mandates. The state of Texas in
the 1970s and early 1980s continued to promote bilingual education
in the face of mounting controversy, yet compromised between the
pedagogy's adherents and its critics.

Before the official recognition of bilingual education, the Texas
Legislature and Governor Price Daniel approached Tejano education by
way of the Pre-School Non-English-Speaking Children program, a legislative outgrowth of the LULAC project called "Little Schools of the
400." Statewide, 22,135 preschool students qualified for the program
in 1959. However, only 720 actual classes and 101 certified teachers
existed; an average of nearly 31 preschoolers per classroom proved un-
acceptable. Professor George I. Sánchez criticized these preschool programs, complaining to public officials that they had a segregatory effect
on Mexican American children, even though the concept for the program had originally been the idea of a former national LULAC president (a position that Sánchez once held), Felix Tijerina of Houston.[1]

These schools were not truly bilingual. There was undoubtedly
some degree of translation between the English and Spanish words in

A LULAC program, the "Little Schools of the 400," was ultimately incorporated into the state's general curriculum for Mexican Americans. The instruction occurred during the summer and attempted to impart enough English to avoid pedagogical segregation. These Corpus Christi students started their day with the pledge. Photo courtesy of the Edmundo E. Mireles Papers at the Nettie Lee Benson Latin American Center, Box 1, Folder 12, XII-133.

the original LULAC pilot program, but the state-run version discouraged any systematic use of Spanish. Officials organized classes in as much of an English-Only framework as possible. Their ultimate goal was "to prepare non-English speaking children for entry into the first grade with a command of the essential English words needed for communicating and receiving instruction from the teacher." In 1963 participating students numbered 18,791. By 1964 the preschools enrolled 20,342 children.[2]

As the federal government in Lyndon Johnson's Great Society became more involved in the education of minorities and the poor, Texas began to classify its own preschool language program for Mexican Americans as part of a statewide effort at "compensatory education." From the mid-1960s, however, the program declined in enrollment and importance. One state report maintained that federal efforts took students away from the state's program: "Although there has been a slight downward trend in enrollments in the summer Preschool Non-

English Speaking Program, more children are being reached in year-long non-English programs funded under Title I of the Elementary and Secondary Education Act." This situation marked a significant shift in responsibility from state to federal government. In the late 1960s and early 1970s the state was abandoning the business of administering the program, as federally sanctioned bilingual education became a viable local option. The state-financed preschool program only enrolled 8,122 students in 1970 and 3,682 students in 1971.[3]

In 1963 the TEA organized another compensatory program: the special migrant education program. Geared to immigrant Mexicans especially, the six-month school (the regular public school term was nine months) intended to conform as neatly as possible to seasonal labor conditions. It lasted five days a week and eight hours a day, whereas the normal school day lasted only six hours. The migrant lessons, much like those of the preschool program for non-English-speaking children, were conducted in an English-Only setting: "Teaching English means practicing phrases and sentences until English word, sound, word form, and word order become automatic."[4] This constant repetition of oral language aped the decades-old direct method of English-Only. This time, however, the audio-lingual techniques were supported by enhanced behaviorist justifications.

By the late 1960s and early 1970s, real bilingual education programs began where the pre-bilingual, statewide compensatory programs had ended. Although the federal legislation did not take effect until 1968, statewide interest in bilingual education dated much earlier. In prepared testimony to the congressional committee assessing the funding of the new bilingual education law during the spring of 1969, Professor Theodore Andersson claimed that in 1957 he had "received from the University of Texas a small amount of money to experiment with bilingual education in selected Austin schools. This experiment met with complete failure, for the public attitude was still such as to be unaware of the educational advantages of bilingual schooling." Despite this early setback, Andersson remained involved with bilingual education in Texas. His Southwest Educational Development Laboratory at the University of Texas was named one of the ESEA Title VII research centers to which funds could be channeled.[5]

Funding for the first bilingual education programs in Texas came from federal and local sources, not the state. The TEA immediately recognized the significance of bilingual instruction after it was accepted on the national level and, not wishing to limit the concept's growth, defined it as broadly as possible: "In bilingual education two languages are used in the instructional program, the language of the child's home and

English. Both are used for a portion of, or all of, the curriculum, except in the teaching of foreign languages." The state initially held that the end pedagogical result of bilingual education was proficiency in both languages for Mexican American and Anglo schoolchildren. This short-lived emphasis on two-way bilingual education immediately gave way as bilingual education became labeled as special, compensatory education. By 1969–70 federal funds supported twenty-seven Texas bilingual projects through Title VII of ESEA. In the academic year 1970–71 the number of Spanish speakers served by bilingual education numbered 12,686, while the number of English-speaking children enrolled was 2,744. Teaching these children were 461 bilingual teachers and 141 monolingual, English-speaking teachers. In 1971–72 the numbers grew to 18,605 Spanish speakers and 3,582 English speakers spread out over forty-one school districts.[6]

The earliest official bilingual education program in the state began in 1964 at the Laredo United Independent School District, representing a rural area on the outskirts of Laredo. Laredo United was ideal in that it maintained a significant Mexican American student body. In 1962 the district hired Harold C. Brantley, a veteran South Texas superintendent who was fluently bilingual. Brantley arrived with a firm conviction regarding English-Only instruction's inadequacy. In 1963 he persuaded the school board to repeal the prohibition of Spanish on school grounds on the basis that it hindered the development of the natural bilingual capacities that he believed should be encouraged. In approaching the TEA regarding his long-held dream of implementing bilingual instruction, Brantley met Dr. Andersson. Andersson alerted Brantley to the presence of the Dade County bilingual program for Cuban refugees in the early 1960s. Brantley believed that the half-Anglo, half-Chicano population of Laredo United schools offered an excellent chance to implement two-way bilingual education. Brantley traveled to Miami, Florida, in 1964 to observe the Dade County bilingual program. He then raided regional private schools to obtain bilingual talent to launch the program. Brantley hired Victor Cruz-Aedo, the superintendent of The Holding Institute, a Methodist institution that, since the 1910s, had served Laredo as a bilingual school. Cruz-Aedo's talent in conceiving of and implementing a bilingual program from scratch was such that he eventually left to join the TEA in developing the statewide bilingual curriculum.[7]

Brantley next sought to smooth over potential public opposition. He expected hostility from two quarters: "first, from the parent of the English-speaking child who might feel her child would be shortchanged in the amount of first grade work he would be able to cover, and second, from the Hispanic parent who was striving to become identified with middle-class Anglo culture." Superintendent Brantley's pilot bilingual program was one of the first in the state and probably one of the most successful. He attributed his success as directly related to his attitude of making bilingual education a total pedagogical approach for *all* children, not a compensatory measure for one group designated as handicapped, disadvantaged, or in need of "special" education. (In 1998 Brantley criticized bilingual education as then practiced as far too limited to non-English speakers and thus stigmatized.) The next year in Texas saw several other bilingual programs funded through the ESEA.[8]

Bilingual education was a central component of the Chicano movement. One Chicano scholar-activist wrote that the relationship between bilingual education programs and the Chicano community was absolutely fundamental for the success of both. Another Chicano scholar-activist urged Chicanos to "take the schools out of the hands of those who are academically suppressing them" to make bilingual-bicultural education a reality, not a paper program with token Chicano input.[9] Student activism and the boycott of schools aided the arrival of bilingual education in Texas. These protests were called school walkouts, or "blowouts." However, the rise of the Chicano movement and its leaders took place shortly after the legalization of bilingual education—not before, as historian Hugh Graham alleges. Texas and the nation had practiced bilingual education for several years before the emergence of so-called Chicano militants.[10]

It took a concerted effort from local pressure groups, mostly the Mexican American community, to successfully demand bilingual education, even when it was funded entirely by the federal government. The TEA, while willing to give some technical assistance to districts trying to create bilingual programs, did not wish to define the issue of bilingual education as a statewide initiative. Dr. Severo Gomez, coordinator of bilingual education for the TEA, testified in 1968 to a congressional hearing that most of the state's bilingual programs that garnered federal support with state approval operated more along the lines of loosely structured ESL programs, not the kind of sophisticated two-way, bilingual programs that had been envisioned by many experts and practiced by Brantley in Laredo.[11]

When TEA did involve itself directly with bilingual education, it demonstrated a tin ear to the implicit biculturalism that the pedagogical approach intended to promote. In the first TEA guidebook for implementing bilingual programs, a "background" section on Mexican American history and society purported to explain how "The *patrón* system rested upon values that for the most part still exist and to a large

By the 1970s, a statewide administrator, Dr. Severo Gomez, was working to integrate official bilingual education into the Texas public school system. Photo courtesy of the Institute of Texan Cultures at University of Texas at San Antonio, No. 71-114.

measure still determine the attitudes of the Mexican American." The document outlined these alleged values: "(1) a blind loyalty toward traditional ethnic leaders, (2) a tendency to desire to enter into dependent but secure positions of dependency upon an employer or a political leader, (3) a reluctance to make decisions and a tendency to postpone decisions as long as possible, (4) a dislike of competition and of personal initiative, (5) a preference for a stable hierarchical social system with well-defined statuses and roles, (6) a preference for friendly person-to-person primary relationship rather than the formal impersonal relationships of the Anglo American world, (7) a strong dislike for and resistance toward social and cultural change." The very attitudes that bilingual education was supposed to help transform were embedded in the state's orientation manual.[12]

Texas did not wait long before it completely overhauled state law to conform more neatly to the national Bilingual Education Act. Texas still had its 1918 English-Only law on the books and very much in force in most school districts. In the first several years of bilingual education's existence in Texas, the TEA granted waivers to the English-Only provisions of the criminal code for those school districts receiving ESEA money for bilingual programs. In order to finesse this discrepancy between law and practice as well as to continue qualifying for federal money, several state legislators, most notably Senator Joe Bernal of San Antonio and Representative Carlos Truan of Kingsville, sought to make bilingual education legal by state statute in 1969. Bernal's initial bilingual education bill, Senate Bill 46, passed overwhelmingly without a dissenting vote. Truan's House Bill 103, also with little opposition, moved more quickly through the House. According to legislative custom in cases where identical bills are passed through both chambers of the legislature, Bernal substituted Truan's House Bill 103 for his own.

Without so much as a whimper, bilingual education in Texas was finally decriminalized in May, 1969, just over half of a century after the public fanfare that christened English-Only as the language policy of the public schools. The bill allowed schools to practice bilingual education without special dispensations from the TEA.[13]

The Texas bilingual statute of 1969 was neither complicated nor controversial, but it was significant. It easily passed both chambers of the legislature because of its limited scope. Also, Truan and Bernal had obtained crucial support for the bill from Lieutenant Governor Ben Barnes, a protégé of Texas governor John B. Connolly, and Speaker of the House of Representatives Gus Mutscher. Barnes and Mutscher both had higher ambitions and courted the Chicano vote. The enabling legislation, in spite of still using only federal dollars, nevertheless gave ultimate control over bilingual programs to the TEA and local schools. In other words, it increased educational services without spending state money—always a popular proposition. Truan and Bernal envisioned future, grander legislation that would earmark state appropriations to match federal dollars. For the moment, however, they were content simply to repeal the old English-Only law.[14]

In 1973 Truan and several of his liberal legislative allies passed another bilingual law—this time more than just enabling legislation. This bill mandated bilingual education through the first six grades in potentially all subjects for any school district with twenty or more students whose test scores indicated that they were of limited English-speaking ability. The money allocated for it came from the general education budget. Although bilingual education remained underfunded throughout the 1970s, it was gaining acceptance from the education community.[15]

As this legislation was being formulated, bilingual education in Texas and across the nation became entangled in the legal efforts by Mexican Americans to challenge educational discrimination in the schools. In the *Cisneros* v. *Corpus Christi Independent School District* decision of 1970, a federal court ruled that Chicanos were an identifiable minority group instead of white, which had been their legal classification since the 1930 *Salvatierra* decision. In addition to the *Brown* v. *Board* legal mechanisms now at the Mexican American community's disposal in the desegregation wars, the idea of bilingual education also came to be regarded a key component for dismantling school segregation.[16]

The *Cisneros* decision opened the door for legal activists to push the boundaries of civil rights law. As the history of educational discrimination against Mexican Americans involved curricular justifications for segregation, it only followed that notions of school integration for Mexican Americans involved not just the shifting of bodies but also a complete overhaul of the standard curriculum that had enabled such discrimination in the first place. Bilingual-bicultural education was viewed as a possible remedy along with busing and the redrawing of school districts in school integration plans. Both federal judges and legal strategists accepted this reasoning. For example, Peter D. Roos, director of education litigation for the Mexican American Legal Defense and Education Fund, in a 1978 law article wrote, "In recent years Chicano communities have sought judicial desegregation throughout the Southwest, and many communities will continue to demand an end to state-imposed ethnic isolation. Nonetheless, for the moment and for the foreseeable future bilingual-bicultural education will be seen as the sword for severing the bonds that hold back Hispanic children." Another legal scholar in 1975 wrote that for Mexican Americans, "Bilingual education thus emerges with strong credentials as a means of providing equal educational benefits to the 'problem population' identified by Herschel Manuel 40 years ago."[17]

Judge William Wayne Justice handed down the next major court decision regarding bilingual education and school desegregation on December 6, 1971. In *United States of America* v. *State of Texas*, the federal court contended that the San Felipe Del Rio Consolidated Independent School District "had made no sincere or good faith effort to obtain federal funding" for a comprehensive educational plan ordered by the court. Such a plan was to include "sufficient educational safeguards to insure that all students in the San Felipe Del Rio Consolidated Independent School District will be offered equal educational opportunities," which included "bilingual and bicultural programs" among other curricular innovations. The plan Judge Justice referred to, approved by HEW, called for a curricular overhaul as part of a desegregation plan offering "all children a bilingual-bicultural instructional program which utilizes the child's language system (English, Spanish, or a blend of both) as the medium of instruction as proficiency in one or more additional language systems is developed."[18]

The U.S. Justice Department also explored bilingual education's uses. On May 25, 1970, the Office of Civil Rights issued a memo stating that it considered the categorical grouping of language minorities into special education classes for slow or retarded children to be a civil rights violation. The memo also suggested that schools were legally bound to notify the parents of language-minority children of all the vernacular instructional possibilities and that they were required to take affirmative steps to open the curriculum to non-English speakers. The Office of Civil Rights would gradually expand these recommendations with internal compliance rules advocating affirmative action for teacher recruitment, specialized training, and cultural diversity as a curricular goal.[19]

Within months Chinese Americans in California filed a lawsuit in federal court. Ultimately decided in 1974, *Lau* v. *Nichols* ruled that a school must provide equal access to bilingual education for all language minorities, provided they were numerically significant. In *Lau* the Supreme Court did not reach the equal protection clause of the Fourteenth Amendment in mandating the implementation of bilingual education programs. Instead, the pro-bilingual stance was deduced by invoking Title VI of the 1964 Civil Rights Act, outlawing discrimination in federally supported programs. *Lau* was a landmark decision in the eventual popularization of bilingual education. However, several crucial points remained murky. For one, the justices did not mandate any specific type of bilingual education. Also, the ruling neglected to mandate a definite numerical threshold at which bilingual education should be adopted in order to establish compliance with Title VI. The Office of Civil Rights jumped into the fray in August, 1975, with the "Lau Remedies," offering specific guidelines to dispel this murkiness. Timetables were issued and recalcitrant school districts were forced to draft "Lau plans" to remedy curricular and administrative deficiencies. Meanwhile, Senators Edward Kennedy of Massachusetts and Walter Mondale of Minnesota passed federal legislation to expand bilingual education.[20]

As bilingual education in Texas became more widespread, it also became more controversial. A six-part investigative series in 1974 by the *San Antonio Light* illustrates the common tack taken by critics of bilingual education. For some, bilingual education fostered segregation, an especially ironic allegation given its use as a lever of desegregation by the federal judiciary and Mexican American civil rights groups. Opponents also charged that bilingual programs instructed too much in Spanish and, thus, failed to emphasize English enough. This instance, if true, would have violated the state's 1973 Bilingual Education Law, which stressed both English and the second language. Other critics worried that the emphasis upon Spanish and biculturalism might teach Mexican American children to be "professional Mexicans, with the Chicano view" at the expense of proper Americanism. A final charge deemed bilingual education to be still too much in the ether of educational theory to be a successful and practical pedagogical approach, ignoring the decades of academic development toward bilingual education.[21]

This growth of negative opinion of bilingual education in Texas also occurred throughout the nation as the pedagogical approach that had been greeted with so much enthusiasm in the prior decade began to experience the first wave of backlash. In 1975 Representative Carlos Truan attempted to increase support for bilingual education. Instead, bilingual education in Texas was watered down from the 1973 mandates, with legislative action making participation by the upper elementary grades optional. Truan was elected to the Senate in the next session in 1977; there his bilingual education bill failed to get out of committee. In 1979 Truan and Senator Jack Ogg of Houston passed Senate Bill 195 to support additional bilingual education. However, Representative Matt Garcia of San Antonio failed to move his House colleagues to take action on the bill. This culminated nearly a decade of legislative stall on Texas bilingual education. It became more controversial nationally as well. An important American Institutes for Research study and a major monograph by critic Noel Epstein titled *Language, Ethnicity, and the Schools* in 1977 represented the first serious salvos lobbed by critics of bilingual education. The Reagan administration's distaste for enforcing Carter-era regulations on bilingual education and civil rights further eroded its position in the 1980s.[22]

Despite the rise to prominence of neoconservative opponents, Texas bilingual education would see its greatest triumph with major legislation in 1981. Judge William Justice ruled in January of that year in another *United States* v. *Texas* case that the state's bilingual education program was wholly inadequate for the purposes of furthering Mexican American efforts to eliminate racial discrimination in the public schools. Justice outlined a plan for remedying the state's bilingual education system, drawing the ire of many establishment political leaders. The state's bilingual education community and the Mexican American leadership responded to the ruling by scrambling to provide an alternative course of action. Senator Carlos Truan and others urged the Texas Legislature to "bite the bullet" regarding the state's antiquated and inadequate bilingual system. Truan suggested that it would be far better for the legislature to put forth its own bilingual education bill than be dictated to by the courts, a source of great irritation among legislators and Governor William Clements.[23]

This sudden flurry of action on bilingual education resulted in the 1981 bilingual education law that, in tandem with the watered-down 1973 legislation, would determine the legal status of bilingual education in Texas throughout the 1980s and 1990s. Truan limited his 1981 bill out of political necessity when he agreed to accept recommendations from a statewide task force on bilingual education that favored increased funding but also put special emphasis upon English acquisition, especially in grades seven through twelve where the task force preferred ESL techniques. This transition-oriented bilingual program fell short of Truan's and others' original vision of unlimited bilingual education for all grades—a much more encompassing system. However, the task force consensus was badly fractured even on this compromise, and advocates were generally heartened that some significant expansion of bilingual education was recommended.[24]

Senate Bill 477, authored by Carlos Truan and cosponsored by Senators Hector Uribe of Brownsville, R. E. Vale of San Antonio, H. T. Santiesteban of El Paso, and Chet Brooks of Pasadena, was sponsored in the House by Representative Matt Garcia. Senator W. E. Snelson, a member of the Senate Education Committee who originally opposed the legislation from within committee, continued his attempts to cripple the bill, as did legislators in the House. After several successful damaging amendments were either withdrawn or excised in conference committee, however, the bill eventually met Truan's satisfaction and was signed by Governor Bill Clements on June 15, 1981.[25]

The remainder of the 1980s and most of the 1990s would be a time of stasis for bilingual education in Texas. The Reagan and Bush administrations would continue to de-emphasize bilingual education at the federal level. Later in the 1990s, however, bilingual education experienced some reversal of fortunes from the Clinton administration. The backlash against bilingual education, evident in Texas by the 1970s, intensified across the nation as twenty states adopted English-Only enactments during the 1980s and 1990s (three other states still maintained such policies from previous eras). Another four states in this period conversely adopted English-Plus enactments, official pronouncements of support for multilingualism.[26] Texas, signaling a spirit of compromise evident with its 1981 bilingual education legislation, chose during the 1980s and 1990s neither a return to English-Only nor a full and total embrace of bilingual education in all its possibilities.

The State of Texas has dealt with bilingual education in a cautiously open manner since its legalization by the federal government in 1968. The state has not enthusiastically welcomed all innovations, but neither has it seriously sought to slam the door shut on bilingual education. The state's 1969 effort was simply enabling legislation, and its 1973 bill, which came to be watered down by the next legislature in 1975, offered only a basic, rudimentary level of bilingual education. Neither of these acts mandated too much, largely because bilingual education was still developing its pedagogical boundaries as well as its own professional constituency. The Chicano Generation viewed bilingual education as equally bicultural. More established leaders of the Mexican American Generation recognized an opportunity for their children to escape the age-old language pedagogy trap of segregation in the public schools. The federal courts, the Justice Department, and the Office of Civil Rights wielded bilingual education as a useful weapon in the desegregation wars. After some false starts later in the 1970s and after some prodding by the federal judiciary, the state finally enacted a major statewide bilingual education law in 1981. This 1981 compromise measure favored more limited, transitional forms of bilingual education over more comprehensive, encompassing ones. This compromise became the underlying framework for bilingual education in the state today, a reconnection to a long thread of Texas history.

Conclusion

The bilingual tradition in Texas during the nineteenth century was rich and vibrant, involving several different ethnic and immigrant groups such as Tejanos, German Americans, and Czech Americans. Policy-makers and ethnic communities saw bilingual education's greatest potential as that of Americanizing children. Progressive Education curtailed this bilingual tradition by centralizing educational policy and administration. Previously, local school officials had decided whether to obey or ignore abstract English-Only sentiments. Texas Progressives implemented curricular mandates, overhauled the teacher certification process, and reformed the way in which schools were organized to outlaw the one method of organization—the community system—that sheltered the bilingual tradition.

The broad, intellectual paradigm of Progressive Education generated the curricular approaches of Americanization and English-Only. Americanization of the early twentieth century followed a "subtractive" model, which neglected the non-English-speaking child's home culture and language; this countered prior "additive" practices of bilingual education. Pedagogues and officials who perceived a need to "Americanize" during World War I advocated the harsh 1918 Texas English-Only law that criminalized bilingual education. Mexican Americans found Americanization during the next decades to be synonymous with racial segregation; its curricular adjunct, English-Only pedagogy, became the pedagogical tool to ensure the legality of such segregation. English-Only proponents regarded bilingual education as educationally backward, ineffective, and un-American, and required teachers to instruct language minorities in English, without any reference to or use of native languages.

Support for English-Only declined during the 1940s and '50s. After a brief, failed effort to reform English-Only during the Good Neighbor days of World War II, the frustrated Mexican American community forcefully challenged the continuing educational segregation. Academicians reevaluated English-Only by questioning the nature and existence of the so-called "language handicap"; they also considered evolving interpretations regarding how children acquire languages. In a pincer-like action, both groups—the Mexican American activist community and the academic community—discredited English-Only pedagogy by the 1960s.

Mexican American leaders and pedagogical experts effectively cooperated with the federal government, initially under Texas Senator Ralph Yarborough and then under President Lyndon Baines Johnson, to decriminalize bilingual education in 1968. Although the Johnson administration expressed initial ambivalence about the program's bureaucratic fit, it eventually supported bilingual education. Through federal court cases and Justice Department actions in the 1970s, bilingual education expanded. Older, established Mexican American Generation leaders came to support bilingual education; so did the younger, more militant Chicano Generation of leadership. A lasting establishment for bilingual education was provided in 1981, thus reconnecting Texas to its bilingual past.

Across the nation, bilingual education has faced fierce resistance and hostility from many quarters. Significant blows include allegations of the instructional technique's ineffectiveness regarding test scores, charges that it fosters ethnic separatism, and a belief among some that it represents linguistic segregation.[1] Since the 1980s and '90s the number of states that have adopted English-Only declarations of principle has multiplied. On June 2, 1998, the state of California passed a statewide measure called Proposition 227 that, in the words of one observer, "virtually outlawed bilingual education in California." By a margin of 61 to 39 percent, Proposition 227 sailed past California voters.[2] People against bilingual education commonly perceive it as a failed, elitist intrusion into the "natural" American experience of rapid linguistic acculturation and shedding of ethnicity. This conclusion stands at stark odds with the historical analysis of bilingual education's history in Texas as well as with findings of many published academic works.

Although Texas bilingual education has not taken the California path, it is free neither of controversy nor problems. All observers can agree that it serves a rapidly growing number of non-English-speaking children. Widely reported data from the 2000 census indicates that the number of language-minority students in Texas has grown rapidly. For example, nearly 10 percent of Texas school-age children, between the ages of five and seventeen, are unable to speak English proficiently.[3] A 1998 Texas Education Agency report notes the acute rise in the "limited English proficiency" (LEP) population. In the 1981–82 school year the LEP percentage of total Texas enrollment in the public schools was

7 percent; in 1996–97 it rose to 13 percent. In raw numbers, the LEP population in those fifteen years has increased by 158 percent compared to the non-LEP population's rise of 30 percent. There are also socioeconomic dimensions to bilingual education in Texas. For the 1992–93 school year 51 percent of all first graders were classified as "economically disadvantaged." Of all the students classified as LEP, 87 percent were simultaneously classified as "economically disadvantaged." The total number of first-grade students in the state that year was 275,142; the LEP students numbered 50,352.[4] Clearly, linguistic minorities have more to deal with in Texas schools than just language difference. Were the social problems of poverty and discrimination finally alleviated, perhaps bilingual education could be more fairly evaluated. Bilingual education students are often the most defenseless and vulnerable of all served by the public schools. Bilingual education critics seldom consider these factors.

Bilingual instruction in Texas was highly regarded by many as an educational tool to reach greater numbers of students. Supporters also believed that it furthered the process of social, civil, and economic integration. These were mighty expectations. Bilingual advocates of the past, however, also noted the irrelevance of educational bilingualism unless accompanied by good teachers, proper resources, and the support of parents and the community. The institutionalization of English-Only and its negative attendants—subtractive Americanization, racial and linguistic segregation, and an uncaring, hypocritical English-Only pedagogy completely disconnected from ethnic or immigrant communities—created lingering problems for language-minority children that modern bilingual education must, at least partially, attempt to overcome. Bilingual education, rather than being a magical sword to cut the shackles of past wrongs and present difficulties, is merely a pedagogical tool to bring the school to the child, positively, instead of forcing the child to the school, negatively. It is one of the few existing official commitments to such children that recognizes their home culture and enhances their opportunity to learn English. In its reconnection to the bilingual past, the United States and Texas have returned their public schools to early, fragmentary roots of tolerance, pluralism, and the will to create opportunity, representing the pinnacle of the classic ideals of American public education. Bilingual education is thoroughly American education.

Notes

Chapter 1

1. Carlos E. Castañeda, *The Mission Era: The Missions at Work, 1731–1761. Volume III, Our Catholic Heritage in Texas, 1519–1936*, p. 33.
2. N. Thomas Greenberg, "Culture Begins With the A. B. C.'s: Education Came to San Antonio With the Cross, the Rifle, the Plow and the Tool Chest," in *San Antonio . . . A History for Tomorrow*, ed. by Sam Woolford, p. 46, Institute of Texan Cultures (hereafter this repository will be abbreviated as ITC), Education in Texas File.
3. Carlos Castañeda, *The Mission Era: The Winning of Texas, 1693–1731. Volume II, Our Catholic Heritage in Texas: 1519–1936*, p. 205.
4. Castañeda, *The Mission Era: The Missions at Work*, pp. 32–33; and Marion A. Habig, *San Antonio's Mission San Jose: State and National Site, 1720–1968*, p. 76.
5. Meyer Weinberg, *A Chance to Learn: The History of Race and Education in the United States*, p. 141.
6. Donald E. Chipman, *Spanish Texas, 1519–1821*, p. 202.
7. Daniel Tyler, "The Mexican Teacher," *Red River Valley Historical Review* 1 (Autumn, 1974): 207–21; and David J. Weber, *The Mexican Frontier, 1821–1846: The American Southwest Under Mexico*, p. 234.
8. "Decree 92" and "Decree 144," in H. P. N. Gammel, *The Laws of Texas, 1822–1897. Volume I*, pp. 237–40 and 267.
9. Andres Tijerina, *Tejanos & Texas Under the Mexican Flag, 1821–1836*, p. 60; and I. J. Cox, "Educational Efforts in San Fernando de Bexar," *Quarterly of the Texas State Historical Association* 6 (July, 1902): 54–55. This journal was later renamed the *Southwestern Historical Quarterly*.
10. "Constitution of the State of Coahuila and Texas: Preliminary Provisions," in Frederick Eby, *Education in Texas: Source Materials. The University of Texas Bulletin, No. 1824*, p. 30.
11. "Contract with the Government of the State for the Colonization of Five Hundred Families. Executive Department of the State of Coahuila and Texas, Decree No. 22," in Gammel, *Laws of Texas. Volume I*, p. 48.
12. "Decree No. 240," in ibid., p. 49. This enactment was issued on May 2, 1833, the day after another bill was passed that stipulated the manner in which legal testimony could be given to courts in a "foreign language," compensation for interpreters, and how the process was to be administered.
13. Mattie Austin Hatcher, "Plan of Stephen F. Austin for an Institute of Modern Languages at San Felipe de Austin," *The Quarterly of the Texas State Historical Association* 12 (Jan., 1909): 231. It is unknown whether this bill was ever presented to or considered by the state legislature. Max Berger, "Stephen F. Austin and Education in Early Texas, 1821–1835," *Southwestern Historical Quarterly* 48 (Jan., 1945): 394.
14. Eugene C. Barker, *The Life of Stephen F. Austin: Founder of Texas, 1793–1836. A Chapter in the Westward Movement of the Anglo-American People*, p. 244; and Paul D. Lack, *The Texas Revolutionary Experience: A Political and Social History, 1835–1836*, pp. 57–58.

15. "Stephen F. Austin's Plan for a College," in Eby, *Education in Texas*, p. 112 (quotations) and 113.

16. "Letters of Buchetti to Austin," in ibid., p. 105; Barker, *Life of Stephen F. Austin*, pp. 349–50; and "To His Excellency, the Governor, and the Honorable, the Legislature of the free and Sovereign State of Coahuila and Texas," *Laws of Texas. Volume I*, p. 493 (quotations).

17. "Municipal Ordinance, Chapter 1: Of the Installation and Interior Rules of the Ayuntamiento, and the Appointment of Committees," in Eby, *Education in Texas*, p. 118.

18. "Contributions for Building Church and School," in ibid., pp. 45–46.

19. Frederick Eby, *The Development of Education in Texas*, pp. 76–77; and "Almonte's Report: Colonel Juan Nepomuceno Almonte," in Eby, *Education in Texas*, p. 93 (quotations).

20. Gregg Cantrell, *Stephen F. Austin: Empresario of Texas*, p. 194.

21. Eby, *Development of Education in Texas*, pp. 108–109; "An Act to Establish Public Schools in the County of Galveston," *Laws of Texas. Volume III, Part I*, pp. 331–34; and "An Act: Incorporating the City of San Antonio and Other Towns Therein Named," in Gammel, *Laws of Texas. Volume I*, p. 1379.

22. "An Act: To Incorporate the Town of Nacogdoches and Other Towns Herein Named," in Gammel, *Laws of Texas. Volume I*, p. 1298.

23. "An Act: Entitled an Act Appropriating Certain Lands for the Establishment of a General System of Education," in Gammel, *Laws of Texas. Volume II, Part II*, pp. 134–36; and "An Act: In Relation to Common Schools and Academies, and to Provide for Securing the Lands Formerly Appropriated for the Purpose of Education," in Gammel, *Laws of Texas. Volume II, Part I*, pp. 320–22 (quotation).

24. Maurine M. O'Banion, "The History of Caldwell County," pp. 194–95.

25. Eby, *The Development of Education in Texas*, pp. 92 and 105 (quotation).

26. "Chapter XVIII: An Act to Establish a System of Schools," in Gammel, *Laws of Texas. Volume III, Part I*, pp. 1461–64; "Chapter CLXXX: An Act Providing for the Support of Schools," in Gammel, *Laws of Texas. Volume IV, Part II*, pp. 525–29 (quotation); and Eby, *Development of Education in Texas*, pp. 96–98.

27. "Chapter 98: An Act to be entitled An Act supplementary to and amendatory of an Act Providing for the support of Schools, Approved 29th August, A.D. 1858," in Gammel, *Laws of Texas. Volume IV, Part III*, p. 999.

28. Michael Allen White, "History of Education in Texas, 1860–1884," chapter 4; and "Chapter CXLVI: An Act Regulating the Public Schools," in Gammel, *Laws of Texas. Volume V, Part II*, p. 1092 (quotation).

29. Jacob C. De Gress, *First Annual Report of the Superintendent of Public Instruction of the State of Texas, 1871*, p. 4 (first quotation); and "Rules and Regulations for the Government of the Public Free Schools in the State of Texas," in Eby, *Education in Texas*, p. 540 (second quotation). See also Eby, *The Development of Education in Texas*, pp. 159–62.

30. During Reconstruction Texas was very much within the standard parameters of the national bilingual tradition. For constitutional and/or statutory provisions protecting bilingual instruction in the states of Indiana, Illinois, Michigan, Wisconsin, Massachusetts, Louisiana, and New Mexico during the nineteenth century see Arthur Charles Aaronson, "The Involvement of the Federal Government in Providing Public Instruction for Non-English-Speaking Pupils from 1800 to 1980," p. 27; Wiebe, *The Search for Order, 1877–1920*, p. 58; Kaestle, *Pillars of the Republic: Common Schools and American Society, 1780–1860*; Kloss, *The American Bilingual Tradition*, pp. 108–13; and Lynne Marie Getz, *Schools of Their Own: The Education of Hispanos in New Mexico, 1850–1940*, p. 17.

31. De Gress, *First Annual Report*, p. 10 (first and second quotations); and De Gress,

Second Annual Report of the Superintendent of Public Instruction of the State of Texas for the Year 1872, p. 14 (third quotation).

32. De Gress, *First Annual Report*, pp. 48–49 (first quotation) and 49 (second quotation). Italics added.

33. "Chapter LXIII: An Act to establish and maintain a System of Public Free Schools in the State of Texas," *Laws of Texas. Volume VII*, p. 543.

34. In 1879 De Gress was elected mayor of Austin as a Greenback candidate. See Alwyn Barr, *Reconstruction to Reform: Texas Politics, 1876–1906*, p. 56.

35. Barry A. Crouch and L. J. Schultz, "Crisis in Color: Racial Separation in Texas During Reconstruction," *Civil War History* 16 (Spring, 1970): 41.

36. Chapter CLVI: An Act to amend sections nine (9), ten (10) . . . of an Act to establish and maintain a system of Public Free Schools in the State of Texas; passed April 30, 1873," in Gammel, *Laws of Texas. Volume VIII*, p. 212 (quotation); and Chapter CXX: An Act to establish and provide for the support and maintenance of an efficient system of Public Free Schools," in Gammel, *Laws of Texas. Volume VIII*, p. 1043.

37. "Chapter CLIV: An Act amendatory of and supplemental to Chapter 3, Title 78 of the Revised Civil Statutes of the State of Texas, adopted at the present session of the 16th legislature," in Gammel, *Laws of Texas. Volume VIII*, p. 1474.

38. Elvie Lou Luetge, "Shelby: A Rural School in a German Immigrant Setting," *East Texas Historical Journal* 18 (1980): 32–33.

Chapter 2

1. These ethnic groups will generally be referred to as Mexican American or Tejano, German American, and Czech American. Those Hispanics on or near the border may be called Mexican or Mexicano. Anglo refers to English-speaking whites of the dominant Anglo American culture.

2. Terry G. Jordan, "A Century and a Half of Ethnic Change in Texas, 1836–1986," *Southwestern Historical Quarterly* 89 (Apr., 1986): 393–96.

3. Guadalupe San Miguel, Jr., *"Let All of Them Take Heed": Mexican Americans and the Campaign for Educational Equality, 1910–1981*, pp. 8–9.

4. J. T. Cummings, "General Report," unpublished report to the superintendent of public instruction, 1892–93, Brownsville File, Box 701-16, State Department of Education Papers (hereafter cited as SDE), Texas State Archives (hereafter cited as TSA), Austin (quotations); and Milo Kearney, Alfonso Gomez Arguelles, and Yolanda Z. Gonzalez, *A Brief History of Education in Brownsville and Matamoros*, p. 5.

5. Melinda Rankin, *Texas in 1850*, p. viii.

6. Guadalupe San Miguel, Jr., "Culture and Education in the American Southwest: Towards an Explanation of Chicano School Attendance, 1850–1940," *Journal of American Ethnic History* 7 (Spring, 1988): 7.

7. San Miguel, "Culture and Education," p. 8; J. S. Kendall, *Twelfth Biennial Report of the State Superintendent of Public Instruction For the Scholastic Years Ending August 31, 1899, and August 31, 1900*, folded insert between pp. lviii and lix; and F. A. Parker, "General Report," unpublished report to superintendent of public instruction, 1892–93, Laredo File, Box 701-86, SDE, TSA (quotation).

8. San Miguel, "Culture and Education," p. 8; San Miguel, *"Let All of Them Take Heed,"* p. 9; Kendall, *Twelfth Biennial Report*, folded insert between pp. lviii and lix; "J. M. J. Letters: From Our Beloved Sisters; Who Quitted St. Mary's, April 17th, 1852, to Commence the Mission of San Antonio. Ursuline Convent Saint Mary's, 1853," Education in Texas File—Religious, ITC (quotation); and Arnoldo De León, *Ethnicity in the Sunbelt: Mexican Americans in Houston*, p. 12.

9. San Miguel, "Culture and Education," p. 10; and Jovita Gonzalez, "Social Life in Cameron, Starr, and Zapata Counties," pp. 69–75.

10.   Emilio Zamora, *The World of the Mexican Worker in Texas*, pp. 100–103; and F. A. Parker, "General Report," unpublished report to the superintendent of public instruction, 1892–93, Laredo File, Box 701-86, SDE, TSA (quotations).

11.   Benjamin Baker, "Remarks," unpublished report to the superintendent of public instruction, 1884–85, Cameron County File, Box 4-23/233, SDE, TSA.

12.   J. M. De La Viña, "General Report," unpublished report to the superintendent of public instruction, 1897–98, Hidalgo County File, Box 4-23/269, SDE, TSA.

13.   Lynne Marie Getz, *Schools of Their Own: The Education of Hispanos in New Mexico, 1850–1940,* 17 and 27; Richard Griswold del Castillo, *The Treaty of Guadalupe Hidalgo: A Legacy of Conflict,* pp. 71, 86, 103–106, and 189–90; and G. W. Huffman, "General Report," unpublished report to the superintendent of public instruction, 1893–94, Ysleta File, Box 701-62, SDE, TSA (quotation).

14.   G. W. Huffman, "General Report," unpublished report to the superintendent of public instruction, 1897–98, El Paso County File, Box 4-23/249, SDE, TSA.

15.   L. A. G. Navarro, "Remarks," unpublished report to the superintendent of public instruction, 1882–83, Zapata County File, Box 4-23/209, SDE, TSA.

16.   A. P. Spohn, "General Report," unpublished report to the superintendent of public instruction, 1897–98, Zapata County File, Box 4-23/209, SDE, TSA.

17.   A. P. Spohn, "General Remarks" and "General Report," unpublished report to superintendent of public instruction, 1900–1901, Zapata County File, Box 4-23/209, SDE, TSA.

18.   W. K. Jones, "General Report," unpublished report to the superintendent of public instruction, 1893–94, Val Verde County File, Box 4-23/224, SDE, TSA.

19.   J. A. Bonnet, "General Report," "General Report," and "General Report," unpublished reports to the superintendent of public instruction, 1896–97, 1898–99, and 1899–1900, Maverick County File, Box 4-23/193, SDE, TSA.

20.   Joseph FitzSimmons, "Remarks," and "Remarks," unpublished reports to the superintendent of public instruction, 1881–82 and 1885–86, Nueces County File, Box 4-23/198, SDE, TSA.

21.   FitzSimmons, "Remarks," unpublished report to the superintendent of public instruction, 1888–89, Nueces County File, Box 4-23/198, SDE, TSA.

22.   FitzSimmons, 1889–90, Nueces County File, Box 4-23/198, SDE, TSA (first quotation); and Joseph FitzSimmons, "Nueces County," in Oscar H. Cooper, *Sixth Biennial Report of the Superintendent of Public Instruction of the Scholastic Years Ending August 31, 1887, and July 1, 1888, Being the Thirteenth Report from the Department of Education,* p. 309 (second quotation).

23.   James O. Luby, "Duval County—1880," in O. N. Hollingsworth, *Second Biennial Report of the State Board of Education for the Scholastic Years Ending August 31, 1879, and 1880,* p. 13.

24.   Arnoldo De Leon, *The Tejano Community, 1836–1900,* pp. 188–90; and Andrés Sáenz, *Early Tejano Ranching: Daily Life at Ranchos San José & El Fresnillo,* introduction by Andrés Tijerina, p. 124.

25.   Jordan, "A Century and a Half of Ethnic Change," pp. 409–11; and Jordan, "The German Element in Texas: An Overview," *Rice University Studies* 63 (Summer, 1977): 9.

26.   Eby, *The Development of Education in Texas,* pp. 130–31; and *State Gazette,* Oct. 24, 1857 (quotations).

27.   "Chapter 43: An Act to Incorporate the German Free school Association of the City of Austin," *Laws of Texas. Volume IV, Part III,* pp. 1223–24; *State Gazette,* July 3, 1858.

28.   *New Braunfels Herald,* June 12, 1975, German Public Schools—New Braunfels File (hereafter this file cited as GPSNB), ITC. See also Eby, *The Development of Education in Texas,* pp. 133–34.

29.   "Chapter 88: An Act to Incorporate the New Braunfels Academy," *Laws of Texas. Volume IV, Part III,* 1274 (first quotation); *New Braunfels Herald,* Nov. 9, 1972, GPSNB,

ITC; and H. E. Fischer, "Remarks," unpublished report to the superintendent of public instruction, 1886–87, New Braunfels File, 701-109, SDE, TSA (second quotation).

30. *New Braunfels Herald,* Nov. 23 and 30, 1972, and Feb. 22, 1973 (quotation), GPSNB, ITC.

31. Elvie Lou Luetge, "Shelby: A Rural School in a German Immigrant Setting," *East Texas Historical Review* 18 (1980): 30 (quotation) and 34.

32. D. W. Trenckmann, "Bellville," *Sixth Biennial Report,* p. 284.

33. J. L. Dupree, "General Report," unpublished report to superintendent of public instruction, 1893–94, Victoria County File, Box 4-23/223, SDE, TSA. Dupree encountered legal action by the ethnic trustees of private schools. See also J. M. Carlisle, *Eleventh Biennial Report of the State Superintendent of Public Instruction for the Scholastic Years Ending August 31, 1897, and August 31, 1898,* pp. 364–90.

34. J. L. Dupree, "General Report," unpublished report to the superintendent of public instruction, 1894–95, Victoria County File, Box 4-23/223, SDE, TSA.

35. J. T. Estill, "General Report," unpublished report to the superintendent of public instruction, 1894–95, Gillespie County File, Box 4-23/262, SDE, TSA (quotations); and W. S. Sutton, "Financial Statement," unpublished report to the superintendent of public instruction, 1887–88, Houston File, Box 701-74, SDE, TSA.

36. Charles H. Schroeder, "General Report," unpublished report to the superintendent of public instruction, 1899–1900, La Grange File, Box 701-84, SDE, TSA.

37. W. T. Nobbitt, "General Report," unpublished report to the superintendent of public instruction, 1902–1903, Kerrville File, Box 701-82, SDE, TSA.

38. Horace W. Morelock, "General Report," unpublished report to the superintendent of public instruction, 1906–1907, Kerrville File, 701-82, SDE, TSA.

39. Christa Carvajal and Annelise M. Duncan, "The German-English School in San Antonio: Transplanting German Humanistic Education to the Texas Frontier," *Yearbook of German-American Studies* 16 (1981): 92 (first quotation) and 96 (second quotation).

40. L. E. Wolfe, "General Report," unpublished report to the superintendent of public instruction, 1902–1903, San Antonio File, Box 701-133, SDE, TSA; Glen E. Lich, *The German Texans,* pp. 129–33; and Joseph William Schmitz, *The Society of Mary in Texas,* pp. 70–71. German Americans in several United States cities—St. Louis, Cleveland, Cincinnati, Indianapolis, and Baltimore—maintained effective bilingual programs in their public schools. See Kloss, *The American Bilingual Tradition;* Schlossman, "Is There an American Tradition of Bilingual Education"; Troen, *The Public and the Schools;* Cunz, *The Maryland Germans: A History.*

41. Jonathan Zimmerman, "Ethnics Against Ethnicity: European Immigrants and Foreign-Language Instruction, 1890–1940," *Journal of American History* 88 (Mar., 2002): 1383–404; Timothy L. Smith, "Immigrant Social Aspirations and American Education, 1880–1930," *American Quarterly* 21 (Fall, 1969), 523–43; and T. Lindsey Baker, "The Early History of Panna Maria, Texas," *Graduate Studies, Texas Tech University* 9 (Oct., 1975): 46–47.

42. E. E. Davis and C. T. Gray, *A Study of Rural Schools in Karnes County. University of Texas Bulletin, No. 2246,* p. 8; and E. P. Curry, "General Report," unpublished report to the superintendent of public instruction, 1896–97, Washington County File, Box 4-23/260, SDE, TSA.

43. *Nederland Diamond Jubilee, 1898–1973,* p. 45, ITC, General File—Education in Texas, State Dutch. This type of instruction—a monolingual teacher or one who does not understand the second language in question aided by an uncertified assistant who acts as interpreter—is common today for schools that do not attract enough certified bilingual teachers to adequately serve their need.

44. Jordan, "A Century and a Half of Ethnic Change," pp. 411–12; Jan L. Perkowski, "A Survey of the West Slavic Immigrant Languages in Texas," unpublished

manuscript, estimated date of 1967 or 1968, Czech File-Languages, ITC; and Glenn G. Gilbert, "Origin and Present Day Location of German Speakers in Texas: A Statistical Interpretation," *Rice University Studies* 63 (Summer, 1977): 22–23.

45. Wesley Valek, "Czech-Moravian Pioneers of Ellis County, Texas: 1873–1917," *Panhandle-Plains Historical Review* 56 (1983): 62; and Clinton Machann and James W. Mendl, *Krasna Amerika: A Study of the Texas Czechs, 1851–1939,* pp. 174–75.

46. G. A. Stierling, "General Report," unpublished report to the superintendent of public instruction, 1905–1906, Fayette County File, Box 4-23/260, SDE, TSA.

47. Valek, "Czech-Moravian Pioneers," p. 62.

48. Estelle Hudson and Henry R. Maresh, *Czech Pioneers of the Southwest,* pp. 176–77.

49. Machann and Mendl, *Krasna Amerika,* p. 226.

Chapter 3

1. For the national Progressive movement and education policy, see Lawrence T. Cremin, *The Transformation of the School: Progressivism in American Education, 1876–1957;* and David Tyack, *The One Best System: A History of American Urban Education.* For Progressive Education in Texas, see Lewis L. Gould, *Progressives & Prohibitionists: Texas Democrats in the Wilson Era;* Norman D. Brown, *Hood, Bonnet, and Little Brown Jug: Texas Politics, 1921–1928;* and Debbie Mauldin Cottrell, *Pioneer Woman Educator in Texas: The Progressive Spirit of Annie Webb Blanton.*

2. Benjamin M. Baker, *Fifth Biennial Report of the Superintendent of Public Instruction for the Scholastic Years Ending August 31, 1885, and August 31, 1886,* pp. 9–10.

3. Thad Sitton and Milam C. Rowold, *Ringing the Children In: Texas Country Schools,* pp. 6–11. For a firsthand account of such schools see William A. Owens, *This Stubborn Soil: A Frontier Boyhood,* pp. 59–61.

4. Oscar H. Cooper, *Special Report of the Superintendent of Public Instruction for the Years Ending Aug. 31, 1887,* pp. 27–31; and R. B. Cousins, *Sixteenth Biennial Report of the State Superintendent of Public Instruction for the Years Ending August 31, 1907, and August 31, 1908,* p. 16.

5. Eby, *Education in Texas,* p. 830; Sitton and Rowold, *Ringing the Children In,* pp. 6–8; Michael Allen White, "History of Education in Texas," chapter 6; Lee Wayne White, "Popular Education and the State Superintendent," chapter 5; and John Stricklin Spratt, *The Road to Spindletop: Economic Change in Texas, 1875–1901,* p. 14 (quotation).

6. "Chapter CXX: An Act to Establish and Provide for the Support and Maintenance of an Efficient System of Public Free Schools," *Laws of Texas. Volume VIII,* pp. 1041–43.

7. "Chapter XXV: An Act to Establish and Maintain a System of Public Free Schools for the State of Texas," *Laws of Texas. Volume IX,* pp. 52–53 and 66; and Lawrence D. Rice, *The Negro in Texas, 1874–1900,* p. 217.

8. Mary Generosa Callahan, *The History of the Sisters of the Divine Providence, San Antonio, Texas,* pp. 111–12; T. P. Huff, "General Report," unpublished report to the superintendent of public instruction, 1897–98, Bexar County File, 4-23/247, SDE, TSA; and Joseph FitzSimmons, "Remarks," unpublished report to the superintendent of public instruction, 1881–82, Nueces County File, 4-23/198, SDE, TSA.

9. Cooper, *Special Report,* p. 29.

10. Oscar H. Cooper, *Seventh Biennial Report of the Superintendent of Public Instruction for the Scholastic Years Ending August 31, 1889, and August 31, 1890, Being the Fourteenth Report from the Department of Education,* p. viii.

11. J. M. Carlisle, *Eighth Biennial Report of the State Superintendent of Public Instruction for the Scholastic Years Ending August 31, 1891, and August 31, 1892,* p. xi (first quotation); and Carlisle, *Eleventh Biennial Report,* p. xlii (second quotation).

12. Cooper, *Seventh Biennial Report,* p. li; and R. B. Cousins, "Public Education in Texas," in *Proceedings of the Texas State Teachers Association. Nineteenth Annual Session. Galveston, Texas, June 29th and 30th and July 1st, 1898,* Texas State Teachers Association Collection (hereafter cited as TSTA), SDE (quotations).

13.   Eby, *The Development of Education in Texas*, p. 211; and S. M. N. Marrs, "Report on Independent Districts and School Legislation," in *Texas State Teachers Association: Report of the Committee on Educational Progress Within the State During the Scholastic Years 1904–05 and 1905–06*, p. 31, TSTA, SDE.

14.   R. B. Cousins, *Fifteenth Biennial Report of the State Superintendent of Public Instruction for the Years Ending August 31, 1905, and August 31, 1906*, p. 13; and "School Districts—Amendment. Chapter CLXXXIII," in Gammel, *Laws of Texas. Volume XI*, p. 322 (quotation).

15.   Cousins, *Fifteenth Biennial Report*, p. 13; and Arthur Lefevre, *Fourteenth Biennial Report of the State Superintendent of Public Instruction for the Years Ending August 31, 1903, and August 31, 1904*, pp. 8–9. They were Cameron, Camp, De Witt, Duval, Fayette, Houston, Lee, Limestone, Matagorda, Panola, Trinity, Washington, and Webb Counties.

16.   F. M. Bralley, *Seventeenth Biennial Report of the State Department of Education for the Years Ending August, 31, 1909, and August 31, 1910*, p. 11.

17.   Ernst Koebig, "Remarks," unpublished report to the superintendent of public instruction, 1881–82, Comal County File, 4-23/255, SDE, TSA.

18.   A. Giesecke, "General Report," unpublished report to the superintendent of public instruction, 1892–93, Comal County File, 4-23/255, SDE, TSA.

19.   W. K. Jones, "Remarks," and "Remarks," unpublished reports to the superintendent of public instruction, 1887–88 and 1888–89, Val Verde County File, 4-23/224, SDE, TSA; and E. H. Goodrich, "General Report," unpublished report to the superintendent of public instruction, 1894–95, Cameron County File, 4-23/233, SDE, TSA.

20.   De Gress, *Second Annual Report*, p. 13.

21.   "Chapter CXX: An Act to establish and provide for the support and maintenance of an efficient system of Public Free Schools," *Laws of Texas. Volume VIII*, p. 1043.

22.   "Chapter XXV: An Act to establish and maintain a system of public free schools for the State of Texas," *Laws of Texas. Volume IX*, p. 48.

23.   Roscoe Martin, *The People's Party in Texas: A Study in Third-Party Politics*, pp. 183–84.

24.   J. E. Smith, "Annual Report," unpublished report to the superintendent of public instruction, 1895–96, San Antonio File, 701-133, SDE, TSA (first quotation); and G. W. Huffman, "General Report," unpublished report to the superintendent of public instruction, 1897–98, El Paso County File, 4-23/249, SDE, TSA (second quotation).

25.   James Clarke, "General Report," unpublished report to the superintendent of public instruction, 1893–94, Starr County File, 4-23/204, SDE, TSA.

26.   R. A. Marsh, "General Report," unpublished report to the superintendent of public instruction, 1904–1905, Hidalgo County File, 4-23/269, SDE, TSA.

27.   Baker, *Fifth Biennial Report*, pp. 9–10; and "Chapter 116: An act to provide for the issuance of certificates to teachers in the public schools of Texas, and prescribing their duties as such," *Laws of Texas. Volume X*, pp. 184 (first and second quotations) and 186 (third quotation).

28.   "Chapter 122: An act to provide for a more efficient system of public free schools for the State of Texas," *Laws of Texas. Volume X*, p. 630 (quotation); and "Chapter 124: An Act to provide for a more efficient system of public free schools for the State of Texas," *Laws of Texas. Volume XII*, p. 291.

29.   Kendall, *Twelfth Biennial Report*, pp. xxi–xxii; and personal letter, F. E. Hunter to J. M. Carlisle, superintendent of public instruction, Nov. 7, 1895, Ysleta File, 701-162, SDE, TSA (quotation).

30.   J. R. Mason, "Remarks," unpublished report to the superintendent of public instruction, 1882–83, Bexar County File, 4-23/247, SDE, TSA.

31.   "Chapter 122: An act to provide for a more efficient system of public free schools for the State of Texas," *Laws of Texas. Volume X*, pp. 632–33.

32.   Ibid., pp. 632 (first and second quotations) and 633 (third quotation).

33.   "An Act to provide for a more efficient system of public free schools for the State of Texas," *Laws of Texas. Volume XII*, p. *290.*

34.   José E. Limón, *"El Primer Congreso Mexicanista de 1911: A Precursor to Contemporary Chicanismo," Aztlan* 5 (Spring–Fall, 1974): 90–94.

35.   W. W. Jenkins, "General Report," and "General Report," unpublished reports to the superintendent of public instruction, 1906–1907 (quotation) and 1907–1908, Williamson County File, 4-23/221, SDE, TSA.

36.   R. B. Cousins, *Sixteenth Biennial Report of the State Superintendent of Public Instruction for the Years Ending August 31, 1907 and August 31, 1908,* p. 19. Original italics included.

37.   Ibid. Italics added.

Chapter 4

1.   The "New" immigrants were from southern and eastern Europe and arrived between the Civil War and World War I.

2.   For one success thesis see Edward George Hartmann, *The Movement to Americanize the Immigrant.* For the classic statement on the Americanization movement see Higham, *Strangers in the Land.* For recent studies see Eileen H. Tamura, *Americanization, Acculturation, and Ethnic Identity: The Nisei Generation in Hawaii;* Lizbeth Cohen, *Making a New Deal: Industrial Workers in Chicago, 1919–1939;* and George J. Sánchez, *Becoming Mexican American: Ethnicity, Culture and Identity in Chicano Los Angeles, 1900–1945.* For Texas see San Miguel, *"Let All of Them Take Heed";* Thomas E. Simmons, "The Citizen Factories: The Americanization of Mexican Students in Texas Public Schools, 1920–1945"; Richard A. Garcia, *Rise of the Mexican American Middle Class: San Antonio, 1929–1941;* and María Cristina García, "Agents of Americanization: Rusk Settlement and the Houston Mexicano Community, 1907–1950," in *Mexican Americans in Texas History,* ed. by Emilio Zamora, Cynthia Orozco, and Rodolfo Rocha, pp. 121–37.

3.   Guadalupe San Miguel, Jr., and Richard R. Valencia, "From the Treaty of Guadalupe Hidalgo to *Hopwood:* The Educational Plight and Struggle of Mexican Americans in the Southwest," *Harvard Educational Review* 68 (Fall, 1998): 358.

4.   Jane Addams, *Twenty Years at Hull-House with Autobiographical Notes, Introduction by James Hurt;* and John Dewey, *Democracy and Education.*

5.   Ellwood P. Cubberley, *Changing Conceptions of Education;* Emory S. Bogardus, *Essentials of Americanization.*

6.   FitzSimmons, "Nueces County," in *Sixth Biennial Report,* p. 309.

7.   A. P. Spohn, "General Report," unpublished report to the superintendent of public instruction, 1908–1909, Zapata County File, 4-23/209, SDE, TSA (quotation); J. F. Bobbitt, *Report on the Survey of the San Antonio Public School System,* pp. 159–66; Garcia, *Rise of the Mexican American Middle Class,* pp. 176–77; Troen, *The Public and the Schools,* pp. 60–61; and Paul Rudolph Fessler, "Speaking in Tongues: German-Americans and the Heritage of Bilingual Education in American Public Schools," pp. 104–106.

8.   San Miguel, "Culture and Education in the American Southwest," p. 8; González, "Social Life," p. 70 (quotation); and B. G. Cole, "Compulsory Education," in *Minutes of the Texas State Teachers Association. Eleventh Annual Session, Galveston, June 25, 26, 27, 1890,* p. 12, TSTAC, TSA.

9.   "Chapter 8: An act to limit and regulate the ownership by aliens of real estate in the State of Texas . . ." in Gammel, *Laws of Texas. Volume X,* pp. 370–72; J. A. Bonnet, "General Report," unpublished report to the superintendent of public instruction, 1896–97, Maverick County File, 4-203/193, SDE, TSA; William Gatewood, "General Report," unpublished report to the superintendent of public instruction, 1892–93, Eagle Pass File, 701-46, SDE, TSA; and C. C. Thomas, "General Report,"

unpublished report to superintendent of public instruction, 1898–99, El Paso
County File, 4-23/249, SDE, TSA.

10. "Chapter 122: An act to provide for a more efficient system of public free schools for
the State of Texas," *Laws of Texas. Volume X*, pp. 632–33; "An Act to provide for a
more efficient system of public free schools for the State of Texas," *Laws of Texas.
Volume XII*, p. 290; and Cousins, *Sixteenth Biennial Report*, p. 19 (quotation).

11. E. E. Davis, *A Study of Rural Schools in Travis County, Texas. Bulletin of the University
of Texas, no. 67*, pp. 15 (quotation) and 36.

12. *Houston Post*, Mar. 4, 1918.

13. Kloss, *The American Bilingual Tradition*, p. 61; *Houston Post*, Mar. 3, 1918; and Eby,
Development of Education in Texas, p. 227–28 (quotations).

14. Quoted in Sitton and Rowold, *Ringing the Children In*, p. 123.

15. *Houston Post*, Mar. 6, 1918; W. F. Doughty, *Twenty-First Biennial Report, State Superintendent of Public Instruction, State of Texas, September 1, 1916, to August 31, 1918*, p. 5
(quotations); and Zamora, *World of the Mexican Worker in Texas*, pp. 136–39.

16. Gould, *Progressives & Prohibitionists*, pp. 185–88; and *Houston Post*, June 21, 1918.

17. Cottrell, *Pioneer Woman Educator*, pp. 48–49; and campaign flyer, "Concerning the
Race for State superintendent of public instruction," Annie Webb Blanton Vertical
File, Center for American History, Austin, Tex. (quotations).

18. *Journal of the House of Representatives of the Fourth Called Session of the Thirty-Fifth
Legislature*, pp. 86–87.

19. Ibid., p. 295.

20. Quoted in Simmons, "The Citizen Factories," p. 81.

21. *Houston Post*, Mar. 9, 1918.

22. Ibid., Mar. 6, 1918.

23. Annie Webb Blanton and R. L. Ragsdale, *Texas High Schools: History and the Social
Sciences. Bulletin 124*, p. 9.

24. David G. Gutiérrez, *Walls and Mirrors: Mexican Americans, Mexican Immigrants, and
the Politics of Ethnicity*, pp. 52 and 56–57.

25. Annie Webb Blanton, *Report on Education in Texas and Recommendations Made to
the Governor and the Thirty-Seventh Legislature*, pp. 21–22 (quotations); Annie Webb
Blanton, "Texas Conditions and Demands," *The Texas Outlook* 5 (July, 1921): 8; and
Jacquelyn Dowd Hall, *Revolt Against Chivalry: Jessie Daniel Ames and the Women's
Campaign Against Lynching, Revised Edition*, p. 46. The white primary in Texas had
existed since 1903 and 1905. See J. Morgan Kousser, *The Shaping of Southern Politics: Suffrage Restriction and the Establishment of the One-Party South, 1880–1910*,
pp. 207–208.

26. Annie Webb Blanton, *A Hand Book of Information as to Education in Texas, 1918–1922.
Bulletin 157*, p. 23.

27. Davis, *Study of Rural Schools in Williamson County*, p. 8.

28. Annie Webb Blanton, *Historical and Statistical Data as to Education in Texas, January 1,
1919–January 1, 1921. Bulletin 133*, p. 44.

29. S. M. N. Marrs and Opal Gilstrap, *Texas High Schools: The Teaching of Spanish, German,
and French. Bulletin 230*, p. 81.

30. Quoted in Sitton and Utley, *From Can See to Can't*, p. 54 (quotation); and Brown,
Hood, Bonnet, pp. 114–17.

31. Walter D. Kamphoefner, "German-American Bilingualism: *Cui Malo?* Mother
Tongue and Socioeconomic Status Among the Second Generation in 1940," *International Migration Review* 28 (Winter, 1994): 861–62.

32. Alwyn Barr, "Occupational and Geographic Mobility in San Antonio, 1870–1900,"
Social Science Quarterly 51 (Sept., 1970): 403.

33. Paul Schuster Taylor, *An American-Mexican Frontier: Nueces County, Texas*, p. 303.
The world *pelado* literally means "shorn," "bald," "crewcut" according to Velas-
quez's dictionary. Elsewhere Taylor claims that the word means something akin

to "penniless Indian." For a brief exposition of the racialization process see Montejano, *Anglos and Mexicans in the Making of Texas 1836–1981*, pp. 159–61.

34.   Paul Schuster Taylor, "Mexican Labor in the United States Dimmit County, Winter
Garden District, South Texas," in *Mexican Labor in the United States, Volume I*, p. 441.

35.   Quoted in Richard Griswold del Castillo, "The 'Mexican Problem': A Critical View
of the Alliance of Academics and Politicians During the Debate Over Mexican
Immigration in the 1920s," *Borderlands* 4 (Spring, 1981): 259–60.

36.   E. Davis, *A Report on Illiteracy in Texas. University of Texas Bulletin, No. 2328*, p. 17 (first
quotation); and Taylor, *American-Mexican Frontier*, p. 202 (second quotation).

37.   Mrs. J. T. Taylor, "The Americanization of Harlingen's Mexican School Population," *The Texas Outlook* 18 (Sept., 1934): 37

38.   R. A. Marsh, "General Report," unpublished report to the superintendent of
public instruction, 1904–1905, Hidalgo County File, 4-23/269, SDE, TSA; and
D. B. Burrows, "General Report," unpublished report to the superintendent of
public instruction, 1910–11, San Diego File, 701-134, SDE, TSA (quotation).

39.   Wilson Little, *Spanish Speaking Children in Texas*, p. 61.

40.   Basil Armour, "Problems in the Education of the Mexican Child," *The Texas Outlook*
16 (Dec., 1932): 29.

41.   E. E. Davis, "King Cotton Leads Mexicans Into Texas," *The Texas Outlook* 9
(Apr., 1925): 8.

42.   Carlos Kevin Blanton, "'They Cannot Master Abstractions, but They Can Often
Be Made Efficient Workers': Race and Class in the Intelligence Testing of Mexican
Americans and African Americans in Texas during the 1920s," *Social Science Quar-
terly* 81 (Dec., 2000): 1014–26; and Carlos Kevin Blanton, "From Intellectual
Deficiency to Cultural Deficiency: Mexican Americans, Testing, and Public School
Policy in the American Southwest, 1920–1940," *Pacific Historical Review* 72, (Feb.,
2003): 39–62.

43.   Taylor, *American-Mexican Frontier*, p. 202.

44.   E. R. Tanner, "General Report," unpublished report to the superintendent of public instruction, 1900–1901, Webb County File, 4-23/222, SDE, TSA (quotation);
and Carlos Kevin Blanton, "Race, Labor, and the Limits of Progressive Reform: A
Preliminary Analysis of the Enforcement of Compulsory Attendance in South
Texas During the 1920s," *The Journal of South Texas* 13 (Fall, 2000): 207–19.

45.   S. M. N. Marrs, *Twenty-Fifth Biennial Report, State Department of Education, 1926–
1928. No. 251*, p. 9.

Chapter 5

1.   Colman Brez Stein, Jr., *Sink or Swim: The Politics of Bilingual Education*, p. 2.

2.   James Crawford, *Hold Your Tongue: Bilingualism and the Politics of "English-Only,"*
chapter 2; and Judith Lessow-Hurley, *The Foundations of Dual Language Instruction,
Second Edition*, pp. 71–73.

3.   Kloss, *The American Bilingual Tradition*, pp. 72–73.

4.   Frederick Eby and Charles Flinn Arrowood, *The History and Philosophy of Education
Ancient and Medieval*, p. 832; and Charles Hart Handschin, *The Teaching of Modern
Languages in the United States. United States Department of the Interior, Bureau of Educa-
tion Bulletin, 1913, No. 3*, p. 94.

5.   G. Stanley Hall, "The Ideal School as Based on Child Study," *The Forum* 32 (Sept.,
1901): 29–30; and Weber, *Peasants into Frenchmen*, pp. 67–72.

6.   Francois Gouin, *The Art of Teaching and Studying Languages, Ninth Edition*, trans. by
Howard Swan and Victor Betis, pp. 10–34; and Handschin, *Teaching of Languages in
the United States*, pp. 97–100.

7.   Frank V. Thompson, *Schooling of the Immigrant* in *Americanization Studies: The Acculturation of Immigrant Groups into American Society, Patterson Smith Reprint Series in
Criminology, Law Enforcement, and Social Problems, volume I*, William S. Bernard, ed.,

pp. 188–89 (first quotation); and Henry H. Goldberger, *Teaching English to the Foreign Born. United States Department of the Interior, Bureau of Education Bulletin, 1919, No. 80,* p. 14 (second quotation).

8. J. T. Estill, "General Report," unpublished report to the superintendent of public instruction, 1894–95, Gillespie County File, 4-23/262, SDE, TSA; R. A Marsh, "General Report," and "General Report," unpublished reports to the superintendent of public instruction, 1904–1905 and 1905–1906, Hidalgo County File, 4-23/269, SDE, TSA.

9. "Relating to Teaching German in the Public Schools," *Journal of the House of Representatives of the Fourth Called Session of the Thirty-Fifth Legislature,* p. 86.

10. Annie Webb Blanton, *Texas School Laws. A Brief Compilation for Teachers of Laws Relating to Teachers and Pupils, Bulletin No. 122;* and William M. McKinney, *Texas Jurisprudence: A Complete Statement of the Law and Practice of the State of Texas,* pp. 177–78.

11. Annie Webb Blanton, *Texas High Schools: History and the Social Sciences. Bulletin 124,* p. 8.

12. Annie Webb Blanton, *A Hand Book of Information,* p. 23 (first quotation); Ibid., *Report on Education in Texas,* p. 21 (second quotation); and Ibid., *Texas Compulsory School Attendance Law. Bulletin 137,* p. 4 (third quotation).

13. Annie Webb Blanton, *A Hand Book of Information,* p. 22 (quotation); S. L. Staples, *General Laws of the State of Texas Passed by the Thirty-Eighth Legislature at the Regular Session Convened at the City of Austin, January 9, 1923, and Adjourned March 14, 1923,* p. 256; and S. M. N. Marrs, *Texas Compulsory School Attendance Law. Bulletin 174,* p. 5.

14. "Chapter Three, Teachers and Schools. Article 288. Shall Use the English Language," in *1928 Complete Texas Statutes Covering the Revised Civil and Criminal Statutes, 1925,* p. 1066.

15. "Spanish Language May be Taught in Schools in Certain Counties, Chapter 188," in Emma Grigsby Meharg, *General Laws of the State of Texas Passed by the Thirty-Ninth Legislature at the First Called Session Convened at the City of Austin, September 13, 1926, and Adjourned October 8, 1926,* 267.

16. "Title 7–Religion and Education. Art. 288," in *1934 Supplement to the 1928 Complete Texas Statutes,* p. 397; and L. A. Woods and Sam B. McAlister, *Public School Laws of the State of Texas, 1938. Bulletin No. 382,* p. 240.

17. L. A. Wilder, "Problems in the Teaching of Mexican Children," *The Texas Outlook* 20 (Aug., 1936): 9 (first quotation); and S. M. N. Marrs, *Texas High Schools, Course of Study. Bulletin, State Department of Education, No. 196,* p. 89 (second quotation).

18. Cousins, *Sixteenth Biennial Report,* p. 19 (quotations); and Herbert Adolphus Miller, *The School and the Immigrant, Cleveland Educational Survey,* p. 57.

19. Elma A. Neal, "Adapting the Curriculum to the Non-English Speaking Child," *The Texas Outlook* 11 (June, 1927): 40.

20. S. M. N. Marrs, Thomas J. Yoe, and M. Perrie Wygal, *A Course in English for the Non-English-Speaking Pupils, Grades I–III Bulletin No. 268,* pp. 19 (first and second quotations) and 33 (third quotation). Original italics.

21. Margaret E. Noonan, "City Schools," in Noonan, Orville G. Brim, and Clarence T. Gray, *Texas Educational Survey Report, Volume V. Courses of Study and Instruction,* pp. 39–41.

22. L. A. Woods and W. A. Stigler, *Handbook for Curriculum Development. Bulletin No. 354,* 17 (quotation); and W. J. Knox, "Teaching Foreigners," and Lizzie M. Barbour, "Primary Work With Non-English-Speaking Children," in *Proceedings and Addresses of the Texas State Teachers Association. Thirty-Seventh Annual Meeting, November 25, 26, and 27, 1915, Corpus Christi, Texas,* TSTAC, TSA.

23. George A. Works, "Chapter XIII: The Non-English Speaking Children and the Public School," *The Texas Outlook* 9 (Aug., 1925): 26 (first quotation); J. Lee Stambaugh, "The Valley Superintendents," *The Texas Outlook* 9 (June, 1925): 29; and

E. C. Dodd, "The Lower Rio Grande Valley Elementary Principals Association," *The Texas Outlook* 12 (June, 1928): 30 (second quotation).

24.   Marrs, Yoe, and Wygal, *A Course in English*, pp. 9 and 11 (quotation).

25.   Ibid., p. 20.

26.   Knox, "Teaching Foreigners," pp. 295 (first quotation) and 296 (second quotation).

27.   Barbour, "Primary Work With Non-English-Speaking Children," p. 325.

28.   Sadie Perry, "They Must Think in English," *The Texas Outlook* 26 (June, 1942): 13; and Emma P. Weir, "The Mexican Child," *The Texas Outlook* 20 (June, 1936): 23 (quotation).

29.   A. H. Hughey, "Speaking English at School," *The Texas Outlook* 28 (Nov., 1944): 36.

30.   Marrs, Yoe, and Wygal, *A Course in English*, p. 34 (quotation); and "One Man and a Boy!" *Vulcan Mold's Pit and Pour* 5 (Apr., 1964), "PP 13-5, Education," White House Central Files, Box 108, Lyndon B. Johnson Presidential Library, Austin, Tex.

31.   L. A. Woods, Eduard Micek, Alois J. Petrusek, and Jesse J. Jochec, *Tentative Course of Study in Czech. Bulletin No. 387*, p. 9; and Marrs, Yoe, and Wygal, *A Course in English*, p. 34 (quotations).

32.   W. F. Doughty, *Manual and Course of Study for the Public Schools of Texas, 1914. Bulletin No. 46*, p. 98 (first quotation); and W. F. Doughty and Rebecca Switzer, *Texas High Schools, Modern Languages. Bulletin No. 82*, p. 7 (second and third quotations).

33.   W. F. Doughty and J. P. Buck, *Texas High Schools, Latin. Bulletin No. 81*, p. 16.

34.   Junius L. Meriam, *Learning English Incidentally: A Study of Bilingual Children. Department of the Interior, Office of Education, Bulletin 1937, No. 15*, p. 6 (first quotation); and Algernon Coleman, *English Teaching in the Southwest: Organization and Materials for Instructing Spanish-Speaking Children*, p. 75 (second quotation).

35.   Annie Webb Blanton, *Texas High Schools, Course of Study. Bulletin No. 151*, p. 92; and S. M. N. Marrs, *Manual and Course of Study, Elementary Grades, Public Schools of Texas, 1924–25. Bulletin 184*, p. 11.

36.   Marrs and Gilstrap, *Texas High Schools*, pp. 12, 13 (first and second quotations) and 17 (third quotation).

37.   Annie Reynolds, *The Education of Spanish-Speaking Children in Five Southwestern States. Bulletin 1933, No. 11*, pp. 45–46; Little, *Spanish-Speaking Children in Texas*, p. 39; and Herschel T. Manuel, *The Education of the Mexican and Spanish-Speaking Children in Texas*, p. 49.

38.   Lucy Claire Hoard, "Chapter VIII: Teaching Beginning Mexican Children," in Woods and Stigler, *Handbook for Curriculum Development*, p. 163.

39.   Dorothy M. Kress, "The Spanish-Speaking School Child in Texas," *The Texas Outlook* 18 (Dec., 1934): 24.

40.   D. B. Burrows, "General Report," unpublished report to the superintendent of public instruction, 1910–11, San Diego File, 701-134, SDE, TSA; and B. Richardson, "General Report," unpublished report to the superintendent of public instruction, 1902–1903, Webb County File, 4-23/222, SDE, TSA (quotation).

41.   Wilder, "Problems in the Teaching of the Mexican Child," p. 10 (quotation); and T. H. Shelby, B. F. Pittenger, J. O. Marberry, and Fred C. Ayer, *Preliminary Survey of the Laredo Public Schools. University of Texas Bulletin, No. 2912*, pp. 45–46.

42.   See C. Blanton, "From Intellectual Deficiency to Cultural Deficiency."

43.   J. Austin Burkhart, "I Teach in a Border Town," *The Texas Outlook* 23 (Dec., 1939): 34. For more on this notion in a national context see Richard Hofstadter, *Anti-Intellectualism in American Life*, p. 350.

44.   "Kingsville Opens," *The Texas Outlook* 9 (June, 1925): 16; *The South Texan*, May 23 and Oct. 12, 26, and Nov. 23, 1926; and Katherine M. Cook, *Opportunities for the Preparation of Teachers of Children of Native and Minority Groups. United States Department of the Interior, Office of Education, Pamphlet No. 77*, p. 10.

45.   Laura Frances Murphy, "An Experiment in Americanization," *The Texas Outlook* 23

(Nov., 1939): 23 (first quotation); and Taylor, "The Americanization of Harlingen's Mexican School Population," p. 37 (second quotation).

46. Meriam, *Learning English Incidentally,* pp. 22–24; and Davis, *Rural Schools in Travis County,* p. 12 (quotation).

47. *Inhabitants of Del Rio Independent School District* v. *Jesus Salvatierra.*

48. Armour, "Problems in the Education of the Mexican Child," p. 29.

49. C. G. Hallmark, "Supplemental Report," unpublished report to the superintendent of public instruction, 1910–11, Brownsville File, 701-16, SDE, TSA; G. B. Snyder, "General Report," unpublished report to the superintendent of public instruction, 1904–1905, Eagle Pass File, 701-46, SDE, TSA; and Charles Grassley, "General Report," unpublished report to the superintendent of public instruction, 1896–97, Corpus Christi File, 701-33, SDE, TSA (quotation).

50. "Robert T. Meyer, plff. in Err., v. State of Nebraska," in *American Law Reports, Annotated. Volume 29,* ed. by Burdett A. Rich and M. Blair Whailes, pp. 1450–51.

51. S. M. N. Marrs and Mary Nash, "History and the Status of the Teaching of Spanish in Texas," *The Texas Outlook* 14 (Feb., 1930): 3.

52. Evangelina Ximenez Bazan, "'La Señorita' Taught Pride," *San Antonio Express,* May 2, 1993, General File-Education, ITC; and San Miguel, "Culture and Education in the American Southwest," pp. 8–10.

53. "Sons of America of Alice, TX, Minutes," pp. 5–6. Sons of America File, The League of United Latin American Citizens Records (hereafter cited as SAF), Nettie Lee Benson Latin American Collection, University of Texas, Austin (hereafter cited as NLB).

Chapter 6

1. Mario T. García, *Mexican Americans: Leadership, Ideology, & Identity, 1930–1960,* 1. Throughout the 1930s and 1940s Tejanos were often referred to as "Latin Americans."

2. Emilio Zamora, "The Failed Promise of Wartime Opportunity for Mexicans in the Texas Oil Industry," *Southwestern Historical Quarterly* 95 (Jan., 1992): 221–36.

3. R. Garcia, *Rise of the Mexican American Middle Class,* p. 272.

4. Benjamin Heber Johnson, "Sedition and Citizenship in South Texas, 1900–1930," pp. 11–12; and M. García, *Mexican Americans,* pp. 17–19. For an indictment of some Chicano-era history see David G. Gutierrez, "Significant to Whom? Mexican Americans and the History of the American West," *Western Historical Quarterly* 24 (Nov., 1993): 519–39.

5. "Sons of America of Alice, TX, Minutes," SAF, NLB, p. 5. These are hastily scribbled minutes to what appears to have been lively meetings. I will refrain from making corrections unless absolutely necessary.

6. Ibid., pp. 5 (first quotation) and 5–6 (second quotation), SAF, NLB.

7. Cynthia E. Orozco, "The Origins of the League of United Latin American Citizens (LULAC) and the Mexican American Civil Rights Movement in Texas With an Analysis of Women's Political Participation in a Gendered Context, 1910–1929," pp. 175–81; and R. Garcia, *Rise of the Mexican American Middle Class,* p. 256.

8. R. Garcia, *Rise of the Mexican American Middle Class,* pp. 256–57; Orozco, "The Origins of the League of United Latin American Citizens," p. 291; and González, "Social Life in Cameron, Starr, and Zapata Counties," pp. 97–99.

9. M. García, *Mexican Americans,* p. 32 (quotations); and R. Garcia, *Rise of the Mexican American Middle Class,* p. 375.

10. O. Douglas Weeks, "The League of United Latin-American Citizens: A Texas-Mexican Civic Organization," *The Southwestern Political and Social Science Quarterly* 10 (Dec., 1929): 278.

11. *Salvatierra,* pp. 793 (quotation) and 795–96. Italics added.

12. M. García, *Mexican Americans,* pp. 65–73; R. Garcia, *Rise of the Mexican American*

Middle Class, pp. 190–91; and Guadalupe San Miguel, Jr., "The Struggle Against Separate and Unequal Schools: Middle Class Mexican Americans and the Desegregation Campaign in Texas, 1929–1957," *History of Education Quarterly* 23 (Fall, 1983): 349.

13. C. R. Van Nice, "Adapting the School Public Relations Program to the War Emergency," *The Texas Outlook* 27 (Mar., 1943): 24.

14. Bryce Wood, *The Making of the Good Neighbor Policy*, pp. 123–35.

15. Anna Woodfin, "Our Mexican Obligation," *The Texas Outlook* 25 (Aug., 1941): 19.

16. Madge Stephenson, "Education Will Make Good Neighbors," *The Texas Outlook* 27 (Mar., 1943): 26.

17. Donald W. Rowland and Harold B. Gotaas, *History of the Office of the Coordinator of Inter-American Affairs: Historical Reports on War Administration*, pp. 5–8 and 109–10; and H. Stephen Helton, *Preliminary inventory of the records of the Office of Inter-American Affairs. Record Group 229*, p. 89.

18. J. Luz Saenz, "Has Time Come?" *The Texas Outlook* 26 (Apr., 1942): 44.

19. Edgar Ellen Wilson and Myrtle L. Tanner, *Meet Latin America: Curriculum Enrichment Materials for Elementary and Junior High Schools, 1945, Bulletin No. 465*, p. 6.

20. L. A. Woods, *Thirty Third Biennial Report. State Department of Education, 1942–1943, 1943–1944, No. 447*, pp. 9–10; and Kibbe, *Latin Americans in Texas*, p. 104.

21. San Miguel also articulates these themes in *"Let All of Them Take Heed,"* chapter 4.

22. Clarice T. Whittenburg and George I. Sánchez, *Materials Relating to the Education of Spanish-Speaking People: A Bibliography. Inter-American Education Occasional papers, 2*, pp. 1–38; Little, *Spanish-Speaking Children in Texas*, p. 3; and San Miguel, *"Let All of Them Take Heed,"* p. 95.

23. Little, *Spanish-Speaking Children in Texas*, p. 62.

24. Kibbe, *Latin Americans in Texas*, pp. 107–108.

25. Myrtle L. Tanner, *Teacher Training Workshop, Inter-American Relations Education: Program, Personnel, Reports, Recommendations, Summaries. University of Texas, Austin, Texas, April 17–22, 1944*, pages not numbered.

26. L. S. Tireman, "Rights and Responsibilities," in *Report on Conferences on Professional Relations and Inter-American Education at the Southwest Texas State Teachers College, San Marcos, Texas, June 30, 1944*, p. 8.

27. "Inter-American Workshop," *The Texas Outlook* 29 (Mar., 1945): 48; and Byron England, "El Paso Develops Aids for Teachers of Bilinguals," *The Texas Outlook* (Oct., 1945): 42, 44.

28. E. C. Dodd and L. A. Woods, *Tentative Course of Study for the Teaching of Spanish in Grades 3 to 8 Inclusive, Bulletin No 426*, xi and xii (quotation).

29. T. Earle Hamilton and Charles B. Qualia, "Spanish in the Grades," *The Texas Observer* 25 (June, 1941): 50 (first quotation) and 51 (second quotation); and Yetta Mae Slayton, "Why Not Spanish Readers?" *The Texas Observer* 26 (July, 1942): 40.

30. K. Rocque Wellborne, "Spanish for Children of Hispano Descent," *The Texas Outlook* 25 (Dec., 1941): 33.

31. Leticia M. Garza-Falcón, *Gente Decente: A Borderlands Response to the Rhetoric of Dominance*, pp. 95–97; "S. B. No. 67, March 31, 1941," Box 1, Folder 1, Item 17, E. E. Mireles Papers (hereafter cited as EEM), NLB; "Comments from Educators," Box 1, Folder 1, Item 8, EEM, NLB (quotation); and Letter from Thurmond Krueger to Marvin P. Baker, Feb. 24, 1942, Box 1, Folder 1, Item 11, EEM, NLB.

32. "Habla Ud. Inglés?" *Time*, Feb. 14, 1944, p. 72, EEM, NLB.

33. "Conversational Spanish Group, E. E. Mireles, Leader Outline," 1944, Box 1, Folder 1, Item 9, EEM, NLB.

34. L. A. Woods, "Recommendations and Suggestions on Improving the Teaching of Spanish at the High School Level," 1945, Box 1, Folder 1, Item 25, EEM, NLB.

35. "Philosophy," 1944, Box 1, Folder 1, Item 12, EEM, NLB.

36. Montgomery, "Pan-Americanism in Texas Schools," pp. 17 (quotations) and 18.

37. Autalee Notgrass, "Down Mexico Way: Middle Grade Unit," *Texas Outlook* (Aug., 1941): 53.

38. George I. Sánchez and Henry J. Otto, *A Guide For Teachers of Spanish Speaking Children in the Primary Grades, 1946. Bulletin No., 464*, pp. 16–17, 19–20, and 34–35.

39. Hughey, "Teaching Spanish in the Elementary Grades," pp. 21–22.

40. "A Report on The Program of Teaching English as a Second Language at the University of Texas, Austin, Texas, From July 5 to August 28, 1943," Box 61, Folder 11, "Inter-American Relations," George I. Sánchez Papers (hereafter cited as GIS), NLB.

41. George I. Sánchez, "The Crux of the Dual Language Handicap," *New Mexico School Review* 38 (Mar., 1954): 38. Original italics included.

42. H. T. Manuel, "Progress in Inter-American Education and Plans in Prospect," *The Texas Outlook* 29 (Mar., 1945): 13 (first quotation) and 14 (second and third quotations).

43. Guadalupe San Miguel, Jr., *Brown, Not White: School Integration and the Chicano Movement in Houston*, p. 56.

44. Patrick J. Carroll, "Tejano Living and Educational Conditions in World War II South Texas," *Victoria College Conference on South Texas Studies* (1994): 94–95.

45. J. Luz Saenz, "Racial Discrimination: A Number One Problem of Texas Schools," *The Texas Outlook* 30 (Dec., 1946): 12 (first three quotations) and 40 (fourth quotation). Saenz referred to Mississippi senator Theodore Bilbo, a racist demagogue then infamous for his white supremacist theories.

Chapter 7

1. San Miguel, *"Let All of Them Take Heed";* and Elliot L. Judd, "Factors Affecting the Passage of the Bilingual Education Act of 1967."

2. George I. Sánchez, "History, Culture and Education," in *La Raza: Forgotten Americans*, ed. by Julian Samora, p. 18; and Division of Research, *Report of Pupils in Texas Public Schools Having Spanish Surnames, 1955–56*, p. 6. Texas Education Agency Library, Austin, Texas (hereafter cited as TEA).

3. Carl Allsup, *The American G.I. Forum: Origins and Evolution. Monograph No. 6*, pp. 158–59.

4. Alonso Perales, ed., *Are We Good Neighbors?*

5. George I. Sánchez, *Concerning Segregation of Spanish-Speaking Children in the Public Schools. Inter-American Education Occasional Papers, IX*, p. 39 (quotations); and Everett Ross Clinchy, Jr., "Equality of Opportunity for Latin-Americans in Texas," pp. 170–73.

6. *Westminster School District of Orange County et al.* v. *Mendez et al.*, pp. 784–85.

7. Carl Allsup, "Education is Our Freedom: The American G. I. Forum and Mexican American School Segregation in Texas, 1948–1957," *Aztlan* 8 (Fall, 1977): 32; and Letter from Joe R. Greenhill, assistant to the Attorney General, to Price Daniel, Attorney General, Apr. 8, 1947, "Segregation in Schools, 1943, 1947–48," Folder 7, Box 38, GIS, NLB (quotation). Italics added.

8. Letter from Sánchez to Greenhill, May 8, 1947, "segregation in Schools, 1943, 1947–48," Folder 7, Box 38, GIS, NLB, pp. 1 (first quotation), 2, and 3 (second quotation).

9. Allsup, "Education is Our Freedom," pp. 32–33.

10. San Miguel, *"Let All of Them Take Heed,"* pp. 124–25; Guadalupe Salinas, "Mexican Americans and the Desegregation of Schools in the Southwest," *Houston Law Review* 8 (1971): 941; and Carlos M. Alcala and Jorge C. Rangel, "Project Report: De Jure Segregation of Chicanos in the Texas Public Schools," *Harvard Civil Rights-Civil Liberties Law Review* 7 (Mar., 1972): 336–37.

11. L. A. Woods, *Statement, Discussion, and Decision on the Segregation in the Del Rio Public Schools*, pp. 4–5.

12.   Woods, *With Texas Public Schools, Bulletin, State Department of Education, September 1948*, p. 2. Original underlining included.

13.   San Miguel, "The Struggle Against Separate and Unequal Schools," p. 351; and J. W. Edgar, *Thirty-Sixth Biennial Report, 1948–49, 1949–50*, pp. 11–15.

14.   Woods, *With Texas Public Schools*, p. 2; and Texas Committee of Ten, *Report Number One of the Survey of Administrative Practices and Board Policies in Texas Public Schools: Pupil Personnel Practices in Texas Public Schools*, pp. 11–12.

15.   San Miguel, *"Let Them All Take Heed,"* pp. 133–34.

16.   *Hermino Hernandez* v. *Driscoll Consolidated Independent School District*, p. 12. Original underlining included. These are Allred's remarks and final judgment given on January 14, 1957. Folder "1384 Hermino Hernandez v Driscoll Consolidated I.S.D., et al.," Box 232, National Archives and Records Administration-Southwest Regional Archives, Fort Worth, Tex. See also Steven Harmon Wilson, "Proceed to Judgment: Aspects of Judicial Management of Growth, Change, and Conflict in the United States District Court for the Southern District of Texas, 1960–2000."

17.   *Hernandez* v. *Driscoll*, p. 13-A (there were two page thirteens, page 13 and page 13-A).

18.   Ozzie G. Simmons, "Anglo Americans and Mexican Americans in South Texas: A Study in Dominant-Subordinate Group Relations," p. 134; and "Exhibit No. 12: Copy of Spanish Detention Slip, El Paso, Texas," in *Hearing Before the United States Commission on Civil Rights. Hearing Held in San Antonio, Texas, December 9–14, 1968*, p. 881 (quotation).

19.   Judd, "Factors Affecting the Passage of the Bilingual Education Act of 1967," pp. 26–32; and Carlos Kevin Blanton, "The Strange Career of Bilingual Education: A History of the Political and Pedagogical Debate Over Language Instruction in American Public Education, 1890–1990," pp. 310–71.

20.   Natalie T. Darcy, "The Effect of Bilingualism Upon the Measurement of the Intelligence of Children of Preschool Age," *The Journal of Educational Psychology* 37 (Feb., 1946): 23–25; and Dorothy H. Eichorn and Harold E. Jones, "Development of Mental Functions," *Review of Educational Research* 22 (Dec., 1952): 421 (quotation).

21.   Natalie T. Darcy, "The Performance of Bilingual Puerto Rican Children on Verbal and on Non-Language Tests of Intelligence," *Journal of Educational Research* 45 (Dec., 1952): 506; Selma E. Herr, "The Effect of Pre-First-Grade Training Upon Reading Readiness and Reading Achievement Among Spanish-American Children," *The Journal of Educational Psychology* 37 (Feb., 1946): 87 and 100; and Natalie T. Darcy, "A Review of the Literature on the Effects of Bilingualism Upon the Measurement of Intelligence," *The Journal of Genetic Psychology* 82 (Mar., 1953): 21–39.

22.   Darcy, "A Review of the Literature," pp. 39–50; Seth Arsenian, "Bilingualism in the Post-War World," *Psychological Bulletin* 42 (Feb., 1945): 74 (first quotation); and C. L. Yarbrough, "Age-Grade Status of Texas Children of Latin-American Descent," *Journal of Educational Research* 40 (Sept., 1946): 26 (second quotation).

23.   Mary Arthur Carrow, "Linguistic Functioning of Bilingual and Monolingual Children," *The Journal of Speech and Hearing Disorders* 22 (Sept., 1957): 371–72; Ralph D. Norman and Donald F. Mead, "Spanish-American Bilingualism and the Ammons Full-Range Picture-Vocabulary Test," *The Journal of Social Psychology* 51 (May, 1960): 326–27; Boris M. Levinson, "A Comparative Study of the Verbal and Performance Ability of Monolingual and Bilingual Native Born Jewish Preschool Children of Traditional Parentage," *The Journal of Genetic Psychology* 97 (Sept., 1960): 110–11; and Jack E. Kittell, "Bilingualism and Language—Non-Language Intelligence Scores of Third-Grade Children," *Journal of Educational Research* 52 (Mar., 1959): 267.

24.   Anne Anastasi, "Introductory Remarks," in *Psychological Testing of Hispanics*, ed. by Kurt F. Geisinger, pp. 3–4; and Anne Anastasi and Cruz de Jesus, "Language Development and Nonverbal IQ of Puerto Rican Preschool Children in New York

City," *The Journal of Abnormal and Social Psychology* 48 (July, 1953): 361 (quotation) and 365.

25. Stanley W. Caplan and Ronald A. Ruble, "A Study of Culturally Imposed Factors on School Achievement in a Metropolitan Area," *The Journal of Educational Research* 58 (Sept., 1964): 19 (first quotation); and Hilda P. Lewis and Edward R. Lewis, "Written Language Performance of Sixth-Grade Children of Low Socio-Economic Status From Bilingual and Monolingual Backgrounds," *The Journal of Experimental Education* 33 (Spring, 1965): 239 (second quotation).

26. Louis Lerea and Suzanna Kohut, "A Comparative Study of Monolinguals and Bilinguals in a Verbal Task Performance," *Journal of Clinical Psychology* 17 (Jan., 1961): 52.

27. Elizabeth Peal and Wallace E. Lambert, *The Relation of Bilingualism to Intelligence. Psychological Monographs: General and Applied, Vol. 76, No. 27,* 16 (first quotation) and 14 (second, third, and fourth quotations).

28. Crawford, *Bilingual Education,* pp. 119–20.

29. Charles C. Fries, *Teaching & Learning English as a Foreign Language,* pp. 6–7.

30. Ofelia Garcia, "A Gathering of Voices, a 'Legion of Scholarly Decency' and Bilingual Education: Fishman's Biographemes as Introduction," in *Bilingual Education: Focusschrift in Honor of Joshua A. Fishman on the Occasion of His 65th Birthday, Volume I,* ed. by Ofelia Garcia, 8; Theodore Andersson, "Spanish, Language of the Americas," *Hispania* 47 (Sept., 1959): 347–51; and Andersson, "The Role of Foreign Languages in International Understanding," *The Bulletin of the National Association of Secondary School Principals* 41 (Dec., 1957): 56–62.

31. Crawford, *Bilingual Education,* pp. 120–22.

32. Texas Committee of Ten, *School Program Practices in Texas Public Schools. Report Number Three of the Texas Committee of Ten,* p. 14.

33. J. W. Edgar, *What Do We Know About . . . Foreign Language Instruction? Bulletin 621,* pp. viii–ix.

34. Hale-Aiken Committee of Twenty-Four for the Study of Texas Public Schools, *Tentative Draft of the Final Report,* p. iv, TEA; San Miguel, *"Let All of Them Take Heed,"* pp. 140–47; and Thomas H. Kreneck, *Mexican American Odyssey: Felix Tijerina, Entrepreneur & Civic Leader, 1905–1965,* p. 271.

35. Hale-Aiken Committee of Twenty-Four, *Tentative Draft of the Final Report,* 2; and Division of Administrative Services, *Laws and Resolutions Affecting Public Education Enacted by the 56th Legislature, Regular Session, 1959,* p. 47.

36. William T. Poulos, "They Learn Basic English *Before* School Starts," *Texas Outlook* 43 (July, 1959): 32; E. E. Mireles, "Summer English Program for Pre-School Non-English Speaking Children," 1962, Box 1, Folder 3, Item 68, EEM, NLB; E. E. Mireles, "Summer English Program, Common Expressions," 1956–57, Box 1, Folder 3, Item 73, EEM, NLB; and Letter from Mireles to Paul Haas, Mar. 1, 1963, Box 1, Folder 3, Item 83, EEM, NLB.

Chapter 8

1. Gail P. Kelly, "Contemporary American Policies and Practices in the Education of Immigrant Children," in *Educating Immigrants,* ed. by Joti Bhatnagar, pp. 227–29; David M. Reimers, *Still the Golden Door: The Third World Comes to America,* 81–86; Milton M. Gordon, *Assimilation in American Life: The Role of Race, Religion, and National Origins;* Nathan Glazer and Daniel Patrick Moynihan, eds., *Beyond the Melting Pot: The Negroes, Puerto Ricans, Jews, Italians, and Irish of New York City;* and E. Digby Baltzell, *The Protestant Establishment: Aristocracy & Caste in America.*

2. Testimony of Commissioner of Education Before Special Subcommittee on Education, House Committee on Education and Labor, Feb. 3, 1964, "LE/EA 2, 7/1/64–10/13/64," White House Central Files (hereafter cited WHCF), Box 37, Lyndon Baines Johnson Presidential Library (hereafter cited as LBJ), Austin, Tex.; and

James E. Alatis, "Our Own Language Barrier," *American Education* 1 (Jan., 1965): 13 (quotations).

3.   Annie Stemmler, "An Experimental Approach to the Teaching of Oral Language and Reading," *Harvard Educational Review* 36 (Summer, 1966): 43 and 45 (quotation).

4.   Carlos J. Ovando and Virginia P. Collier, *Bilingual and ESL Classrooms: Teaching in Multicultural Contexts,* p. 25; and Marjorie C. Johnston and Elizabeth Keesee, *Modern Foreign Languages and Your Child,* pp. 1–7.

5.   Theodore Andersson, "Foreign Languages and Intercultural Understanding," *The National Elementary Principal* 5 (Feb., 1957): 32–33 and 35.

6.   J. J. Osuna, "Report on Visits to New York City Schools," in *Puerto Rican Children in Mainland Schools: A Source Book for Teachers,* ed. by Francesco Cordasco and Eugene Bucchioni, pp. 227–39; and Mary Jenkins, *Bilingual Education in New York City,* p. 14 (quotations).

7.   María Cristina García, *Havana USA: Cuban Exiles and Cuban Americans in South Florida, 1959–1994,* pp. 23–28; Maria de los Angeles Torres, "From Exiles to Minorities: The Politics of Cuban-Americans," in *Latinos and the Political System,* ed. by F. Chris Garcia, p. 83 (quotations); and Memo, Alden Lillywhite, acting director of the Division of School Assistance, to John F. Thomas, director, Cuban Refugee Program, Oct., 12, 1964, "BESE-Financial Assistance and Education of Cuban Refugees," HEW Records, Box 162, LBJ.

8.   U. S. Commission on Civil Rights, *Stranger in One's Land. U. S. Commission on Civil Rights Clearinghouse Publication No. 19, May 1970,* pp. 28 (quotation) and 23.

9.   Manuel Ramírez III and Alfredo Castañeda, *Cultural Democracy: Bicognitive Development, and Education,* p. 22.

10. "Testimony of Dr. George I. Sánchez, Austin, Texas," in *Hearing Before the United States Commission on Civil Rights,* p. 92.

11. "Testimony of Mr. Homero Sigala and Fermin Calderon, M.D., Del Rio, Texas," in ibid., pp. 295 and 308 (quotation). Original italics used.

12. Ignacio M. García, *Viva Kennedy: Mexican Americans in Search of Camelot,* pp. 165–69; Montejano, *Anglos and Mexicans in the Making of Texas,* p. 282; San Miguel, *"Let All of Them Take Heed,"* pp. 165–66; Allsup, *The American G. I. Forum,* pp. 133–39.

13. Juan Gómez Quiñones, *Chicano Politics: Reality & Promise, 1940–1990,* p. 108.

14. Julie Leininger Pycior, *LBJ & Mexican Americans: The Paradox of Power,* pp. 200–201 and 206–207.

15. José E Vega, *Education, Politics, and Bilingualism in Texas,* pp. 31–32; Quiñones, *Chicano Politics,* pp. 109–10; and Richard Griswold Del Castillo and Richard A. Garcia, *César Chávez: A Triumph of the Spirit,* p. 16.

16. Armando Navarro, *Mexican American Youth Organization: Avant-Garde of the Chicano Movement in Texas,* pp. 118–48; and Quiñones, *Chicano Politics,* pp. 118–23.

17. Chicano Coordinating Council on Higher Education, *El Plan de Santa Barbara: A Chicano Plan for Higher Education,* p. 78.

18. Sánchez, "History, Culture, and Education," p. 12.

19. Chicano Coordinating Council, *El Plan de Santa Barbara,* p. 9; and José E. Limón, "El Meeting: History, Folk Spanish, and Ethnic Nationalism in a Chicano Student Community," in *Spanish in the United States: Sociolingual Aspects,* ed. by Jon Amastae and Lucía Elías-Olivares, pp. 313–20.

20. Robert Dallek, *Lone Star Rising: Lyndon Johnson and His Times, 1908–1960,* p. 79 (quotations); Transcript, Wilton Woods and Virginia Woods Oral History Interview, 1983, AC 83-46 and 47, pp. 6–7, LBJ.

21. Letter, Lyndon Johnson to Rebekah Johnson, Oct., 17, 1928, Family Correspondence, "Rebekah Johnson Correspondence," Box 1, LBJ.

22. Stuart Eskenazi, "Raw View of Poverty at Cotulla School Shaped LBJ," *Austin American Statesman,* Nov. 26, 1995, "Cotulla" Reference File, LBJ.

23. Jim Strodes, "One Man's Evaluation of LBJ: Ear Pincher!" *Durham Morning Herald,* Jan. 20, 1964, "PP-13-5, Education," White House Central Files (hereafter cited as WHCF), Box 108, LBJ (first two quotations); and "One Man and a Boy!" *Vulcan Mold's Pit and Pour,* 5 (Apr., 1964), PP 13-5, "PP 13-5, Education," WHCF, Box 108, LBJ, unnumbered (third quotation).

24. Strodes, "Ear Pincher!" "PP 13-5, Education," WHCF, Box 108, LBJ.

25. Tom Johnson, "Former Pupils Praise Johnson," *Washington Post,* Jan. 27, 1967, "PA—Biographical Information, Teacher," LBJA Subject File, Box 73, LBJ.

26. "Message on Education and Health in America," p. 5, "SP 2-3/1967/ED," WHCF, Box 82, LBJ.

27. Speech, "Remarks of the President at Cotulla, Texas," "EX-SP 3-165," WHCF, Box 185, LBJ.

28. Graham, *Uncertain Triumph,* pp. 155–59 and 217–21.

29. Letter, Sánchez to Joe Alaniz, May 26, 1967, Folder 12, "Yarborough," Box 46, GIS, NLB; and "S. 428. A Bill to Amend the Elementary and Secondary Education Act of 1965 . . . ," pp. 2 (first quotation) and 1, "LE/FA 2, 5/24/67–1/2/68," WHCF, Box 39, LBJ.

30. Judd, "Factors Affecting the Passage of the Bilingual Education Act of 1967," pp. 121–22; Memo, Howe to Cater, "Senator Yarborough's Bilingual Education Bill (S.428)," "May–June 1967," Cater Name Files, Box 21, LBJ; and Francesco Cordasco, "The Bilingual Education Act," *Phi Delta Kappan* 51 (Oct., 1969): 75.

31. Graham, *The Uncertain Triumph,* pp. 159 and 219.

32. Theodore Andersson, "Testimony Presented on HR 9840 and HR 10224 to Authorize Bilingual Programs in Elementary and Secondary Schools Before the House General Subcommittee on Education and Labor, 29 June 1967," Folder 14, "Testimony: National Bilingual Education Act," Box 1, Theodore Andersson Papers (hereafter cited as TAP), NLB.

33. Pycior, *LBJ and Mexican Americans,* 184–87.

34. Memo, John Gardner to Lister Hill, undated, 2 (quotation) and 3, "LE/FA 2, 5/24/67–1/2/68," WHCF, Box 39, LBJ.

35. Memo, Harold Howe II to Douglass Cater, June 26, 1967, "May–June 1967," Cater Name Files, Box 21, LBJ.

36. Memo, John Gardner to Lister Hill, undated, pp. 5–6, "LE/FA 2, 5/24/67–1/2/68," WHCF, Box 39, LBJ; and Memo, Harold Howe II to Douglass Cater, June 26, 1967, "May–June 1967," Cater Name Files, Box 21, LBJ (quotation).

37. Memo, Jim Gaither to Joe Califano, Aug. 15, 1967, "LE/FA 2, 5/2/64–1/2/68," WHCF, Box 39, LBJ.

38. Ibid. (quotation); and Allen J. Matusow, *The Unraveling of America: A History of Liberalism in the 1960s,* p. 191.

39. Memo, Ralph Huitt to Douglass Cater and Barefoot Sanders, Aug. 8, 1967, "LE/FA 2, 5/24/67–1/2/68," WHCF, Box 39, LBJ (first quotation); and Memos, Barefoot Sanders to Joe Califano, and Califano to Jim Gaithers, Aug. 9, 10, 1967, "LE/FA 2, 5/24/67–1/2/68," WHCF, Box 39, LBJ (second and third quotations).

40. Statement by Lyndon Johnson, "Signing H.R. 7819—The Elementary and Secondary Education Amendments," "P.L. 90-247, HR 7819, 1/2/68," Enrolled Legislation, Box 60, LBJ.

41. "ESEA-1967 Conference Report," Dec., 15, 1967, 37, "P.L. 90-247, HR 7819," Enrolled Legislation, Box 60, LBJ; and Maria M. Swanson, "Bilingual Education: The National Perspective," in *Responding to New Realities,* ed. by Gilbert A. Jarvis, pp. 95–96.

42. Annual Report by National Advisory Council on the Education of Disadvantaged Children, Jan. 31, 1968, "FG 764, 1/1/67–2/29/68," WHCF, Box 410, LBJ.

43. National Advisory Committee on Mexican American Education of the U. S. Office of Education, "Cowboys, Indians and American Education," address by Harold

Howe II, U.S. commissioner of education. National Conference on Educational Opportunities for Mexican Americans, Austin, Tex., Apr. 25, 1968, unnumbered.

44.   "60 Education Laws Enacted During President Johnson's Administration," "60 Education Laws," Califano Name File, Box 85, LBJ; Julie Leininger Pycior, "From Hope to Frustration: Mexican Americans and Lyndon Johnson in 1967," *Western Historical Quarterly* 24 (Nov., 1993): 470; and Gene B. Preuss, "Cotulla Revisited: A Reassessment of Lyndon Johnson's Year as a Public School Teacher," *Journal of South Texas* 10 (1997): 28–29.

Chapter 9

1.   J. W. Edgar, *Public Education in Texas, 1958–1960: A Report to the Governor and the Legislature. 41st Biennial Report, Texas Education Agency, Bulletin No. 610*, pp. 49–51; Donald Denum, "Official Agenda State Board of Education, September 12, 1959," Minutes of the State Board of Education, TEA; and Letter, Sánchez to Senators John Tower, Ralph Yarborough, and Congressman Jake Pickle, May 24, 1968, Box 46, Folder 12, "Correspondence 1966–68," GIS, NLB.

2.   J. W. Edgar, *42nd Biennial Report, 1960–1962. Bulletin No. 630*, p. 38 (quotation); Edgar, *43rd Biennial Report, 1962–1964. Bulletin No. 654*, p. 30; and Edgar, *44th Biennial Report, 1964–1966*, p. 22.

3.   J. W. Edgar, *45th Biennial Report, 1966–1968. No. 678*, p. 47 (quotation); and Edgar, *47th Biennial Report, 1970–1972. No. 729*, p. 43.

4.   R. P. Ward, *Proposed Curriculum Program for Texas Migratory Children*, pp. 2–3; and J. W. Edgar, *Preschool Instructional Program For Non-English-Speaking Children. Bulletin No. 642*, pp. 30–31 (quotation).

5.   Statement from Theodore Andersson to House Committee on Education and Labor, Feb. 19, 1969, Folder 14, "Testimony: National Bilingual Education Act," Box 1, TAP, NLB; Andersson, "Spanish, Language of the Americas," p. 350 (quotation); and Edgar, *45th Biennial Report*, p. 79.

6.   J. W. Edgar, *46th Biennial Report, 1968–1970*, pp. 78 (quotation) and 79; and Edgar, *47th Biennial Report*, p. 77.

7.   Robert L. Hardgrave, Jr. and Santiago Hinojosa, *The Politics of Bilingual Education: A Study of Four Southwest Texas Communities*, pp. 16–19; and Harold C. Brantley, interview by author, Nov. 2, 1998, San Marcos, Tex. (hereafter cited as Brantley interview).

8.   Harold C. Brantley, "The Implementation of a Program of Bilingual Instruction," in *Educating the Mexican American*, ed. by Henry Sioux Johnson and William J. Hernández—M., p. 253 (quotation); Brantley interview; Doris Wright, "S.A. Was Forerunner in Dual Language Study," *San Antonio Light,* May 20, 1974, Mexican File—Language, ITC; and Hardgrave and Hinojosa, *The Politics of Bilingual Education.*

9.   Ernesto Galaraza, "The Humanization of Bilingual-Bicultural Schooling," in *Humanidad: Essays in Honor of George I. Sánchez*, ed. by Américo Paredes, pp. 71–72; and Philip D. Ortego, "Schools for Mexican-Americans: Between Two Cultures," *Saturday Review, Education Supplement*, Apr. 17, 1971, 81, "Mexican File, Education," ITC (quotation).

10.   Navarro, *Mexican American Youth Organization*, chapter 4; Guadalupe San Miguel, Jr., "'The Community is Beginning to Rumble': The Origins of Chicano Educational Protest in Houston, 1965–1970," *The Houston Review* 13 (summer, 1991): 136–46; San Miguel, Jr., *Brown, Not White;* and Graham, *Uncertain Triumph*, pp. 159 and 219.

11.   "Testimony of Dr. James Winfred Edgar, Texas State Commissioner of Education; Dr. Severo Gomez, Assistant Commissioner for Bilingual and International Education; and Mr. Leon Grimm, Assistant Commissioner for Administration, Austin, Texas," in *Hearing Before the United States Commission on Civil Rights*, p. 390.

12. J. W. Edgar, *A Resource Manual for Implementing Bilingual Education Programs,* pp. 23–24. Original underlining.

13. Vega, *Education, Politics, and Bilingualism,* pp. 64–77; *Journal of the House of Representatives of the Regular Session of the Sixty-First Legislature,* pp. 172–73, 435, 469–71, 489, 1715, 1735–37, and 1961–62; and *Journal of the Senate of the State of Texas, Regular Session of the Sixty-First Legislature,* pp. 94–95, 210, 335, 435–36, 387, 407, 2421.

14. Vega, *Education, Politics, and Bilingualism,* pp. 77–78.

15. *Journal of the House of Representatives of the Regular Session of the Sixty-Third Legislature,* pp. 2752, 2784, 3231, 3705–10, 4017, 4533, 4555, 4750, 5628; *Journal of the Senate of the State of Texas, Regular Session of the Sixty-Third Legislature,* pp. 115, 699, 834, 850, 852, 861, 1425, 1429, 1525, 1551, 1803; and San Miguel, *"Let All of Them Take Heed,"* pp. 196–97.

16. San Miguel, *"Let All of Them Take Heed,"* p. 181.

17. Peter D. Roos, "Bilingual Education: The Hispanic Response to Unequal Educational Equality," *Law and Contemporary Problems* 42 (Autumn, 1978): 112 (first quotation); and Leo J. Juarez, "Equal Access or Equal Benefits: Court and Legislative Mandates on Bilingual Education," *Texas Tech Journal of Education* 2 (Fall, 1975): 189 (second quotation).

18. *United States of America* v. *State of Texas et al.,* pp. 28 (first three quotations) and 31 (fourth quotation).

19. Guadalupe San Miguel, Jr., "Conflict and Controversy in the Evolution of Bilingual Education in the United States—An Interpretation," *Social Science Quarterly* 65 (June, 1984): 507; and Juarez, "Equal Access or Equal Benefits," p. 184.

20. Crawford, *Bilingual Education,* pp. 45–47.

21. Doris Wright, "Language Segregation a Problem," *San Antonio Light,* May 19, 1974, "Mexican File, Language," ITC; Wright, "Learning Basic Subject is not Delayed," *San Antonio Light,* May 22, 1974, "Mexican File, Language," ITC; Wright, "Spanish-Speaking Have Highest Drop-Out Rate," *San Antonio Light,* May 24, 1974, "Mexican File, Language," ITC (quotation); and Mario Benitez, "Point—Counterpoint," *San Antonio Express-News,* Sept. 28, 1980, "Mexican File, Education," ITC.

22. San Miguel, *"Let All of Them Take Heed,"* pp. 197–200; *Journal of the House of Representatives of the Regular Session of the Sixty-Sixth Legislature of the State of Texas,* pp. 5613, 4495–96; and Crawford, *Bilingual Education,* pp. 49–53.

23. Frank Kemerer and Jim Walsh, *The Educator's Guide to Texas School Law, Fourth Edition,* pp. 72–73; and San Miguel, *"Let All of Them Take Heed,"* pp. 201–203 and 203(quotation).

24. San Miguel, *"Let All of Them Take Heed,"* pp. 206–207.

25. *Journal of the Senate of the State of Texas. Regular Session of the Sixty-Seventh Legislature,* 1414–29, 1558–63, 2030–31, 2147–55, and 2217; *Journal of the House of Representatives of the Regular Session of the Sixty-Seventh Legislature of the State of Texas,* pp. 4024–30, 4149, 4231, and 4418; and San Miguel, *"Let All of Them Take Heed,"* pp. 207–209.

26. Raymond Tatalovich, "Official Language: English-Only Versus English-Plus," in *Moral Controversies in American Politics: Cases in Social Regulatory Policy,* ed. by Tatalovich and Byron W. Daynes, pp. 198–99; and Bill Piatt *¿Only English? Law & Language Policy in the United States,* pp. 20–26. English-Only states are Alabama (1990), Arizona (1988), Arkansas (1987), California (1986), Colorado (1988), Florida (1988), Georgia (1996), Hawaii (1978), Illinois (1969), Indiana (1984), Kentucky (1984), Louisiana (1991), Mississippi (1987), Montana (1995), Nebraska (1920), New Hampshire (1995), North Carolina (1987), North Dakota (1987), South Carolina (1987), South Dakota (1995), Tennessee (1984), Virginia (1981), and Wyoming (1996). English-Plus states are New Mexico (1989), Oregon (1989), Rhode Island (1992), and Washington (1989).

Conclusion

1. For non-academic criticism see Wayne Lutton and John Tanton, *The Immigrant Invasion,* p. 57; Robert Rienow and Leona Rienow, *The Great Unwanteds Want Us. Illegal Aliens: Too Late to Close the Gates?* p. 30; and Richard D. Lamm and Gary Imhoff, *The Immigration Time Bomb: The Fragmenting of America,* pp. 103–109. For academic criticism see Graham, *The Uncertain Triumph,* p. 219; and Schlesinger, *The Disuniting of America,* p. 108.
2. Crawford, *Bilingual Education,* pp. 243 (quotation) and 256.
3. Mark Babineck, "Texas Less Proficient in English. State Ranks Lower than National Rate," *Houston Chronicle,* Aug. 6, 2001.
4. Texas Education Agency Office of Policy Planning and Research, Academic Achievement of Elementary Students with Limited English Proficiency in Texas Public Schools, Report No. 10, Jan., 1998, pp. 29 and 14.

Bibliography

Archival Collections 179

Center for American History. University of Texas. Austin. Annie Webb Blanton Vertical File.

Institute of Texan Cultures. San Antonio.

Czech File—Languages; Education in Texas File; Education in Texas File—Dutch; Education in Texas File—Religious; General File—Education; German Public Schools—New Braunfels; Mexican File—Language; Mexican File—Education.

Lyndon Baines Johnson Presidential Library. University of Texas, Austin.

Califano Name File; Cater Name File; Cotulla Reference File; Enrolled Legislation File; Family Correspondence; HEW Files; LBJA Subject File; Oral Histories; White House Central Files.

Nettie Lee Benson Latin American Collection. University of Texas, Austin.

E. E. Mireles Papers; George I. Sánchez Papers; League of United Latin American Citizens Records, Sons of America File; Theodore Andersson Papers.

South Texas Archives. Texas A&M University—Kingsville.

Texas Education Agency Library. Austin.

Texas State Archives. Austin.

State Department of Education Files: Bexar County; Brownsville; Cameron County; Comal County; Corpus Christi; Eagle Pass; El Paso County; Fayette County; Gillespie County; Hidalgo County; Houston; Kerrville; La Grange; Laredo; Maverick County; New Braunfels; Nueces County; San Antonio; San Diego; Starr County; Val Verde County; Victoria County; Washington County; Webb County; Williamson County; Ysleta; Zapata County.

———. Texas State Teachers Association Collection.

Theses, Dissertations, and Interviews

Aaronson, Arthur Charles. "The Involvement of the Federal Government in Providing Public Instruction for Non-English-Speaking Pupils from 1800 to 1980." Ph.D. diss., Virginia Polytechnic Institute and State University, 1980.

Blanton, Carlos Kevin. "The Strange Career of Bilingual Education: A History of the Political and Pedagogical Debate Over Language Instruction in American Public Education, 1890–1990. Ph.D. diss., Rice University, 1999.

Brantley, Harold C. Interview by author, November 2, 1998, tape recording, residence, San Marcos, Texas.

Clinchy, Everett Ross, Jr. "Equality of Opportunity for Latin-Americans in Texas." Ph.D. diss., Columbia University, 1954; reprint, New York: Arno Press, 1974.

Fessler, Paul Rudolph. "Speaking in Tongues: German-Americans and the Heritage of Bilingual Education in American Public Schools." Ph.D. diss., Texas A&M University, 1997.

González, Jovita. "Social Life in Cameron, Starr, and Zapata Counties." M.A. thesis, University of Texas, 1930.

Johnson, Benjamin Heber. "Sedition and Citizenship in South Texas, 1900–1930." Ph.D. diss., Yale University, 2000.

Judd, Elliot L. "Factors Affecting the Passage of the Bilingual Education Act of 1967." Ph.D. diss., New York University, 1977.

O'Banion, Maurine. "The History of Caldwell County." M.A. thesis, University of Texas, 1931.

Orozco, Cynthia E. "The Origins of the League of United Latin American Citizens (LULAC) and the Mexican American Civil Rights Movement in Texas with an Analysis of Women's Political Participation in a Gendered Context, 1910–1929." Ph.D. diss., University of California at Los Angeles, 1992.

Simmons, Ozzie G. "Anglo Americans and Mexican Americans in South Texas: A Study in Dominant-Subordinate Group Relations." Ph.D. diss., Harvard University, 1952.

Simmons, Thomas E. "The Citizen Factories: The Americanization of Mexican Students in Texas Public Schools, 1920–1945." Ph.D. diss., Texas A&M University, 1976.

White, Lee Wayne. "Popular Education and the State Superintendent of Public Instruction in Texas, 1860–1899." Ph.D. diss., University of Texas, 1974.

White, Michael Allen. "History of Education in Texas, 1860–1884." Ed.D., diss., Baylor University, 1969.

Wilson, Steven Harmon. "Proceed to Judgment: Aspects of Judicial Management of Growth, Change, and Conflict in the United States District Court for the Southern District of Texas, 1960–2000." Ph.D. diss., Rice University, 2000.

Books and Articles

1928 Complete Texas Statutes Covering the Revised Civil and Criminal Statutes, 1925. Kansas City: Vernon Law Book Company, 1928.

1934 Supplement to the 1928 Complete Texas Statutes. Kansas City: Vernon Law Book Company, 1934.

Addams, Jane. *Twenty Years at Hull-House with Autobiographical Notes.* Introduction by James Hurt. Chicago: University of Illinois Press, 1990.

Alatis, James E. "Our Own Language Barrier." *American Education* 1 (January, 1965): 12–13.

Alcala, Carlos M., and Jorge C. Rangel. "Project Report: De Jure Segregation of Chicanos in the Texas Public Schools." *Harvard Civil Rights-Civil Liberties Law Review* 7 (March, 1972): 307–91.

Allsup, Carl. "Education is Our Freedom: The American G.I. Forum and Mexican American School Segregation in Texas, 1948–1957." *Aztlan* 8 (Fall, 1977): 27–50.

———. *The American G.I. Forum: Origins and Evolution. Monograph No. 6.* Austin: Center for Mexican American Studies, 1982.

Amastae, Jon, and Lucía Elías-Olivares, eds. *Spanish in the United States: Sociolingual Aspects.* New York: Cambridge University Press, 1982.

Anastasi, Anne, and Cruz deJesus. "Language Development and Nonverbal IQ of Puerto Rican Preschool Children in New York City." *The Journal of Abnormal and Social Psychology* 48 (July, 1953): 357–66.

Andersson, Theodore, and Mildred Boyer. *Bilingual Schooling in the United States:*

History, Rationale, Implications, and Planning, Volume I. Austin: Southwest Educational Development Laboratory, 1970; reprint, Detroit: Blaine-Ethridge Books, 1976.

————. "Foreign Languages and Intercultural Understanding." *The National Elementary Principal* 5 (February, 1957): 32–37.

————. "Spanish, Language of the Americas." *Hispania* 47 (September, 1959): 347–51.

————. "The Role of Foreign Languages in International Understanding." *The Bulletin of the National Association of Secondary School Principals* 41 (December, 1957): 56–62.

Armour, Basil. "Problems in the Education of the Mexican Child." *The Texas Outlook* 16 (December, 1932): 29–31.

Arsenian, Seth. "Bilingualism in the Post-War World." *Psychological Bulletin* 42 (February, 1945): 65–86.

Baker, Benjamin M. *Fifth Biennial Report of the Superintendent of Public Instruction for the Scholastic Years Ending August 31, 1885, and August 31, 1886.* Austin: State Printing Office, 1886.

Baker, T. Lindsey. "The Early History of Panna Maria, Texas." *Graduate Studies, Texas Tech University* 9 (October, 1975): 1–69.

Baltzell, E. Digby, *The Protestant Establishment: Aristocracy & Caste in America.* New York: Random House, Inc., 1964; reprint, New Haven: Yale University Press, 1987.

Barker, Eugene C. *The Life of Stephen F. Austin: Founder of Texas, 1793–1836. A Chapter in the Westward Movement of the Anglo-American People.* Austin: Texas State Historical Association, 1949.

Barr, Alwyn. "Occupational and Geographic Mobility in San Antonio, 1870–1900." *Social Science Quarterly* 51 (September, 1970): 396–403.

————. *Reconstruction to Reform: Texas Politics, 1876–1906.* Austin: University of Texas Press, 1971.

Berger, Max. "Stephen F. Austin and Education in Early Texas, 1821–1835." *Southwestern Historical Quarterly* 48 (January, 1945): 387–94.

Bhatnagar, Joti, ed. *Educating Immigrants.* New York: St. Martin's Press, 1981.

Blanton, Annie Webb, and R. L. Ragsdale. *Texas High Schools: History and the Social Sciences. Bulletin 124.* Austin: Department of Education, State of Texas, 1920.

Blanton, Annie Webb. *A Hand Book of Information as to Education in Texas, 1918–1922. Bulletin 157.* Austin: Department of Education, State of Texas, 1923.

————. *Historical and Statistical Data as to Education in Texas, January 1, 1919–January 1, 1921. Bulletin 133.* Austin: Department of Education, State of Texas, 1921.

————. *Report on Education in Texas and Recommendations Made to the Governor and the Thirty-Seventh Legislature.* Austin: State Printing Office, 1921.

————. *Texas Compulsory School Attendance Law. Bulletin 137.* Austin: Department of Education, State of Texas, 1922.

————. "Texas Conditions and Demands." *The Texas Outlook* 5 (July, 1921): 6–9.

————. *Texas High Schools: History and the Social Sciences. Bulletin 124.* Austin: Department of Education, State of Texas, 1920.

————. *Texas High Schools, Course of Study. Bulletin No. 151.* Austin: State Department of Education, State of Texas, 1922.

————. *Texas School Laws. A Brief Compilation for Teachers of Laws Relating to Teachers and Pupils, Bulletin No. 122.* Austin: Department of Education, State of Texas, 1920.

Blanton, Carlos Kevin. "From Intellectual Deficiency to Cultural Deficiency: Mexican Americans, Testing, and Public School Policy in the American

Southwest, 1920–1940." *Pacific Historical Review* 72 (February, 2003): 39–62.

———. "Race, Labor, and the Limits of Progressive Reform: A Preliminary Analysis of the Enforcement of Compulsory Attendance in South Texas During the 1920s." *Journal of South Texas* 13 (Fall, 2000): 207–19.

———. "'They Cannot Master Abstractions But They Can Often Be Made Efficient Workers': Race and Class in the Intelligence Testing of Mexican Americans and African Americans in Texas During the 1920s." *Social Science Quarterly* 81 (December, 2000): 1014–26.

Bobbitt, J. F. *Report on the Survey of the San Antonio Public School System.* San Antonio: San Antonio School Board, 1915.

Bogardus, Emory S. *Essentials of Americanization.* Los Angeles: University of Southern California Press, 1920.

Bralley, F. M. *Seventeenth Biennial Report of the State Department of Education for the Years Ending August 31, 1909, and August 31, 1910.* Austin: Austin Printing Co., Printers, 1911.

Brown, Norman D. *Hood, Bonnet, and Little Brown Jug: Texas Politics, 1921–1928.* College Station: Texas A&M University Press, 1984.

Burkhart, J. Austin. "I Teach in a Border Town." *The Texas Outlook* 23 (December, 1939): 34.

Callahan, Mary Generosa. *The History of the Sisters of the Divine Providence, San Antonio, Texas.* Milwaukee: Catholic Life Publications, 1955.

Cantrell, Gregg. *Stephen F. Austin, Empresario of Texas.* New Haven: Yale University Press, 1999.

Caplan, Stanley W., and Ronald A. Ruble. "A Study of Culturally Imposed Factors on School Achievement in a Metropolitan Area." *The Journal of Educational Research* 58 (September, 1964): 16–21.

Carlisle, J. M. *Eighth Biennial Report of the State Superintendent of Public Instruction for the Scholastic Years Ending August 31, 1891, and August 31, 1892.* Austin: Ben C. Jones & Co., State Printers, 1893.

———. *Eleventh Biennial Report of the State Superintendent of Public Instruction for the Scholastic Years Ending August 31, 1897, and August 31, 1898.* Austin: Ben C. Jones & Co., State Printers, 1898.

Carroll, Patrick J. "Tejano Living and Educational Conditions in World War II South Texas." *Victoria College Conference on South Texas Studies* (1994): 82–103.

Carrow, Mary Arthur. "Linguistic Functioning of Bilingual and Monolingual Children." *The Journal of Speech and Hearing Disorders* 22 (September, 1957): 371–80.

Carvajal, Christa, and Annelise M. Duncan. "The German-English School in San Antonio: Transplanting German Humanistic Education to the Texas Frontier." *Yearbook of German-American Studies* 16 (1981): 89–102.

Castañeda, Carlos E. *The Mission Era: The Missions at Work, 1731–1761. Volume III, Our Catholic Heritage in Texas, 1519–1936.* Austin: Von Boeckmann–Jones Company, 1936.

———. *The Mission Era: The Winning of Texas, 1693–1731. Volume II, Our Catholic Heritage in Texas, 1519–1936.* Austin: Von Boeckmann–Jones Company, 1936.

Chicano Coordinating Council on Higher Education. *El Plan de Santa Barbara: A Chicano Plan for Higher Education.* Oakland: La Causa Publications, 1969.

Chipman, Donald E. *Spanish Texas, 1519–1821.* Austin: University of Texas Press, 1992.

Cohen, Lizbeth. *Making a New Deal: Industrial Workers in Chicago, 1919–1939.* New York: Cambridge University Press, 1992.

Coleman, Algernon. *English Teaching in the Southwest: Organization and Materials for Instructing Spanish-Speaking Children.* Washington: American Council on Education, 1940.

Cook, Katherine M. *Opportunities for the Preparation of Teachers of Children of Native and Minority Groups. United States Department of the Interior, Office of Education, Pamphlet No. 77.* Washington: Government Printing Office, 1937.

Cooper, Oscar H. *Seventh Biennial Report of the Superintendent of Public Instruction for the Scholastic Years Ending, August 31, 1889, and August 31, 1890, Being the Fourteenth Report from the Department of Education.* Austin: State Printing Office, 1890.

————. *Sixth Biennial Report of the Superintendent of Public Instruction of the Scholastic Years Ending August 31, 1887, and July 1, 1888, Being the Thirteenth Report from the Department of Education.* Austin: State Printing Office, 1889.

————. *Special Report of the Superintendent of Public Instruction for the Years Ending Aug., 31, 1887.* Austin: State Printing Office, 1888.

Cordasco, Francesco, and Eugene Bucchioni, eds. *Puerto Rican Children in Mainland Schools: A Source Book for Teachers.* Metuchen, N.J.: Scarecrow Press, Inc., 1968.

Cordasco, Francesco. "The Bilingual Education Act." Phi Delta Kappan 51 (October, 1969): 75.

Cottrell, Debbie Mauldin. *Pioneer Woman Educator in Texas: The Progressive Spirit of Annie Webb Blanton.* College Station: Texas A&M University Press, 1993.

Cousins, R. B. *Fifteenth Biennial Report of the State Superintendent of Public Instruction for the Years Ending August, 31, 1905, and August 31, 1906.* Austin: Von Boeckmann–Jones Co., Printers, 1906.

————. *School Laws of Texas, 1909. Bulletin No. 1.* Austin: Von Boeckmann–Jones Co., Printers, 1909.

————. *Sixteenth Biennial Report of the State Superintendent of Public Instruction for the Years Ending August 31, 1907 and August 31, 1908.* Austin: Von Boeckmann–Jones Co., Printers, 1909.

Cox, I. J. "Educational Efforts in San Fernando de Bexar." *Quarterly of the Texas State Historical Association* 6 (July, 1902): 27–63.

Crawford, James. *Bilingual Education: History, Politics, Theory, and Practice. Fourth Edition, Revised and Expanded.* Los Angeles: Bilingual Educational Services, Inc., 1999.

————. *Hold Your Tongue: Bilingualism and the Politics of "English-Only."* Reading, Mass.: Addison Wesley Publishing Company, 1992.

Cremin, Lawrence T. *The Transformation of the School: Progressivism in American Education, 1876–1957.* New York: Alfred A. Knopf, 1961; reprint, Vintage Books, 1964.

Crouch, Barry A., and L. J. Schultz. "Crisis in Color: Racial Separation in Texas During Reconstruction." *Civil War History* 16 (Spring, 1970): 37–49.

Cubberley, Ellwood P. *Changing Conceptions of Education.* Boston: Houghton Mifflin Company, 1909.

Cunz, Dieter. *The Maryland Germans: A History.* Princeton: Princeton University Press, 1948.

Dallek, Robert. *Lone Star Rising: Lyndon Johnson and His Times, 1908–1960.* New York: Oxford University Press, 1991.

Darcy, Natalie T. "A Review of the Literature on the Effects of Bilingualism Upon the Measurement of Intelligence." *The Journal of Genetic Psychology* 82 (March, 1953): 21–57.

————. The Effect on Bilingualism Upon the Measurement of the Intelligence of Children of Preschool Age." *The Journal of Educational Psychology* 37 (February, 1946): 21–44.

———. "The Performance of Bilingual Puerto Rican Children on Verbal and on Non-Language Tests of Intelligence." *Journal of Educational Research* 45 (December, 1952): 499–506.

Davis, E. E., and C. T. Gray. *A Study of Rural Schools in Karnes County. University of Texas Bulletin, No. 2246.* Austin: Publications of the University of Texas, 1922.

Davis, E. E. *A Report on Illiteracy in Texas. University of Texas Bulletin, No. 2328.* Austin: University of Texas Publications, 1923.

———. *A Study of Rural Schools in Travis County, Texas: Bulletin of the University of Texas, No. 67.* Austin: Publications of the University of Texas, 1916.

———. "King Cotton Leads Mexicans Into Texas." *The Texas Outlook* 9 (April, 1925): 7–9.

De Gress, Jacob C. *First Annual Report of the Superintendent of Public Instruction of the State of Texas, 1871.* Austin: J. G. Tracy, State Printer, 1872.

———. *Second Annual Report of the Superintendent of Public Instruction of the State of Texas for the Year 1872.* Austin: James P. Newcombe & Co., 1873.

De León, Arnoldo. *Ethnicity in the Sunbelt: Mexican Americans in Houston.* College Station: Texas A&M University Press, 2001.

———. *The Tejano Community, 1836–1900.* Albuquerque: University of New Mexico Press; reprint, Dallas: Southern Methodist University Press, 1997.

Del Castillo, Richard Griswold, and Richard A. Garcia. *César Chávez: A Triumph of the Spirit.* Norman: University of Oklahoma Press, 1995.

Del Castillo, Richard Griswold. "The 'Mexican Problem': A Critical View of the Alliance of Academics and Politicians During the Debate Over Mexican Immigration in the 1920s." *Borderlands* 4 (Spring, 1981): 251–74.

———. *The Treaty of Guadalupe Hidalgo: A Legacy of Conflict.* Norman: University of Oklahoma Press, 1990.

Dewey, John. *Democracy and Education.* New York: Macmillan Company, 1916; reprint, The Free Press, 1966.

Division of Administrative Services. *Laws and Resolutions Affecting Public Education Enacted by the 56th Legislature, Regular Session, 1959.* Austin: Texas Education Agency, 1959.

Dodd, E. C., and L. A. Woods. *Tentative Course of Study for the Teaching of Spanish in Grades 3 to 8 Inclusive, Bulletin No. 426.* Austin: State Department of Education, 1943.

Dodd, E. C. "The Lower Rio Grande Valley Elementary Principals Association." *The Texas Outlook* 12 (June, 1928): 30–31.

Doughty, W. F., and J. P. Buck. *Texas High Schools, Latin. Bulletin No. 81.* Austin: Department of Education, State of Texas, 1918.

Doughty, W. F., and Rebecca Switzer. *Texas High Schools, Modern Languages. Bulletin No. 82.* Austin: Department of Education, State of Texas, 1918.

Doughty, W. F. *Manual and Course of Study for the Public Schools of Texas, 1914. Bulletin No. 46.* Austin: Department of Education, State of Texas, 1915.

———. *Twenty-First Biennial Report, State Superintendent of Public Instruction, State of Texas, September 1, 1916, to August 31, 1918.* Austin: State Board of Education, 1918.

Eby, Frederick, and Charles Flinn Arrowood. *The History and Philosophy of Education Ancient and Medieval.* New York: Prentice-Hall, Inc., 1940.

Eby, Frederick, ed. *Education in Texas: Source Materials. University of Texas Bulletin, No. 1824.* Austin: University of Texas, 1918.

———. *The Development of Education in Texas.* New York: Macmillan Company, 1925.

Edgar, J. W. *42nd Biennial Report, 1960–1962. Bulletin No. 630.* Austin: Texas Education Agency, 1963.

———. *43rd Biennial Report, 1962–1964. Bulletin No. 654.* Austin: Texas Education Agency, 1965.

———. *44th Biennial Report, 1964–1966.* Austin: Texas Education Agency, 1967.

———. *45th Biennial Report, 1966–1968. No. 678.* Austin: Texas Education Agency, 1969.

———. *46th Biennial Report, 1968–1970.* Austin: Texas Education Agency, 1971.

———. *47th Biennial Report, 1970–1972. No. 729.* Austin: Texas Education Agency, 1973.

———. *A Resource Manual for Implementing Bilingual Education Programs.* Austin: Texas Education Agency, 1970.

———. *Preschool Instructional Program for Non-English-Speaking Children. Bulletin No. 642.* Austin: Texas Education Agency, 1964.

———. *Public Education in Texas, 1958–1960: A Report to the Governor and the Legislature. 41st Biennial Report, Texas Education Agency, Bulletin No. 610.* Austin: Texas Education Agency, 1961.

———. *Thirty-Sixth Biennial Report, 1948–49, 1949–50.* Austin: Texas Education Agency.

———. *What Do We Know About . . . Foreign Language Instruction? Bulletin 621.* Austin: Texas Education Agency, 1962.

Eichorn, Dorothy H., and Harold E. Jones. "Development of Mental Functions." *Review of Educational Research* 22 (December, 1952): 421–38.

England, Byron. "El Paso Develops Aids for Teachers of Bilinguals." *The Texas Outlook* 29 (October, 1945): 42 and 44.

Ferguson, Charles A., and Shirley Brice Heath, eds. *Language in the USA.* New York: Cambridge University Press, 1981.

Fishman, Joshua A. *Bilingual Education: An International Sociological Perspective.* Rowley, Mass.: Newbury House Publishers, 1976.

———. *Language and Nationalism: Two Integrative Essays.* Rowley, Mass.: Newbury House Publishers, 1972.

———, ed. *Language Loyalty in the United States: The Maintenance and Perpetuation of Non-English Mother Tongues by American Ethnic and Religious Groups.* The Hague: Netherlands, Mouton & Company, 1966.

Fries, Charles C. *Teaching & Learning English as a Foreign Language.* Ann Arbor: University of Michigan Press, 1945.

Gammel, H. P. N. *The Laws of Texas, 1822-1897. Volumes I, II, III, IV, V, VII, VIII, IX, X, XI, XII.* Austin: Gammel Book Company, 1898.

Garcia, F. Chris, ed. *Latinos and the Political System.* Notre Dame: University of Notre Dame Press, 1988.

García, Ignacio M. *Viva Kennedy: Mexican Americans in Search of Camelot.* College Station: Texas A&M University Press, 2000.

García, María Cristina. *Havana USA: Cuban Exiles and Cuban Americans in South Florida, 1959–1994.* Berkeley: University of California Press, 1996.

García, Mario T. *Mexican Americans: Leadership, Ideology, & Identity, 1930–1960.* New Haven: Yale University Press, 1989.

Garcia, Ofelia, ed. *Bilingual Education: Focusschrift in Honor of Joshua A. Fishman on the Occasion of His 65th Birthday, Volume I.* Philadelphia: John Benjamin's Publishing Company, 1991.

Garcia, Richard A. *Rise of the Mexican American Middle Class: San Antonio, 1929–1941.* College Station: Texas A&M University Press, 1991.

Garza-Falcón, Leticia M. *Gente Decente: A Borderlands Response to the Rhetoric of Dominance.* Austin: University of Texas Press, 1998.

Geisinger, Kurt, ed. *Psychological Testing of Hispanics.* Washington: American Psychological Association, 1992.

Getz, Lynne Marie. *Schools of Their Own: The Education of Hispanos in New Mexico, 1850–1940.* Albuquerque: University of New Mexico Press, 1997.

Gilbert, Glenn G. "Origin and Present Day Location of German Speakers in Texas: A Statistical Interpretation." *Rice University Studies* 63 (Summer, 1977): 21–34.

———, ed. *Texas Studies in Bilingualism: Spanish, French, German, Czech, Polish, Sorbian, and Norwegian in the Southwest.* Berlin: Walter de Gruyter & Co., 1970.

Glazer, Nathan, and Daniel Patrick Moynihan, eds. *Beyond the Melting Pot: The Negroes, Puerto Ricans, Jews, Italians, and Irish of New York City.* Cambridge, Mass.: MIT Press, 1963.

Goldberger, *Teaching English to the Foreign Born. United States Department of the Interior, Bureau of Education Bulletin, 1919, No. 80.* Washington: Government Printing Office, 1920.

Gordon, Milton M. *Assimilation in American Life: The Role of Race, Religion, and National Origins.* New York: Oxford University Press, 1964.

Gouin, Francois. *The Art of Teaching and Studying Languages, Ninth Edition.* Translated by Howard Swan and Victor Betis. New York: Longmans, Green, & Company, 1919.

Gould, Lewis L. *Progressives & Prohibitionists: Texas Democrats in the Wilson Era.* Austin: University of Texas Press, 1973.

Graham, Hugh Davis. *The Uncertain Triumph: Federal Education Policy in the Kennedy and Johnson Years.* Chapel Hill: University of North Carolina Press, 1984.

Gutiérrez, David G. "Significant to Whom? Mexican Americans and the History of the American West." *Western Historical Quarterly* 24 (November, 1993): 519–39.

———. *Walls and Mirrors: Mexican Americans, Mexican Immigrants, and the Politics of Ethnicity.* Berkeley: University of California Press, 1995.

Habig, Marion A. *San Antonio's Mission San Jose: State and National Site, 1720–1968.* San Antonio: The Naylor Company, 1968.

Hall, G. Stanley. "The Ideal School as Based on Child Study." *The Forum* 32 (September, 1901): 24–39.

Hall, Jacquelyn Dowd. *Revolt Against Chivalry: Jessie Daniel Ames and the Women's Campaign Against Lynching, Revised Edition.* New York: Columbia University Press, 1993.

Hamilton, T. Earle, and Charles B. Qualia. "Spanish in the Grades." *The Texas Outlook* 25 (June, 1941): 50–51.

Handschin, Charles Hart. *The Teaching of Modern Languages in the United States. United States Department of the Interior, Bureau of Education Bulletin, 1913, No. 3.* Washington: Government Printing Office, 1913.

Hardgrave, Robert L., Jr., and Santiago Hinojosa. *The Politics of Bilingual Education: A Study of Four Southwest Texas Communities.* Manchaca, Tex.: Sterling Swift Publishing Company, 1975.

Hartmann, Edward George. The Movement to Americanize the Immigrant. New York: Columbia University Press, 1948; reprint, AMS Press, Inc., 1967.

Hatcher, Mattie Austin. "Plan of Stephen F. Austin for an Institute of Modern Languages at San Felipe de Austin." *The Quarterly of the Texas State Historical Association* 12 (January, 1909): 231–39.

Hearing Before the United States Commission on Civil Rights. Hearing Held in San Antonio, Texas, December 9–14, 1968. Washington: Government Printing Office, 1968.

Helton, H. Stephen. *Preliminary Inventory of the Records of the Office of Inter-American*

Affairs. Record Group 229. Washington: National Archives and Record Service, 1952.

Herr, Selma E. "The Effect of Pre-First-Grade Training Upon Reading Readiness and Reading Achievement Among Spanish American Children." *The Journal of Educational Psychology* 37 (February, 1946): 87–102.

Higham, John. *Strangers in the Land: Patterns of American Nativism, 1860–1925.* New Brunswick: Rutgers University Press, 1955.

Hofstadter, Richard. *Anti-Intellectualism in American Life.* New York: Vintage Books, 1963.

Hollingsworth, O. N. *Second Biennial Report of the State Board of Education for the Scholastic Years Ending August 31, 1879 and 1880.* Galveston: Galveston News Steam Book and Job Printing Establishment, 1881.

Hudson, Estelle, and Henry R. Maresh. *Czech Pioneers of the Southwest.* Dallas: South-West Press Inc., 1934.

Hughey, A. H. "Speaking English at School." *The Texas Outlook* 28 (November, 1944): 36.

Inhabitants of Del Rio Independent School District v. *Jesus Salvatierra,* 33 S.W. 2d 790. Texas Civil Appeals, 1930.

"Inter-American Workshop." *The Texas Outlook* 29 (March, 1945): 48.

Jarvis, Gilbert A., ed. *Responding to New Realities.* Skokie: National Textbook Company, 1974.

Jenkins, Mary. *Bilingual Education in New York City.* New York: New York City Board of Education, 1971.

Johnson, Henry Sioux, and William J. Hernández—M. *Educating the Mexican American.* Valley Forge, Pa.: Judson Press, 1970.

Johnston, Marjorie C., and Elizabeth Keesee. *Modern Foreign Languages and Your Child.* Washington: United States Department of Health, Education, and Welfare, Office of Education, 1964.

Jordan, Terry G. "A Century and a Half of Ethnic Change in Texas, 1836–1986." *Southwestern Historical Quarterly* 89 (April, 1986): 385–422.

———. "The German Element in Texas: An Overview." *Rice University Studies* 63 (Summer, 1977): 1–11.

Juárez, Leo J. "Equal Access or Equal Benefits: Court and Legislative Mandates on Bilingual Education." *Texas Tech Journal of Education* 2 (Fall, 1975): 179–91.

Kaestle, Carl E. *Pillars of the Republic: Common Schools and American Society, 1780–1860.* New York: Hill and Wang, 1983.

Kamphoefner, Walter D. "German-American Bilingualism: *Cui Malo?* Mother Tongue and Socioeconomic Status among the Second Generation in 1940." *International Migration Review* 28 (Winter, 1994): 846–64.

Kearney, Milo, Alfonso Gomez Arguelles, and Yolanda Z. Gonzalez. *A Brief History of Education in Brownsville and Matamoros.* Brownsville: University of Texas—Pan American at Brownsville, 1989.

Kemerer, Frank, and Jim Walsh. *The Educator's Guide to Texas School Law, Fourth Edition.* Austin: University of Texas Press, 1996.

Kendall, J. S. *Twelfth Biennial Report of the State Superintendent for the Scholastic Years Ending August 31, 1899, and August 31, 1900.* Austin: Von Boeckmann, Moore, and Schultz, State Printers, 1900.

Kittell, Jack E. "Bilingualism and Language—Non-Language Intelligence Scores of Third-Grade Children." *Journal of Educational Research* 52 (March, 1959): 263–68.

Kloss, Heinz. *The American Bilingual Tradition.* Rowley, Mass.: Newbury House Press, 1977.

Kousser, J. Morgan. *The Shaping of Southern Politics: Suffrage Restriction and the*

Establishment of the One-Party South, 1880–1910. New Haven: Yale University Press, 1974.

Kreneck, Thomas H. *Mexican American Odyssey: Felix Tijerina, Entrepreneur & Civic Leader, 1905–1965.* College Station: Texas A&M University Press, 2001.

Kress, Dorothy, M. "The Spanish-Speaking School Child in Texas." *The Texas Outlook* 18 (December, 1934): 24.

Lack, Paul D. *The Texas Revolutionary Experience: A Political and Social History, 1835–1836.* College Station: Texas A&M University Press, 1992.

Lamm, Richard D., and Gary Imhoff. *The Immigrant Time Bomb: The Fragmenting of America.* New York: Truman Talley Books, E. P. Dutton, 1985.

Lefevre, Arthur. *Fourteenth Biennial Report of the State Superintendent of Public Instruction for the Years Ending August 31, 1903, and August 31, 1904.* Austin: Gammel-Statesman Publishing Co., 1905.

Leibowitz, Arnold H. *Educational Policy and Political Acceptance: The Imposition of English as the Language of Instruction in American Schools.* Washington: Center for Applied Linguistics, 1971.

Lerea, Louis, and Suzanna Kohut. "A Comparative Study of Monolinguals and Bilinguals in a Verbal Task Performance." *Journal of Clinical Psychology* 17 (January, 1961): 49–52.

Lessow-Hurley, Judith. *The Foundations of Dual Language Instruction, Second Edition.* New York: Longman Publishers, 1996.

Levinson, Boris M. "A Comparative Study of the Verbal and Performance Ability of Monolingual and Bilingual Native Born Jewish Preschool Children of Traditional Parentage." *The Journal of Genetic Psychology* 97 (September, 1960): 93–112.

Lewis, Hilda P., and Edward R. Lewis. "Written Language Performance of Sixth-Grade Children of Low Socio-Economic Status from Bilingual and Monolingual Backgrounds." *The Journal of Experimental Education* 33 (Spring, 1965): 237–42.

Lich, Glen E. *The German Texans.* San Antonio: University of Texas Institute of Texan Cultures, 1981.

Limón, José E. "El Primer Congreso Mexicanista de 1911: A Precursor to Contemporary Chicanismo." *Aztlan* 5 (Spring–Fall, 1974): 85–106.

Lissak, Rivka Shpak. *Pluralism and Progressives: Hull House and the New Immigrants, 1890–1919.* Chicago: University of Chicago Press, 1989.

Little, Wilson. *Spanish-Speaking Children in Texas.* Austin: University of Texas Press, 1944.

Luckey, G. W. A. *The Rural Teacher of Nebraska, Bulletin No. 20, 1919.* Washington: Department of the Interior, Bureau of Education, 1919.

Luetge, Elvie Lou. "Shelby: A Rural School in a German Immigrant Setting." *East Texas Historical Review* 18 (1980): 29–40.

Lutton, Wayne, and John Tanton. *The Immigrant Invasion.* Petoskey, Mich.: The Social Contract Press, 1994.

Machann, Clinton, and James W. Mendl. *Krasna Amerika: A Study of the Texas Czechs, 1851–1939.* Austin: Eakin Press, 1983.

Manuel, Herschel T. "Progress in Inter-American Education and Plans in Prospect." *The Texas Outlook* 29 (March, 1945): 13–15.

———. *The Education of the Mexican and Spanish-Speaking Children in Texas.* Austin: Fund for Research in Social Sciences, University of Texas, 1930.

Marrs, S. M. N., and Mary Nash. "History and the Status of the Teaching of Spanish in Texas." *The Texas Outlook* 14 (February, 1930): 3–4.

Marrs, S. M. N., and Opal Gilstrap. *Texas High Schools: The Teaching of Spanish, German, and French. Bulletin 230.* Austin: State Department of Education, 1927.

Marrs, S. M. N., Thomas J. Yoe, and M. Perrie Wygal. *A Course in English for the Non-English-Speaking Pupils, Grades I–III, Bulletin No. 268.* Austin: State Department of Education, 1930.

Marrs, S. M. N. *Manual and Course of Study, Elementary Grades, Public Schools of Texas, 1924–25. Bulletin 184.* Austin: Department of Education, State of Texas, 1924.

———. *Texas Compulsory School Attendance Law. Bulletin 174.* Austin: State Department of Education, State of Texas, 1923.

———. *Texas High Schools, Course of Study. Bulletin, State Department of Education, No. 196.* Austin: State Department of Education, 1925.

———. *Twenty-Fifth Biennial Report, State Department of Education, 1926–1928. No. 251.* Austin: Von Boeckmann–Jones Co., 1929.

Martin, Roscoe. *The People's Party in Texas: A Study in Third-Party Politics.* Austin: University of Texas Press, 1933; reprint, 1970.

Matusow, Allen J. *The Unraveling of America: A History of Liberalism in the 1960s.* New York: Harper & Row, Publishers, 1984.

McKinney, William M. *Texas Jurisprudence: A Complete Statement of the Law and Practice of the State of Texas, Volume XXXVII Robbery to Schools.* San Francisco: Bancroft-Whitney Company, 1935.

Meharg, Emma Grigsby. *General Laws of the State of Texas Passed by the Thirty-Ninth Legislature at the First Called Session Convened at the City of Austin, September 13, 1926, and Adjourned October 8, 1926.* Austin: Secretary of State, 1926.

Merium, Junius L. *Learning English Incidentally: A Study of Bilingual Children. Department of the Interior, Office of Education, Bulletin 1937, No. 15.* Washington: United States Government Printing Office, 1938.

Miller, Herbert Adolphus. *The School and the Immigrant, Cleveland Educational Survey.* Cleveland: Survey Committee of the Cleveland Foundation, 1916.

Mintz, Steven. *Moralists and Modernizers: America's Pre-Civil War Reformers.* Baltimore: Johns Hopkins University Press, 1995.

Montejano, David. *Anglos and Mexicans in the Making of Texas, 1836–1986.* Austin: University of Texas Press, 1987.

Murphy, Laura Francis. "An Experiment in Americanization." *The Texas Outlook* 23 (November, 1939): 23–24.

National Advisory Committee on Mexican American Education of the U.S. Office of Education. "Cowboys, Indians, and American Education." Address by Harold Howe, U.S. Commissioner of Education in Austin, Tex., April 25, 1968.

Navarro, Armando. *Mexican American Youth Organization: Avant-Garde of the Chicano Movement in Texas.* Austin: University of Texas Press, 1995.

Neal, Elma A. "Adapting the Curriculum to the Non-English Speaking Child." *The Texas Outlook* 11 (June, 1927): 39–40 and 63.

Noonan, Margaret E., Orville G. Brim, and Clarence T. Gray. *Texas Educational Survey Report, Volume V. Courses of Study and Instruction.* Austin: Texas Educational Survey Commission, 1924.

Norman, Ralph D., and Donald F. Mead. "Spanish-American Bilingualism and the Ammons Full-Range Picture-Vocabulary Test." *The Journal of Social Psychology* 51 (May, 1960): 319–30.

Notgrass, Autalee. "Down Mexico Way: Middle Grade Unit." *The Texas Outlook* 25 (August, 1941): 53.

Ovando, Carlos J., and Virginia P. Collier. *Bilingual and ESL Classrooms: Teaching in Multicultural Contexts.* New York: McGraw-Hill Book Company, 1985.

Owens, William A. *This Stubborn Soil: A Frontier Boyhood.* New York: Lyons & Burford, 1986.

Paredes, Americo, ed. *Humanidad: Essays in Honor of George I. Sánchez.* Los Angeles: University of California, Chicano Studies Center, 1977.

Peal, Elizabeth, and Wallace E. Lambert. *The Relation of Bilingualism to Intelligence. Psychological Monographs: General and Applied, Vol. 76, No. 27.* Washington: American Psychological Association, 1962.

Perales, Alonso, ed. *Are We Good Neighbors?* San Antonio: Artes Graficas, 1948; reprint, New York: Arno Press, 1974.

Perry, Sadie. "They Must Think in English." *The Texas Outlook* 26 (June, 1942): 13–14.

Piatt, Bill. *¿Only English? Law & Language Policy in the United States.* Albuquerque: University of New Mexico Press, 1990.

Preuss, Gene B. "Cotulla Revisited: A Reassessment of Lyndon Johnson's year as a Public School Teacher." *Journal of South Texas* 10 (1997): 20–37.

Poulos, William T. "They Learn Basic English *Before* School Starts." *The Texas Outlook* 43 (July, 1959): 15–16 and 33–34.

Pycior, Julie Leininger. "From Hope to Frustration: Mexican Americans and Lyndon Johnson in 1967." *Western Historical Quarterly* 24 (November, 1993): 469–94.

———. *LBJ & Mexican Americans: The Paradox of Power.* Austin: University of Texas Press, 1997.

Quiñones, Juan Gómez. *Chicano Politics: Reality & Promise, 1940–1990.* Albuquerque: University of New Mexico Press, 1990.

Ramirez, Manuel, III, and Alfredo Castañeda. *Cultural Democracy, Bicognitive Development, and Education.* New York: Academic Press, 1974.

Rankin, Melinda. *Texas in 1850.* Introduction by John C. Rayburn. Waco: Texian Press, 1966.

Reimers, David M. *Still the Golden Door: The Third World Comes to America.* New York: Columbia University Press, 1985.

Report on Conferences on Professional Relations and Inter-American Education at the Southwest Texas State Teachers College, San Marcos, Texas, June 30, 1944. San Marcos: Southwest Texas Teachers College, 1944.

Reynolds, Annie. *The Education of Spanish-Speaking Children in Five Southwestern States. Bulletin 1933, No. 11.* Washington: United States Department of the Interior, Office of Education, 1933.

Rice, Lawrence D. *The Negro in Texas, 1874–1900.* Baton Rouge: Louisiana State University Press, 1971.

Rich, Burdett A., and M. Blair Whailes, eds. "Robert T. Meyer, plff. In err., v. State of Nebraska." *American Law Reports, Annotated. Volume 29.* Rochester: Lawyers Co-Operative Publishing Company, 1924.

Rienow, Robert, and Leona Rienow. *The Great Unwanteds Want Us. Illegal Aliens: Too Late to Close the Gates?* Monterey, Calif.: Viewpoint Books, 1980.

Roos, Peter D. "Bilingual Education: The Hispanic Response to Unequal Educational Equality." *Law and Contemporary Problems* 42 (Autumn, 1978): 111–40.

Rowland, Donald W., and Harold B. Gotaas. *History of the Office of the Coordinator of Inter-American Affairs: Historical Reports on War Administration.* Washington: United States Printing Office, 1947.

Sáenz, Andrés. *Early Tejano Ranching: Daily Life at Ranchos San José & El Fresnillo.* Introduction by Andrés Tijerina. College Station: Texas A&M University Press, 1999.

Saenz, J. Luz. "Has Time Come?" *The Texas Outlook* 26 (April, 1942): 44.

———. "Racial Discrimination: A Number One Problem of Texas Schools." *The Texas Outlook* 30 (December, 1946): 12 and 40.

Salinas, Guadalupe. "Mexican Americans and the Desegregation of Schools in the Southwest." *Houston Law Review* 8 (1971): 929–51.

Samora, Julian, ed. *La Raza: Forgotten Americans.* Notre Dame: University of Notre Dame Press, 1966.

San Miguel, Guadalupe, Jr., and Richard R. Valencia. "From the Treaty of Guadalupe Hidalgo to *Hopwood:* The Educational Plight and Struggle of Mexican Americans in the Southwest." *Harvard Educational Review* 68 (Fall, 1998): 353–412.

San Miguel, Guadalupe, Jr. *Brown, Not White: School Integration and the Chicano Movement in Houston.* College Station: Texas A&M University Press, 2001.

———. "Conflict and Controversy in the Evolution of Bilingual Education in the United States—An Interpretation." *Social Science Quarterly* 65 (June, 1984): 505–18.

———. "Culture and Education in the American Southwest: Towards an Explanation of Chicano School Attendance, 1850–1940." *Journal of American Ethnic History* 7 (Spring, 1988): 5–21.

———. *"Let All of Them Take Heed": Mexican Americans and the Campaign for Educational Equality in Texas, 1910–1981.* Austin: University of Texas Press, 1987.

———. "'The Community is Beginning to Rumble': The Origins of Chicano Educational Protest in Houston, 1965–1970." *The Houston Review* 13 (Summer, 1991): 136–46.

———. "The Struggle Against Separate and Unequal Schools: Middle Class Mexican Americans and the Desegregation Campaign in Texas, 1929–1957." *History of Education Quarterly* 23 (Fall, 1983): 343–59.

Sánchez, George I., and Henry J. Otto. *A Guide for Teachers of Spanish Speaking Children in the Primary Grades, 1946. Bulletin No. 464.* Austin: State Department of Education, 1946.

Sánchez, George I. *Concerning Segregation of Spanish-Speaking Children in the Public Schools. Inter-American Education Occasional Papers, IX.* Austin: University of Texas Press, 1951; reprint, New York: Arno Press, 1974.

———. "The Crux of the Dual Language Handicap." *New Mexico School Review* 38 (March, 1954): 13–15 and 38.

Sánchez, George J. *Becoming Mexican American: Ethnicity, Culture, and Identity in Chicano Los Angeles, 1900–1945.* New York: Oxford University Press, 1993.

Schlesinger, Arthur M., Jr. *The Disuniting of America: Reflections on a Multiracial Society.* New York: W. W. Norton & Company, 1991.

Schlossman, Steven L. "Is There an American Tradition of Bilingual Education? German in the Public Elementary Schools, 1840–1919." *American Journal of Education* 91 (February, 1983): 139–86.

Schmitz, Joseph William. *The Society of Mary in Texas.* San Antonio: The Naylor Company, 1951.

Shelby, T. H., B. F. Pittenger, J. O. Marberry, and Fred C. Ayer. *Preliminary Survey of the Laredo Public Schools. University of Texas Bulletin, No 2912.* Austin: Publications of the University of Texas, 1929.

Sitton, Thad, and Dan K. Utley. *From Can See to Can't: Texas Farmers on the Southern Plains.* Austin: University of Texas Press, 1997.

Sitton, Thad, and Milam C. Rowold. *Ringing the Children In: Texas Country Schools.* College Station: Texas A&M University Press, 1987.

Smith, Timothy L. "Immigrant Social Aspirations and American Education, 1880–1930." *American Quarterly* 21 (Fall, 1969): 523–43.

Spratt, John Stricklin. *The Road to Spindletop: Economic Change in Texas, 1875–1901.* Dallas: Southern Methodist University Press, 1955; reprint, Austin: University of Texas Press, 1970.

Stambaugh, J. Lee. "The Valley Superintendents." *The Texas Outlook* 9 (June, 1925): 29.

Staples, S. L. *General Laws of the State of Texas Passed by the Thirty-Eighth Legislature at the Regular Session Convened at the City of Austin, January 9, 1923, and Adjourned March 14, 1923.* Austin: A. C. Baldwin & Sons, State Printers, 1923.

Stein, Colman Brez, Jr. *Sink or Swim: The Politics of Bilingual Education.* New York: Praeger Publishers, 1986.

Stemmler, Annie. "An Experimental Approach to the Teaching of Oral Language and Reading." *Harvard Educational Review* 36 (Summer, 1966): 42–59.

Stephenson, Madge. "Education Will Make Good Neighbors." *The Texas Outlook* 27 (March, 1943): 26.

Tamura, Eileen H. *Americanization, Acculturation, and Ethnic Identity: The Nisei Generation in Hawaii.* Urbana: University of Illinois Press, 1994.

Tanner, Myrtle L. *Teacher Training Workshop, Inter-American Relations Education: Program, Personnel, Reports, Recommendations, Summaries. University of Texas, Austin, Texas, April 17–22, 1944.* Austin: State Department of Education, 1944.

Tatalovich, Raymond, and Byron W. Daynes, eds. *Moral Controversies in American Politics: Cases in Social Regulatory Policy.* Armonk, N.Y.: M. E. Sharpe, 1998.

Taylor, J. T. "The Americanization of Harlingen's Mexican School Population." *The Texas Outlook* 18 (September, 1934): 37–38.

Taylor, Paul Schuster. *An American-Mexican Frontier: Nueces County, Texas.* New York: Russell and Russell, 1934.

———. "Mexican Labor in the United States, Dimmit County, Winter Garden District, South Texas." In *Mexican Labor in the United States,* Volume I. Berkeley: University of California Press, 1930.

Texas Committee of Ten. *Report Number One of the Survey of Administrative Practices and Board Policies in Texas Public Schools: Pupil Personnel Practices in Texas Public Schools.* Austin: Texas Committee of Ten, 1957.

———. *School Program Practices in Texas Public Schools. Report Number Three of the Texas Committee of Ten.* Austin: Texas Committee of Ten, 1957.

Texas Education Agency Office of Policy Planning and Research, *Academic Achievement of Elementary Students with Limited English Proficiency in Texas Public Schools, Report No. 10, January 1998.* Austin: Texas Education Agency, 1998.

Texas Legislature. House. *Journal of the House of Representatives of the Fourth Called Session of the Thirty Fifth Legislature.* Austin: Von Boeckmann–Jones Co., Printers, 1918.

———. House. *Journal of the House of Representatives of the Regular Session of the Sixty-First Legislature.* Austin: Nelson Typesetting Company, 1969.

———. Senate. *Journal of the Senate of the State of Texas, Regular Session of the Sixty-First Legislature.* Austin: Von Boeckmann–Jones Co., 1969.

———. House. *Journal of the House of Representatives of the Regular Session of the Sixty-Third Legislature.* Austin: Nelson Typesetting Company, 1973.

———. Senate. *Journal of the Senate of the State of Texas, Regular Session of the Sixty-Third Legislature.* Austin: Von Boeckmann–Jones Co., 1973.

———. House. *Journal of the House of Representatives of the Regular Session of the Sixty-Sixth Legislature of the State of Texas.* Austin, 1979.

———. House. *Journal of the House of Representatives of the Regular Session of the Sixty-Seventh Legislature of the State of Texas.* Austin, 1981.

———. Senate. *Journal of the Senate of the State of Texas. Regular Session of the Sixty-Seventh Legislature.* Austin, 1981.

Thompson, Frank V. *Schooling the Immigrant in Americanization Studies: The Accul-*

turation of Immigrant Groups Into American Society, Patterson Smith Reprint Series in Criminology, Law Enforcement, and Social Problems, Volume I. Ed. by William Bernard. New York: Harper and Brothers, 1920; reprint, Montclair, N.J.: Patterson Smith, 1971.

Tijerina, Andres. *Tejanos & Texans Under the Mexican Flag, 1821–1836.* College Station: Texas A&M University Press, 1994.

Troen, Selwyn K. *The Public and the Schools: The Shaping of the St. Louis System, 1838–1920.* Columbia: University of Missouri Press, 1975.

Tyack, David. *The One Best System: A History of American Urban Education.* Cambridge: Harvard University Press, 1974.

Tyler, Daniel. "The Mexican Teacher." *Red River Valley Historical Review* 1 (Autumn, 1974): 207–21.

U.S. Commission on Civil Rights, Stranger in One's Land. U.S. Commission on Civil Rights Clearinghouse Publication No. 19, May, 1970. Washington: Government Printing Office, 1970.

United States of America v. *State of Texas et al.,* 321 F. Supp. 24. Eastern District of Texas, 1971.

Valek, Wesley. "Czech-Moravian Pioneers of Ellis County, Texas: 1873–1917." *Panhandle-Plains Historical Review* 56 (1983): 49–63.

Van Nice, C. R. "Adapting the School Public Relations Program to the War Emergency." *The Texas Outlook* 27 (March, 1943): 24–26.

Vega, José E. *Education, Politics, and Bilingualism in Texas.* Washington: University Press of America, Inc., 1983.

Ward, R. P. *Proposed Curriculum Program for Texas Migratory Children.* Austin: Texas Education Agency, 1963.

Weber, David J. *The Mexican Frontier, 1821–1846: The American Southwest Under Mexico.* Albuquerque: University of New Mexico Press, 1982.

Weber, Eugen. *Peasants Into Frenchmen: The Modernization of Rural France, 1870–1914.* Stanford: Stanford University Press, 1976.

Weeks, O. Douglas. "The League of United Latin-American Citizens: A Texas-Mexican Civic Organization." *The Southwestern Political and Social Science Quarterly* 10 (December, 1929): 257–78.

Weinberg, Meyer. *A Chance to Learn: The History of Race and Education in the United States.* New York: Cambridge University Press, 1977.

Weir, Emma P. "The Mexican Child." *The Texas Outlook* 20 (June, 1936): 23–24.

Wellborne, K. Rocque. "Spanish for Children of Hispano Descent." *The Texas Outlook* 25 (December, 1941): 33–34.

Westminster School District of Orange County et al. v. Mendez et al., 161 F. 2Nd 774. California Federal District Court, 1947.

Whittenburg, Clarice T., and George I. Sánchez. *Materials Relating to the Education of Spanish-Speaking People: A Bibliography. Inter-American Educational Papers, 2.* Austin: University of Texas Press, 1948.

Wiebe, Robert H. *The Search for Order, 1877–1920.* New York: Hill and Wang, 1967.

Wilder, L. A. "Problems in the Teaching of Mexican Children." *The Texas Outlook* 20 (August, 1936): 9–10.

Wilson, Edgar Ellen, and Myrtle L. Tanner. *Meet Latin America: Curriculum Enrichment Materials for Elementary and Junior High Schools, 1945, Bulletin No. 465.* Austin: State Department of Education, 1945.

Wood, Bryce. *The Making of the Good Neighbor Policy.* New York: W. W. Norton & Company, 1961.

Woodfin, Anna. "Our Mexican Obligation." *The Texas Outlook* 25 (August, 1941): 19.

Woods, L. A., and W. A. Stigler. *Handbook for Curriculum Development. Bulletin No. 354.* Austin: State Department of Education, 1936.

Woods, L. A., and Sam B. McAlister. *Public School Laws of the State of Texas, 1938. Bulletin No. 382.* Austin: State Department of Education, 1938.

Woods, L. A., Eduard Micek, Alois J. Petrusek, and Jesse J. Jochec. *Tentative Course of Study in Czech. Bulletin No. 387.* Austin: State Department of Education, estimated publication date of 1930s.

Woods, L. A. *Statement, Discussion, and Decision on the Segregation in the Del Rio Public Schools.* Austin: State Department of Education, 1949.

———. *Thirty-Third Biennial Report. State Department of Education, 1942–1943, 1943–1944, No. 447.* Austin: State Department of Education, 1944.

———. *With Texas Public Schools, Bulletin, State Department of Education, September 1948.* Austin: State Department of Education, 1948.

Woodward, C. Vann. *The Strange Career of Jim Crow. A Commemorative Edition with a New Afterword by William S. McFeely.* New York: Oxford University Press, 2002.

Works, George A. "Chapter XIII: The Non-English Speaking Children and the Public School." *The Texas Outlook* 9 (August, 1925): 26–29.

———. "The Non-English Speaking Children and the Public School." *Texas Educational Survey, Volume I.* Austin: State Department of Education, 1936.

Yarbrough, C. L. "Age-Grade Status of Texas Children of Latin-American Descent." *Journal of Educational Research* 40 (September, 1946): 14–27.

Zamora, Emilio, Cynthia Orozco, and Rodolfo Rocha, eds. *Mexican Americans in Texas History.* Austin: Texas State Historical Association, 2000.

Zamora, Emilio. "The Failed Promise of Wartime Opportunity for Mexicans in the Texas Oil Industry." *Southwestern Historical Quarterly* 95 (January, 1992): 221–36.

———. *The World of the Mexican Worker in Texas.* College Station: Texas A&M University Press, 1993.

Index

ISBN 1-58544-310-7